DATE DUE

			PRINTED IN U.S.A.

OCT 08 2014

Brazilian Propaganda

UNIVERSITY PRESS OF FLORIDA

Florida A&M University, Tallahassee
Florida Atlantic University, Boca Raton
Florida Gulf Coast University, Ft. Myers
Florida International University, Miami
Florida State University, Tallahassee
New College of Florida, Sarasota
University of Central Florida, Orlando
University of Florida, Gainesville
University of North Florida, Jacksonville
University of South Florida, Tampa
University of West Florida, Pensacola

Brazilian Propaganda

Legitimizing an Authoritarian Regime

Nina Schneider

UNIVERSITY PRESS OF FLORIDA

Gainesville/Tallahassee/Tampa/Boca Raton

Pensacola/Orlando/Miami/Jacksonville/Ft. Myers/Sarasota

This book may be available in an electronic edition.

19 18 17 16 15 14   6 5 4 3 2 1

Library of Congress Cataloging-in-Publication Data
Schneider, Nina, (Postdoctoral researcher), author.
Brazilian propaganda : legitimizing an authoritarian regime / Nina Schneider.
pages cm
Includes bibliographical references and index.
ISBN 978-0-8130-4990-8
1. Brazil—History—1964–1985. 2. Brazil—Politics and government. 3. Brazil—
Propaganda. I. Title.
F2538.25.S36 2014
981.06'3—dc23   2014003466

The University Press of Florida is the scholarly publishing agency for the State University
System of Florida, comprising Florida A&M University, Florida Atlantic University,
Florida Gulf Coast University, Florida International University, Florida State University,
New College of Florida, University of Central Florida, University of Florida, University
of North Florida, University of South Florida, and University of West Florida.

University Press of Florida
15 Northwest 15th Street
Gainesville, FL 32611-2079
http://www.upf.com

This book is dedicated to my Brazilian host family,

Zélia and Pedro L. Durão

and their children, Claudia, Daniel, Bruno, and Vitão,

who introduced me to this wonderful country called Brazil . . .

and also to Max, Tom, and Emi

Contents

Preface

If, by chance, you were born and raised a second- or third-generation post-Nazi German, one question would perplex you throughout your life: how could my ancestors not have prevented the Nazi dictatorship? This is a very complex question. Reams of books have been written on the subject and continue to fill library shelves.

Although it took decades for the country to reckon with its violent past, studying the Nazi dictatorship already formed a major part of the West German curriculum when I went to school in the 1980s and 1990s. We did not just study the Nazis in our history and politics courses. We also read poems and novels in German, French, and English: Erich Fried's *Warngedichte*, Berthold Brecht's "Kälbermarsch," Anne Frank's diary, Hans Peter Richter's *Damals war es Friedrich*, Jean Bruller's *Le Silence de la mer*, Paul Éluard's "Liberté, j'écrit ton nome," George Orwell's *1984*, and Todd Strasser's (pen name Morton Rhue) *The Wave*. We analyzed supposedly "degenerate art" and deconstructed the "race" concept in biology class.

When I first traveled to Brazil in the 1990s as a sixteen-year-old exchange student, I was surprised to find that the relatively recent and enduring military dictatorship (1964–1985) was not part of the curriculum at the renowned high school I attended in Rio de Janeiro. That entire period was silenced. The German and Brazilian experiences are, of course, vastly different, and reckoning with dictatorships usually takes decades. Still, it was this key formative experience—my unmet expectation of learning about the Brazilian dictatorship, and the perplexity I felt as a result—that further fed my curiosity about Brazil's authoritarian period in particular and about repressive regimes and their legacies in general. For the past eleven years, I have sought to understand why societies live by dictatorships, and this reflection has brought me to the examination of propaganda, an element common to both the German and Brazilian experiences.

Alongside violent intimidation and nationalist fervor, propaganda stands out for its key role in bringing the Nazis to power. It is important to understand propaganda and its power to persuade, because if totalitarianism has taught us anything, it has taught us the importance of engaging critically with the discourses (and practices) in which we are immersed. The price of not doing so might be freedom itself.

The Brazilian experiment with propaganda is worth studying, because it upends many commonly held assumptions about this form of discourse, bringing nuance to scholarly understanding of the subject. While writing this book, I discovered not only that the line between authoritarian and democratic propaganda is much blurrier than one might expect but also that the same could be said of the classical difference between state and private agents of propaganda, such as commercial advertisers and the media. Private propaganda agents may be more culpable than they seem.

This book elucidates propaganda in its many shapes and forms, whether produced under democratic or authoritarian rule, by state or by private agents. Used as a tool to constrain human liberties for centuries, propaganda remains as relevant as ever. And yet dissecting propaganda is arguably more difficult now than ever before: as the role of the nation-state continues to evolve, the lines between public and private advertising often get blurred, and in a globalized world it is often unclear where power interests lie.

Acknowledgments

I wish to thank the staff of the National Archives in Rio and Brasília for their help and kindness, in particular Cláudio, Valeria, Pablo, Clovis, Satyr, and Rosane. Furthermore, I would like to warmly thank the staff of the Edgar Leuenroth Archive in Campinas, the São Paulo State Archive, the Center for Research and Documentation of Contemporary Brazilian History (CPDOC) in Rio, and the Marines Archive in Rio, particularly Claudia Drumond and Marcia Prestes. I would also like to thank Professor Carlos Fico and the members of the Study Group on the Military Dictatorship (Grupo de Estudos sobre a ditadura militar, GEDM) at the Federal University of Rio (UFRJ) for letting me participate in their sessions.

I wish to thank all my interviewees for giving their time and for sharing their personal experiences with me. Thanks to General Octávio Pereira da Costa, General José Maria Toledo Camargo, Professor Alberto Rabaça, Professor Gustavo Barbosa, Professor José Cavalieri, ex-Minister Jarbas Passarinho, Professor Alberto Dines, Ambassador João Clemente Baena Soares, Brigadier Rui Moreira Lima, Capitan Corrêa, Vivien Ishaq, Professor Maria Celina D'Araújo, Professor Carlos Fico, Regina Souza, Cleofas Santiago, Ricardo Corrêa, Jane Ferreira, Fridinan Caitano, José Pinto, Seu João, Dona Dalva, Dona Tereza, Clarino Santos, and an anonymous local politician. I also wish to thank Seu Tião of the Conjunto da Maré for his kind assistance in establishing my contacts in the community and in granting me safe passage.

Most important, I wish to thank Dr. Matthias Röhrig Assunção, Professor Edward J. Higgs, Dr. Jeremy Krikler, Professor Anthony W. Pereira, and Professor Kenneth P. Serbin for their valuable comments on this work. I am deeply grateful to the Department of History at the University of Essex, the Arts and Humanities Research Council, and the EU FP7 Marie Curie ZIF Program at the University of Konstanz (grant no. 291784) for their support of this book project. I also warmly thank my acquiring editors at the University Press of

Florida, Amy Gorelick, Meredith Morris-Babb, and Nevil Parker for their much appreciated help and guidance; Lisa McKee for her wonderful proofreading work; Iñaki Rañó, Leila Kazimova, Nadja Ruther, Sylvia Baur, and Julia Masser for their superb technical and graphical support; my friend and colleague Rebecca J. Atencio for her greatly valued advice; and my longtime friend Meike Strüber for her intellectual and moral involvement. Last, I send special thanks to my mother and her partner, Christiane and Götz Osteroth, to my father and his partner, Klaus D. Schneider and Edda Baldauf, and to my grandmother, Christa Peters, for their love and support.

Introduction

Legitimizing an Authoritarian Regime—Brazil

The Brazilian Regime

During the 1960s and 1970s, in the midst of the Cold War, authoritarian regimes seized power throughout most of Latin America. While the case of the former Chilean dictator, Augusto Pinochet, who narrowly escaped prosecution, is legendary, by contrast few people are familiar with the military regime in Brazil.[1] The authoritarian government in Brazil ruled between 1964 and 1985, making it one of the longest-lasting military regimes in the southern cone. While the process of transitioning to democracy was "negotiated," as in most Latin American countries (except in Argentina, where the regime collapsed), the unique aspect of the Brazilian transition was its lengthy and gradual process of political opening, initiated by military president Ernesto Geisel (1974–1979).[2] Geisel instigated the so-called *distensão* (literally "depressurization"),[3] which led to a marked reduction in human-rights crimes prior to the regime's demise. The Brazilian people played a crucial part in the transition process, because large sectors of the population mobilized in support of a return to democracy from 1975 onward. While much of the literature continues to assert that this novel military policy was primarily driven "from above,"[4] other scholars have claimed that it was largely demanded "from below," as the regime's popularity declined in the 1970s.[5] As summarized by Alfred P. Montero, the transition entailed a mixture of government-initiated gradual opening and control and popular mobilization in the form of the so-called Brazilian amnesty movement.[6]

Arguably the most important distinguishing characteristic of the authoritarian regime in Brazil was its fundamentally ambiguous character, which fluctuated between authoritarian principles and democratic pretense.[7] Although the regime was not democratic, it made a great effort to create the appearance of a democracy and to avoid comparisons with a dictatorship. Democratic institutions and procedures were maintained but in a distorted form. The traditional legal system remained, but it was overlaid by an arbitrary "revolutionary" legal system composed of institutional acts.

The regime justified these additional decrees by referring to a diffuse notion of "national security."[8] During the Cold War, national security provided a common and convenient argument for many states to justify authoritarian decrees. They claimed that the threat of communism would jeopardize national security, even though this threat was often spurious and merely used as a pretext for increasing state control. In authoritarian Brazil, Congress continued to sit but was closed when it disobeyed the regime's orders.[9] Indirect elections to Congress were manipulated, yet they continued to be held, unlike in authoritarian Chile (1973–1990) or Argentina (1976–1983). The military regime in Brazil used the word *democracy* as a synonym for *anticommunist state*, rather than to mean a representative system that protected people's rights.

The illegal regime used various methods to maintain its grip on power. It suspended the political rights of its opponents for ten years (*cassações*), forced dissenting civil servants and military officials to retire, and, most importantly, used political repression in the form of exile, prison, torture, murder, and disappearance. According to the first official report by the Brazilian government in 2007, the estimated overall number of dead and disappeared in military Brazil is relatively low, at a total of 474. Compare this with Argentina, where estimates are in the region of 20,000–30,000, and Chile, which saw between 3,000 and 5,000 assassinations.[10] This first figure, however, is currently subject to revision; the number of victims may increase in the final report of the Brazilian Truth Commission, expected in 2014.[11] Yet despite this much smaller number of victims and the fact that repression in Brazil was largely selective (at least to our current knowledge), affecting primarily left-wing groups who opposed the regime, we must not forget that torture nonetheless became a systematic state procedure from 1969/70 onward. Vladimir Safatle and Edson Teles have furthermore argued that the Brazilian dictatorship's death toll was much higher, because it created long-term structures of violence, in the form of police repression and death squads, which increased homicide rates after formal democratization.[12]

Brazilians had experienced torture before, but it was the installation, in 1969/70, of notorious repressive organs—the so-called Center of Internal Defense Operations–Detachment of Intelligence Operations (Centro de Operações de Defesa Interna–Destacamento de Operações de Informações, CODI-DOI)—that institutionalized human-rights violations. In July 1969, the so-called Operation Bandeirantes (OBAN) was installed, which was financed by São Paulo and international businesses and already staffed by the armed forces and local police units. The CODI-DOI institutionalized and expanded the repressive structures of the OBAN on the basis of a secret decree-law passed by the National Security Council.[13] In the literature it is also called DOI-CODI; however, as technically the DOI was under the CODI, this book uses the formally more correct term CODI-DOI.[14] Yet the military regime did not maintain power by force alone but employed more subtle mechanisms for manufacturing consent; these less obvious strategies to control society and legitimize forms of illegal rule have been overlooked.[15] Investigating the official propaganda of authoritarian Brazil tells us how the regime tried to justify its rule and thus provides hints about the true nature of the regime.

The propaganda of authoritarian Brazil also had a long-term effect. Just as there has been much political and legal continuity from authoritarianism to democracy in post-1985 Brazil, vital motives and justifications for authoritarian propaganda still shape the struggle over how Brazilians remember the dictatorship. Analyzing the regime's official propaganda helps us to discover and deconstruct the remnants of authoritarian propaganda in present-day Brazil.

Although, in 1995, the Brazilian state officially assumed responsibility for the victims of this systematic repression, to this day no post-1985 civilian government has prosecuted any military officials implicated in those human-rights violations. The perpetrators were granted full amnesty by the Amnesty Law of 1979, which has never been revoked. In 2008, the Brazilian Lawyers Association (OAB) appealed to the Supreme Court to investigate whether the Amnesty Law was constitutional, but their request was rejected in April 2010.[16] Six months later, the Inter-American Court of Human Rights (IACHR) of the Organization of American States (OAS) ruled that the Brazilian Amnesty Law violated international human-rights law, leading to an open confrontation between Brazil and the international human-rights community.[17] In most other Latin American countries, officials from the repressive organs have been punished, or prosecutions are ongoing. In Brazil, Colonel Brilhante Ustra alone, head of the CODI-DOI in São Paulo between 1970 and 1974, was symbolically tried in 2007 and "morally" condemned for torture in August 2012. In December 2009, the Brazilian Human Rights Minister, Paulo Vannuchi, suggested creating a National Truth Commission to clarify cases of human-rights crimes, but even this non-retributive proposal met with resistance and led to a government crisis.[18] In May 2012, twenty-seven years after the return to formal democracy, a so-called National Truth Commission (Commissão Nacional da Verdade) was instated to shed light on the human-rights abuses committed by agents of the state.

Another key characteristic of the regime in Brazil that is crucial to understanding the authoritarian propaganda that it generated is its internal division into different military camps.[19] Propaganda production constituted a contested field, a battle zone between the "hardliners" (*linha dura*) and "moderates," sometimes also called "softliners" or "Sorbonne." These terms are applicable to both military officers and civilians, and they represent a highly problematic heuristic categorization, but it is the only one currently available.[20] The term "hardliner" denotes those who supported violent repression and favored the continuation of military rule.[21] Hardliners demanded that opponents of the regime be tortured or even killed. They believed that Brazil was engaged in a kind of civil war and that the regime needed to eliminate alleged communists by any means available for the sake of national security. Although hardliners did not believe in the principles underlying liberal democracy, they nonetheless used its rhetoric.[22] The label "moderates" is applied to people who were also authoritarian but rejected repression "in principle," justifying it only in exceptional cases.[23] Moderates furthermore regarded military rule as a transitional phase, with their ultimate goal being the handing over of power to civilians. Anne-Marie Smith has rightly pointed out that the so-called moderates were defined as such only in contrast to the hardliners, not because of their benevolence.[24]

Although the classifications of moderates and hardliners are very general, they are nonetheless useful for describing the friction that occurred between the appointed propaganda officials who belonged to the moderate camp and their hardliner antagonists. Only insiders would know that the arena of propaganda production constituted a highly contested field, because the authoritarian regime tried to portray itself as united and to prevent any information about inner conflicts from reaching the Brazilian public. The official authoritarian propaganda also served as an instrument for concealing problems within the regime.

The Coup

On March 31, 1964, General Olímpio Mourão Filho, commander of the fourth military region in Juiz de Fora, in the state of Minas Gerais, launched a coup against the legally elected president, João Goulart, and forced him into exile. While numerous military officers rejected supporting the coup and later faced repression, those military officials involved called this act a revolution—a euphemistic and politically biased term that is still prevalent among supporters of the regime in modern-day Brazil.[25] The new military government started to arrest, forcibly retire, and dismiss from their jobs thousands of Brazilian citizens. Although many left-wing military officers, who supported Goulart, along with university students, intellectuals, and labor officials, disapproved of the coup, no substantial opposition arose. On the contrary, sectors of the upper and middle classes took to the streets of Rio de Janeiro to celebrate the military intervention. Most people therefore prefer to think of it as a civilian-military, rather than a strictly military, coup.[26] The term "civilian-military coup," however, is also problematic, because it has been used by revisionists who defend the dictatorship, arguing that it was "called for" by the Brazilian people.

The seizure of power had numerous causes.[27] Brazil was confronted with a combination of economic, fiscal, and political crises, namely huge foreign debts, hyperinflation, and, most importantly, an increasingly mobilized labor movement. President Goulart had gradually moved further to the left and promised major reforms, including a historic land reform and the nationalization of private oil companies, thus undermining the benefits enjoyed by large parts of the upper and middle classes.[28]

The Ideological Roots of the Regime's Propaganda

The rhetoric and arguments of the regime's propaganda were rooted in traditional Brazilian authoritarian thought, the National Security Doctrine (NSD) developed by the Superior War School (ESG), and developmentalist ideas, particularly those of the Superior Institute of Brazilian Studies (ISEB).[29] The Superior War School was a civilian-military think tank that, during the early 1960s, gained formal power among the military.[30] It provided the "revolution's" key ideology, the National Security Doctrine, and functioned as a "network of influence," since many civilian and military leaders were ESG graduates.[31] The ESG came under the direct influence of the U.S. War College.[32] The NSD originally evolved after the military dismantled the empire in 1889. Since then, the military had clung to the belief that it should be in charge for the good of the Brazilian nation.[33] At the beginning of the twentieth century, the NSD held that the army was the only force capable of overcoming regional differences and solving the nation's problems.

In the context of the Cold War, the ESG refined the NSD; the major innovation was that it now insisted upon the constant threat from "internal enemies," which laid the basis for an arbitrary system of power and repression. Much like McCarthy's anticommunist witch hunt in the United States, which made all citizens vulnerable to scrutiny, every Brazilian citizen was considered a potential communist and thus a threat to the nation. The new role of the military was no longer to "moderate," nor to resist, an external invasion, but to defy these potential enemies that were believed to be capable of psychologically infiltrating the minds of Brazilians.[34]

Brazil was not an exceptional case. In the context of the Cold War, theories of "total war," which highlighted "internal threats," achieved prominence throughout the whole of Latin America. Labor movements were regarded as "communist subversions." It was believed that in underdeveloped countries more workers would be seduced by communism than in industrialized nations. The Brazilian version of the Security Doctrine contained some insoluble contradictions. The process of aligning with the "Occident" and "democracy" was incompatible with the construction of the ubiquitous internal enemy, which had to be combatted with authoritarian means. Justifying the creation of this security system depended on the construction of an internal enemy, even if none existed.[35] The discrepancy between democratic rhetoric and oppressive reality led to a permanent legitimacy crisis, or to what Lucia Klein has termed "emptiness of legitimacy," which propaganda and censorship attempted to fill.[36] Its profession of adherence to democracy limited the regime's totalitarian actions. Smith has phrased this concisely, stating that the regime was "constrained by a notably ambivalent yet continuous search for legitimacy."[37]

The second main principle espoused by the NSD was that national security depended on development that was regarded as the ideal antidote to communism.[38] Improving living standards was not a by-product but a strategic goal.[39] According to the ESG's key ideologist, Golbery da Silva Couto, the nation's well-being had to be sacrificed for security if necessary. Development theories were partly provided by the ISEB—the think tank of developmentalists between 1954 and 1964. Different ideological streams coexisted among *isebianos*, but core aspects recurred in the regime's propaganda, such as the abolition of class distinctions, social pacification, the goal of national unity, and the realization of the "common good" in order to overcome political, cultural, and economic underdevelopment.[40] The required development was to be led by the state. Other ideas borrowed from the ideology of "developmentism," which was prominent under Juscelino Kubitschek's presidency (1955–1960), were the goals of prosperity, peace, and sovereignty; the emphasis on "order and security" to safeguard development; the highlighting of the democratic and Christian traditions; anticommunism; nationalism; and the belief in "national grandeur" as Brazil's destiny (Brasil Grande).

The NSD held that it was the responsibility of the political elite to lead the masses, who were believed to be susceptible to communism. This vein of traditional authoritarian thought inherent in the NSD is significant in regard to the so-called moderates and hardliners. Friction existed among the three branches of the armed forces (land army, air force, and navy), as well as among those of different military ranks, institutions, economic viewpoints, and ideological camps.[41] Yet, despite these frictions, most of which had roots that preceded the 1964 coup, the regime nonetheless maintained sufficient unity to rule for two decades. Why then did the regime not break down earlier?

While some scholars claim that the NSD was a common denominator, Carlos Fico, in contrast, argues that the military was united not by the doctrine but by an "authoritarian utopia," a term coined by Maria Celina D'Araújo.[42] This "utopia" espoused the superiority of the military over the unprepared masses and the necessity of a certain degree of violence. However, the "authoritarian utopia," which was inherent in the NSD, was so vague that it was able to serve as a basis for both the moderates and the hardliners.[43] Both military factions used NSD rhetoric, although with quite different intentions.[44]

Early Propaganda (1962–1968)

During the first phase, in preparation for the coup, two private organizations launched huge propaganda campaigns: the IPÊS and IBAD. They intended to replace the Goulart government, prevent his reform policies, and reorganize Brazil's economy. These pre-coup propaganda organizations were comprised of both civilians and military officers and were cofinanced by national and international enterprises.[45] Importantly, strong personal affiliations existed between the IPÊS and the Superior War School. One of the key ESG ideologists, General Golbery, was also a leading member of the IPÊS.

The IPÊS was officially founded in February 1962 as a civil association with an interest in "cultural, moral, and civic education."[46] Ruth Leacock and René Dreifuss claim that both institutions were financially supported by the CIA, and the first director-general of the IBAD was suspected to be a CIA agent. The IPÊS probably received funding from U.S. businesses.[47] Dreifuss argues that "multinational and associated interest groups" gradually infiltrated and ultimately took control of the Brazilian state: initially, they expanded networks and organizational structures in order to spread their ideology, starting in approximately 1948 with the founding of the Superior War School. Thus "conservative-modernizing" ideas blossomed in various forms among the "dominant class," in think tanks, like the Getúlio Vargas Foundation, and in civil society organizations, like the Commercial Association of São Paulo (FIESP), long before the coup took place. According to Dreifuss, between 1961 and 1964 new organizations, including the IPÊS and IBAD, were formed with the direct aim of destroying the Goulart government. The campaigns run by the IPÊS and IBAD, which Dreifuss describes as "ideologically bourgeois," directly paved the way for the coup.[48] Thus the coup was not just the result of a political-economic crisis but of an active step by the "multinational and associated block" that was only made possible through the careful orchestration of the massive propaganda campaign launched by the IPÊS and IBAD prior to the coup.

The IPÊS and IBAD used various means to disseminate their message: books and pamphlets, conferences and seminars, "education campaigns," short films, television programs, and advertisements on television and radio.[49] They financed ten television programs and short films with patriotic titles such as *Brazil Needs You*, all of which had a happy ending.[50] It is clear that the IPÊS and IBAD produced large quantities of propaganda, something that was only made possible by the enormous private donations they received.[51] Besides running media campaigns, the IPÊS and IBAD actively infiltrated organizations to spread anticommunist ideas, attack the executive, and promote the notion that the living conditions of the Brazilian people would only improve through the involvement of private businesses, rather than the state. The female wing of the IPÊS organized more than four hundred "marches of the family with God for liberty" which were directed against communism and in defense of "the family and Christian morals."[52] Dreifuss maintains that the IPÊS and IBAD ultimately succeeded in creating an "atmosphere of political inquietude," destabilizing the Goulart government, and convincing parts of the armed forces to actively intervene against "chaos" and "communism."[53] The archives of the IPÊS were later used by the Brazilian intelligence service (Serviço Nacional de Informações, SNI), which provided information to the organs of repression and thus enabled human-rights violations from behind the scenes.

The fact that the first propaganda organs (IPÊS and IBAD) were predominantly supported by business enterprises may explain why most propaganda scholars have automatically assumed that the later propaganda-producing bodies—Assessoria Especial de Relações Públicas (AERP) and Assessoria Especial de Relações Públicas (ARP)—were necessarily linked to business interests, too. However, we will see that the AERP and ARP were in fact led by military officials who apparently retained only negligible links with businessmen. The final report by the AERP, which recapitulates the operating structure and output of the organization since 1968, does not mention any business contacts, and neither does a single oral history interview. In contrast to the IPÊS and IBAD, the available sources suggest that the AERP and ARP were financed exclusively by the state and not by private businesses or the CIA.[54] The AERP and ARP staff maintained complete editorial control: they planned the campaigns, wrote the text, edited the productions if necessary, and checked the final version before it was broadcast.[55] In addition to these crucial institutional differences, the shrewd, subtle philosophy that AERP mastermind Costa adopted toward propaganda contrasted starkly with the blunt and even aggressive propaganda style of the IPÊS and IBAD. Nonetheless, IPÊS' self-proclaimed agenda of "moral and civic education" reappeared in later propaganda produced by the regime and included the following features: the acceleration of the country's development; the improvement of living standards; and the preservation of national unity through a "program of integration" of the various regions of Brazil that had been developing at different rates.

After 1964, although propaganda justifying the coup continued to be produced, it was poorly organized, and no systematic campaigns were launched.[56] The first military president, Humberto de Alencar Castello Branco (1964–1967), had a press secretary, a common position in many democratic regimes, but rejected a formal propaganda institution, like the former Department of Press and Propaganda (DIP). The DIP was the first centralized propaganda organ in the history of Brazil. Between 1939 and 1945, during the dictatorship of Getúlio Vargas, the DIP attempted to gain public support. It was a major organization, with branch offices in every state, but, unlike the AERP and ARP, the DIP was simultaneously responsible for censorship and propaganda.[57] It actively produced propaganda itself, including the newspaper *Cultura Política*. Branco rejected the establishment of a propaganda institution on the grounds that it would make the military regime seem too much like the Vargas dictatorship.

The term used by officials from the authoritarian propaganda organs, AERP and ARP, both in oral history interviews and in their publications, is not "propaganda" but the more neutral "social communication" (*communicação social*). This raises some important questions: Was this a euphemism? Did they actually produce "propaganda" or "civic education campaigns?" And how should propaganda be defined?

Propaganda is a complex category; the term initially referred to institutions that spread a doctrine, but this meaning was later transferred to the dogma itself.[58] In the nineteenth century, it described the technique used to propagate a doctrine. Approaches to propaganda can be divided into broad definitions, which locate propaganda close to information, and narrow definitions. Both narrow and broad approaches have their own particular advantages. The concept of propaganda is like a chameleon that loses its intellectual insight when one tries to force it into an inflexible, oversimplified definition.

Jacques Driencourt and Jacques Ellul, for instance, argue that everything that is said constitutes propaganda and that the strategies and outlets of propaganda remain the same, regardless of whether a democratic or an authoritarian system is producing it.[59] The disadvantage of a broad definition is that in the context of a military regime it is "politically toothless";[60] the distinction between education, information, and propaganda is blurred. Yet this broad perspective on propaganda has the advantage of highlighting historical continuities and illuminating the fact that the main transmitters of propaganda—the media—are often private monopolies, as in the case of Brazil. Scholars like Qualter thus claim that the distinctive feature of propaganda is that it has a specific purpose,[61] and this purpose is always linked with an interest in maximizing the propagandist's power.

Borrowing from Terry Eagleton's work on ideology, this book distinguishes between epistemological and functional falsehood. Epistemological truth is produced if an assertion is valid.[62] For example, the military president, Emilio G. Médici (1969–1974), proclaiming that the inflation rate was 3 percent, when in fact it was 20 percent, can be considered epistemologically false. However, often ideas that are epistemologically true are still used for the "functional maintenance of an oppressive power."[63] For example, while the military regime in Brazil accurately quoted the high percentage of economic growth achieved in the late 1960s and early 1970s, this can nonetheless be considered functionally false, because it justifies the regime's policy, despite its human-rights violations. The purpose is, of course, highly contextual and therefore crucial to propaganda analysis.

To illustrate this point, an apparently apolitical "Don't drink and drive" propaganda short film produced during the military regime might not be considered propaganda today, because it would no longer be functionally false, as it has lost its purpose of distracting Brazilians from being critical of the systematic human-rights breaches by the state that occurred under military rule. In order to comment on "functional propaganda" it is necessary to consider the relationship between the proclamation and its function within a specific historical situation.[64] The idea of "functional" truth also helps to distinguish advertisements from political propaganda, as the purpose of the advertisement is always to sell a product. Looking at both the epistemological and functional truth, this book verifies whether proclamations were factually true or false and ascertains whether the purpose of an assertion was legitimate, with due attention to the historical context.

In order to acknowledge the different kinds of propaganda, I opted to introduce attributes and distinguish among three types: subliminal, blunt, and aggressive pro-regime propaganda. All three forms are used in a negative sense, to describe the deliberate attempt by a politically involved institution or company to strengthen, alter, or form public opinion through the monopolization and transmission of ideas and values, with the intention to make the population react in the way desired by the propagandist. These ideas might be rational or irrational and epistemologically true or false. They are often, but not necessarily, affective and unconscious, and they attempt to naturalize ideas. Propaganda is limited to the "field of signification"; it principally comprises the mass media and symbols, such as flags, but excludes political acts, such as murder.[65]

However, there are crucial differences among these three categories, and they vary in the degree of their negative connotations. Subliminal propaganda, the least negatively connoted form, is defined as an attempt to win general support for the military regime, yet draws a veil over some specific characteristics, most importantly violent repression. I will provide more examples in chapter 2, but, to give a general idea, a subliminal propaganda film would be a "Don't drink and drive" film or one advising people to vaccinate their children. While subliminal propaganda reiterates specific values that lent the regime stability (order, security, patriotism, and striving for economic development, for example), thereby supporting it indirectly, this type of propaganda deliberately refuses to intimidate, threaten, construct enemies, or justify violence. Subliminal-propaganda films do not use slogans like "Beware of the communists around every corner" or "Beware of the naughty student who misbehaves when protesting against this government." Its key characteristics are the omission of violence, of the arbitrary regime and its agents, and the emphasis on the positive aspects of the regime (for example, more babies being vaccinated each year). Subliminal propaganda is indirect and hidden and only recognizable as propaganda with knowledge of its specific historical context. It appears apolitical in its focus on everyday topics and does not show politicians or discuss politics.[66] Most of the AERP and ARP campaigns are best characterized as subliminal pro-regime propaganda.

Blunt propaganda, in contrast, directly praises the arbitrary regime, specifies the names of agents, even to the extent of creating a personality cult, directly hails government programs and actions, and uses stereotypes. It is a form of obvious pro-regime propaganda or, in Brazilian Portuguese, *chapa branca*. To illustrate this, imagine a short film showing the construction of a new highway. The accompanying voice-over declares: "This government has built two hundred thousand kilometers of more highways in the Amazon region. Brazil's progress cannot be stopped." Chapter 3 illustrates how significant parts of the privately owned media, most importantly the Globo network, promoted the military regime much more openly than the official organs of the AERP and ARP, thereby clearly qualifying as blunt propaganda. Both blunt and subliminal propaganda attempted to enhance the self-esteem of the Brazilian population.[67]

Aggressive propaganda is the most negatively connoted and repressive form of propaganda. Aggressive propaganda glorifies the regime by promoting violence, clearly constructing enemies, creating a personality cult around military leaders, and praising organs of repression. The agents behind aggressive propaganda are the most difficult to trace, but they can be located among outbreaks of violence promoting hardliners and their supporters. Aggressive propaganda is closely related to psychological-war propaganda—sometimes also called revolutionary-war propaganda—which uses intimidating campaigns in addition to physical violence. It was based on a radical anticommunism that had traditionally existed within the Brazilian armed forces to some extent but had been significantly sharpened in the context of the Cold War. This revolutionary-war propaganda was likewise characterized by the construction of a clearly defined enemy, expressed in the jargon of the hardliners as "communists," "subversives," or simply "the left" (*a esquerda*), which, in this context, meant a "delinquent" or was intended as an obscenity. Revolutionary-war and psychological-war propaganda are specifically linked to the context of the Cold War and of the military regime; I opted for the more general classification, aggressive propaganda, yet I use these terms as synonyms. Throughout this book I show that aggressive propaganda contrasted strongly with the AERP and ARP philosophy and was mainly produced by hardliners.

In summary, all three types of propaganda—subliminal, blunt, and aggressive pro-regime propaganda—were intended to win support for a military dictatorship that secured its illegal power through targeted (at least to our current knowledge) yet systematic repression and censorship. However, while aggressive propaganda directly promoted violence, subliminal propaganda omitted the arbitrary facets of the regime, thereby lending itself to several interpretations that are examined in this book. Ascribing attributes does not mean that we have to choose between an entirely neutral and a negative definition of propaganda, which would lead to an oversimplification of the complex nature of propaganda. Instead, it allows us to describe a spectrum of propaganda, ranging from subliminal as the least negatively connoted form to aggressive propaganda as the most negatively connoted type.

✳

Within the last fifteen years the civilian-military regime in Brazil has become a vibrant field of research.[68] The Brazilian National Truth Commission (2012–2014) and the more than eighteen local Memory, Truth, and Justice Commissions are expected to expand our knowledge about the regime. The Brazilian government is also giving incentives to scholarly research about lesser-known aspects of the dictatorship, and the fiftieth anniversary of the military coup, in 2014, will generate a wave of new publications. However, our knowledge about the official propaganda of authoritarian Latin America is still very limited.[69] This book investigates the defining characteristics of the official propaganda produced in authoritarian Brazil, drawing on valuable oral history interviews with former propaganda officials, since the full administrative documentation of the AERP and ARP is unavailable.[70] Analyzing the official propaganda enables a greater understanding of how the military regime in Brazil tried to legitimize itself and what was distinctive about this particular regime. This book elucidates the varying degrees of perpetratorship during the military regime in Brazil and aims to kick-start a debate on civil collaboration.

1

Small and "Democratic"?

The Official Propaganda Institution

Development and Function

Propaganda during the military regime can be divided into three phases.[1] In the first phase (1962–1968), propaganda was organized by civilian-military private organizations and initially characterized by anti-Goulart slogans. In the second phase (1968–1974), under President Artur da Costa e Silva (1967–1969) and his successor, Emilio Garrastazú Médici (1969–1974), a systematic propaganda organ was created, shortly before press censorship was introduced, which continued until the establishment of the Geisel government. After an interim period without a formal propaganda organ (1974–1975), the third propaganda phase (1976–1979) commenced under the leadership of Ernesto Geisel. Press censorship declined sharply, and systematic propaganda production was reinstated, albeit using slightly different legitimizations. The most important and organized phases of authoritarian propaganda in Brazil were the second and third phases (1968–1979), which form the core subject of this book.

In military Brazil, a conventional government-led propaganda institution was not installed until 1968. This initial reluctance to create a propaganda organ, along with its institutional structure, methods and content, reflected not only the ideals of the moderate camp but also the regime's fear of appearing authoritarian. Just as the military had justified the seizure of power as being in "defense of democracy," it was important that the whole authoritarian propaganda process should look as democratic as possible.

As the 1964 regime became increasingly unpopular, the need for a systematic propaganda policy became more urgent. An opinion poll by the private Brazilian Institute of Public Opinion (IBOPE) revealed that the military government had a dreadful reputation. Brazilians were dissatisfied with the economic situation and largely disinterested in politics.[2] Thus, in 1967, a small and barely financed agency, called Group for Public Relations, was founded by Hernani d'Aguiar, a close friend of President Costa e Silva, with the aim of enhancing the president's popularity.[3] In order to coordinate the government's public relations work (hereafter PR), a seminar was convened for the PR officials of the sixteen federal ministries. It proposed a propaganda policy that would bring the Brazilian people closer to the government by highlighting its achievements, and on January 15, 1968, the regime finally created the Special Public Relations Consultancy (AERP), which remained in place until 1974.[4] The AERP was founded discreetly and was initially almost unknown but later attracted more frequent mention in the press, which reported on statements made by its leader, Octávio Costa, or announced new campaigns.[5] However, beyond this negligible press readership, the AERP and ARP continued to attract little recognition and, interestingly, until 2007, the AERP remained absent from historical dictionaries and reference works.[6]

The reason why the AERP came into existence at that particular moment is the subject of much debate. Fico argues that the pro-propaganda faction among the military succeeded in overruling the camp that rejected the use of propaganda. As such, propaganda was not a defensive response to the growing political opposition but an inherent strategy to strengthen military rule.[7] In contrast, Sérgio Caparelli relates it to the increasing opposition from students, workers, politicians, intellectuals, and progressive Catholics who held rallies in major cities in the late 1960s.[8] Statements from AERP officials confirm the second hypothesis. In a final report summarizing the work of the AERP shortly before its closure, Costa explains: "Only because social incidents in 1968 put pressure [on the government] was it [AERP] installed on a permanent basis."[9] Odair Lima correctly points out that initially the coup was backed by powerful groups, including businessmen, the press, the middle classes, and the church. It is plausible that propaganda only became perceived as necessary when support vanished in 1967/68.[10] When public opinion took a more favorable turn again, during the period of the economic "miracle," from 1969 onward, the AERP had already established its position.

After the brief leadership of Colonel Hernani D'Aguiar, the AERP was masterminded by Colonel Octávio Costa, who introduced a very different propaganda style. D'Aguiar's films looked like obvious propaganda, with their constant emphasis on the "Great Brazil." Great Brazil (Brasil Grande) is a subcategory characterized by a mixture of subliminal and blunt propaganda. Films of this type exaggerated the natural resources of Brazil and stirred patriotism by pointing to the various potential riches offered by the country but without necessarily directly praising the government. In contrast to subliminal propaganda, the message or feeling conveyed (self-esteem, national pride) is very clear. This type of "ufanistic" propaganda often perpetuated by the media was rejected by the AERP and ARP. Literally, the word "ufanistic" means "boastful nationalism" or "chauvinism." In the case of Brazil it alludes to the country's natural riches.[11]

In contrast, Costa's films—called *filmetes*—did not resemble official propaganda.[12] Apparently, D'Aguiar's "official" propaganda had been unpopular.[13] The AERP films, however, dealt with everyday subjects that people could relate to, such as family, work, and patriotism, and were dominated by images and music, with a small amount of text at the end, often a moral. Costa's new propaganda strategy, officially ratified on November 20, 1970, demanded that the films stick to ostensibly apolitical topics, contain no references to military leaders or politicians (Costa rejected personality cults), transmit positive values and "optimism" instead of constructing enemies (he avoided attacking communists), and be aesthetically appealing and modern, in contrast to the previous formal and uninspiring programs.[14]

Costa's tactics furthermore involved maintaining a democratic appearance, through keeping personnel and financial resources to a minimum, limiting institutional size, and employing an indirect production procedure. The AERP was deliberately small: besides its headquarters in Brasília, it had two branches, one in Rio and one in São Paulo, with a total of fifty employees, of whom the decision-making core constituted a mere six.[15] Colonel Octávio Costa, Colonel José Maria Toledo Camargo, and João Baena Soares were project coordinators, while Alberto Rabaça and the journalist Sérgio Freddy were responsible for the productions in Rio and São Paulo, respectively. The psychologist and philosopher José Cavalieri served as a consultant. The AERP was thus led by a military colonel, but its core team consisted of one military official and four civilian employees. The AERP headquarters in Brasília were located on the fourth floor of the Planalto (the building where the president and the government are based), the branch in Rio in the Treasury Building, and the São Paulo office in the town hall.[16] Its small size was deliberately designed to discourage associations with the former DIP, the much larger propaganda organ of the Vargas dictatorship, with branch offices in every Brazilian regional state. In the press, Costa regularly drew attention to its lack of human and material resources, so as to refute comparisons with the DIP.[17] Thus the institutional structure itself was intended to distract from the authoritarian nature of the regime and maintain a democratic façade.

The democratic pretense was also reflected in the typical production procedure. The AERP and ARP team decided on themes and objectives and hired private media agencies, which competed to produce the films, thereby constituting a kind of outsourcing process.[18] Thus the AERP controlled the content, but it did not produce the films themselves. This allowed the AERP to keep personnel and operational costs to a minimum and maintain a democratic appearance. In contrast to the huge propaganda machines of authoritarian states that directly produced propaganda, like the DIP or the Reichspropagandaamt under the Nazis, the AERP and ARP formed a minimal PR organ that "democratically" made use of private production companies. Costa also instructed other public PR organs to employ private agencies wherever possible. Hiring private production firms had the additional advantage of supporting free market ideas perpetuated by the regime at the time.[19] The knowledge and experience of professionals also improved the aesthetic quality of the films, which was outstandingly high in the case of the AERP and ARP. Moreover, unlike the DIP and the Reichspropagandaamt, the AERP and ARP were not simultaneously responsible for censorship. The official authoritarian propaganda was furthermore distinct from the mobilizing propaganda of the Nazi or Soviet regimes, which operated through completely different channels. The actual "participation" of ordinary Brazilians within the regime was not the desired objective; the intention was to create the illusion that they could participate.[20]

Formally, the AERP was directly linked to the president and disconnected from other official organs, like the Press Secretary or the official news agency, Agência Nacional. Decree Law No. 67,611 of November 19, 1970, established a so-called PR system of the government, and declared that the AERP should function as the central organ of that system.[21] According to the regulations, the PR sections of the state departments were obliged to coordinate all public campaigns with the AERP. In practice, the AERP's coordinating power was regularly sabotaged on two levels: on an institutional level, and on a level perhaps best described as personal-ideological. Institutions that carried out acts of sabotage included state departments, the Cabinet Office, and intelligence organs. In terms of personal-ideological opponents, so-called hardliners opposed Costa's moderate form of propaganda. Often those hardliners belonged to intelligence organs, but not always. They also held positions within other state administrative departments or private businesses. Other PR agencies ran a significant number of campaigns that violated the established AERP rules. They were aggressive, not peaceful; obvious, not subliminal; and, contrary to Costa's principle of "impersonality," worshipped government members or specific programs.

Costa's final report explicitly criticizes the AERP's "lack of status."[22] He complains about coordination problems with several secretaries of state and about their extraordinary expenditures; often they did not even keep records of exactly how much was spent on campaigns. Moreover, he complains that secretaries of state violated his rules by paying for favorable press articles and television reports in ufanistic (boastful) programs. In particular, he criticizes the treasury, arguing that the minister ran campaigns merely to promote himself. The report also complains about other organizations that attempted to fill the AERP's free time slots.[23] In addition to evidence from oral history interviews and Costa's final report, evidence of attempts to sabotage the AERP's leadership role can be found in other sources. For instance, Costa sent a letter to the Marines' PR department, in which he asks them not to "contribute to a publicity orgy" and not to waste money on senseless PR publications planned for the commemoration of the tenth anniversary of the coup.[24] This letter shows that even as late as 1973 the AERP had not succeeded in centralizing the PR system. The final AERP report explicitly states that attempts to cooperate with the secretaries of state were abandoned in 1972, due to a lack of collaboration.

Yet the AERP's most committed antagonists were hardliners residing in the Cabinet Office and intelligence organs, most importantly the Brazilian intelligence system, the SNI. This might seem astounding, since the radical, authoritarian, right-wing camp would naturally be expected to support state propaganda. However, several interviews with former AERP officials, the final report, and even hints from the press provide evidence of frequent conflict. Both the leader of the AERP, Costa, and that of its successor organ, ARP, Camargo, repeatedly mention friction with the SNI and certain radical officials, an argument already put forward by Fico.[25] Interestingly, both portray this experience in terms of a "narrative of suffering." Costa repeatedly described how hardliners disrespected him and his subliminal-propaganda strategy and how powerless the AERP was compared to the SNI.[26] A constant enemy was the hardliner Hugo de Abreu, the leader of the Cabinet Office under Médici.[27] Although officially it was the task of the AERP leader to write speeches for the president, Abreu dismissed Costa from his function as presidential ghostwriter, arguing that Costa's speeches were too lyrical.

More subtle hints alluding to friction can be found in Costa's final report, where his remarks about "repenting terrorists" on television also convey a critical undertone. At the time in question, terrorists who had been arrested were forced to repent in front of television cameras in a kind of mock trial. Costa writes: "The AERP gave technical support to some programs which inter-

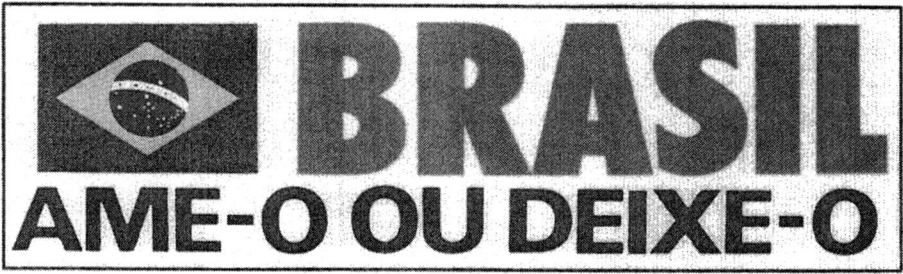

Figure 1.1. Love It or Leave It campaign, 1969–1970.

viewed repenting terrorists, an initiative of either television stations or security sectors."[28] This excerpt shows that he attempted to distance himself from those programs. The wording is very brief and unemotional, and he refutes any responsibility for such actions. This form of aggressive propaganda was designed to cause fear, not promote harmony, and clearly it violated Costa's propaganda rules. In oral history interviews, he affirmed his aversion to these programs.[29]

Another more obvious example of friction is the notorious hardliner campaign "Brazil: Love It or Leave It," which ran during the Bandeirantes Operation (OBAN) in June 1969. Stickers bearing that slogan were widely distributed. The Bandeirantes Operation (OBAN) was launched in São Paulo and aimed to weed out "subversive" suspects. It marked the beginning of the use of a systematic repressive organ, the Center of Internal Defense Operations–Detachment of Intelligence Operations (Centro de Operações de Defesa Interna-Destacamento de Operações de Informações, CODI-DOI).[30]

The OBAN was financed by São Paulo businessmen—something that was acknowledged in the press when one businessman, Boiensen, was assassinated by guerrilla groups in 1971.[31] The exact origin of the "Love It or Leave It" campaign is unclear, but its relationship to the OBAN is striking.[32] There is no evidence to suggest that private companies financed AERP campaigns, which were in fact state-sponsored.

There was constant discord between the intelligence service, SNI, and the AERP and ARP members. While it is more difficult to find concrete evidence of friction in the SNI files, these conflicts are repeatedly described in oral history interviews, and even *Veja* magazine alluded to them.[33] When, in 1971, the AERP was awarded a prize for its short films, *Veja* magazine claimed that these awards also "served to show the SNI and the direct advisers to the president [Hugo de Abreu] its [the AERP's] efficiency, who accompany and record their right and wrong decisions all the time."[34] To summarize, the propaganda organization and the repressive intelligence organs did not work together but, rather, were in a continual state of conflict.

✷

Each year the AERP's campaigns and goals were meticulously planned in advance. For each project, an annual plan established its goal, means, budget, and length and determined who the addressee and project coordinator would be. The budget set in 1970 increased in 1972 and again in 1973, when the AERP spent five times as much as the original budget.[35] According to the final AERP report, the AERP received 2,500,000 cruzeiros from the Civil Cabinet each year and 1,000,000 copy allowances from the National Cinema Institute (INC), hosted by the ministry for education and culture (MEC).[36] The production companies received a document containing detailed instructions, including technical specifications, the intended addressee, and a comment to the producer. Thus the production process operated under what was termed "global monitoring."[37] The AERP generally announced campaigns by sending letters to mayors and schools, with the goal of prompting schools to organize parallel events that would support the campaign.[38]

In addition to propaganda production and the coordination of the communication system, another task assigned to the AERP was to assist foreign journalists and official guests. Until its closure, the AERP gave support to 285 foreign journalists by organizing their accommodations, customs duty, and authorizations and establishing contacts with government officials.[39] Furthermore, in AERP's first year, its officials frequently gave talks at schools and cultural and business associations, intending to "establish a canal of approximation between the government and these areas."[40] For example, Costa delivered a speech at the Superior War School on April 23, 1970, and at the Federal Police Department in July 1970. Sérgio Freddy, the AERP representative in São Paulo, gave a speech at the Shop Owners' Club in Santos in October 1970. They eventually stopped giving talks because the invitations became too frequent to keep up with—on average one per day.[41]

Numerous oral history interviews confirm that military president Médici did not get involved with the AERP's work.[42] Costa was disappointed about Médici's lack of interest and recognition. Nonetheless, despite the permanent vigilance of the SNI and radical officials, Costa was allowed to choose his propaganda strategy independently. The question must be raised as to why hardliners never exerted enough pressure to remove Costa from office. While Costa depicts the AERP as a weak institution, it was nonetheless able to defend its propaganda philosophy. This might have been because Costa was respected among powerful parts of the armed forces and was friendly with important journalists. However, it could also indicate that hardliners lacked sufficient support.

Means and Delivery

The AERP and ARP disseminated propaganda through several channels, which are outlined in the annual production catalogues. One particularly favored method was making short films for television and cinema. The organizations also did radio broadcasts and disseminated publications, mainly of the president's speeches. The AERP experimented with various methods in the early stages. Initially, they distributed Médici's biography and his inaugural speech throughout the interior of Brazil. However, they subsequently stopped, due to criticism depicting them as the "new DIP."[43] They even tried to shoot a prime-time television series (*telenovela*) about Brazilian history, but the project failed due to its poor production quality. An exhibition on government achievements was also abandoned due to lack of interest.[44] The most important and innovative propaganda outlets were television and radio. Although the television audience was growing, radio continued to be the most important propaganda channel, as it was accessible to more people.[45]

According to a Brazilian media research department, in 1972 two-thirds of the Brazilian population could be reached by mass media.[46] Most Brazilians had access to radio, the main form of media in rural areas. According to a 1970 census, 59 percent of all Brazilian households had a radio, and this number had risen to 80 percent by 1972.[47] Slightly more than a third of all Brazilian households and 60 percent of urban homes had television sets in 1972.[48] Those who owned a television formed part of an intensive viewing culture at peak time in the evening, when 70 to 80 percent of all television sets were switched on.[49] It was calculated that between 42 and 48 percent of the urban population watched television during prime time in 1973. The television market increased by 20 percent per year, and even in the slums the number of antennas was growing. Throughout the course of the 1970s, the total number of households with television sets increased from 24 to 56 percent.[50]

In the case of cinema, market research conducted in 1974 showed that in the big urban centers 48 percent of Brazilians over fifteen were regular cinema-goers.[51] Most cinema-goers were younger than thirty (75 percent), came from a wealthy background, and were male (64 percent).[52] Thus, while in the late

Table 1. Total number of means of production, 1969–1977 (calculated based on the AERP and ARP production calendars)

Means	1969	1970	1971	1972	1973	1974	1975	1976	1977
Short Films	0	45	42	32	51	12	24	74	95
Documentaries	0	0	1	4	7	0	0	0	0
Reports	0	0	0	0	0	0	0	0	2
Photos of president	0	0	0	0	0	0	0	2	0
Radio productions	0	56	32	26	17	0	0	79	90
Musical scores	0	0	0	0	0	0	0	1	0
Leaflets and stickers	0	0	3	2	3	0	0	2	0
Posters	0	0	3	19	5	0	0	1	0
Publications	0	8	2	2	5	0	0	7	3
Total	0	109	83	85	88	12	24	166	190

1960s AERP short films largely reached the middle and upper classes, who were cinema-goers or possessed a television, nearly half of the urban population had the means to watch the films on television by 1973. Short films were of particular importance; Camargo called them the "backbone of the communication program."[53] According to AERP personnel and other witnesses, they were remembered vividly and were apparently very popular. During the AERP years the number of short films increased, while radio productions declined.[54] The short films were emblematic of the general campaigns; their themes and slogans were utilized by other media outlets, such as radio and poster productions.

The propaganda short films were shown both in cinemas and on television. The leader of the early AERP, D'Aguiar, had negotiated an agreement with the Brazilian Association for Television and Radio (ABERT), through which he acquired ten minutes of broadcasting time for the government free of charge. PR professionals openly criticized this "gentlemen's agreement."[55] Every fortnight, television broadcasters received two or three new AERP films. Generally, eighty copies of 16 mm film were produced for television: the vast majority, sixty-five copies, for São Paulo, ten for Brasília, and five for Rio. For cinema distribution the AERP produced 135 copies of 35 mm film. As of March 3, 1969, it became obligatory to show the propaganda short films in cinemas before the credits of the main feature, after the censorship certificate. The films arrived at Brazilian cinemas already attached to a copy of the feature film.[56] Thus Brazilian cinema audiences saw the short film first and then the feature film. A similar free-broadcasting policy applied to official radio propaganda. Every fortnight, the AERP provided radio stations with three new programs.[57]

The propaganda films were financed and copied by the ministry of education and culture (MEC), headed by Jarbas Passarinho. Passarinho was never involved in choosing their content or style; this was exclusively done by the AERP, and screenplay suggestions from outside sources were rejected.[58] The AERP maintained full editorial control, enabling them to pursue their subliminal-propaganda strategy. This indirect or hidden financing via the MEC, instead of through a separate budget, was yet another part of the strategy to portray the government as a democratic entity.

✳

The propaganda of the military regime actively catalyzed and benefited from the quantitative and qualitative "revolution" in mass media in the 1960s. The government's support for the distribution of equipment and the development of a media infrastructure was led by an interest in industrial modernization and "national integration," which were central propaganda messages and legitimizations. To maximize its audience, the regime distributed four thousand loudspeakers throughout the country to be used in public places.[59] At the time, mass media, and television in particular, were conceived of as innovations. Development theorists and politicians still believed in their unlimited power to manipulate and the crucial role they could play in "development."[60] A book by development theorist Wilbur Schramm strongly influenced both Costa and Camargo. Camargo even called Schramm's book the bible of the ARP's propaganda philosophy.[61] Costa's main propaganda principle—"motivation for development"—mirrors Schramm's belief that development was less a matter of economic conditions than of psychological motivation. Development theories emphasizing the potential of the media were also absorbed by the advertising sector at the time. The foremost publicity magazine, *Propaganda*, published reviews of development theorists' work, including a book by Daniel Lerner, and concluded that these books were "indispensable" to understanding the current era.[62]

The ARP

The closure of the AERP in early 1974 under Geisel was followed by a brief interim phase without a formal propaganda institution. Similarly to Castelo Branco, the moderate Geisel initially rejected a propaganda organ as superfluous and "totalitarian" and criticized the propaganda style of the former AERP.[63] However, in 1975, the Press and Public Relations Consultancy (AIRP) was founded, combining the presidential press service with governmental PR under one umbrella.[64] The AIRP coordinated government information but did not produce propaganda campaigns. The event that proved decisive in changing this policy was the 1974 election, in which Geisel suffered a terrible humiliation. In the run-up to the 1976 election, a similar propaganda organ, with only a slightly different name, was created: the Public Relations Consultancy (ARP), from whose inception the beginning of the third propaganda phase can be dated (1976–1980).[65]

The new propaganda institution was now led by former AERP official Toledo Camargo, who revived the most popular campaigns of the AERP. The ARP was structured in a similar way to the AERP, with representatives in Rio and São Paulo, and its operation and principles also remained broadly the same. Yet the political and economic context had changed decisively in the process of Geisel's "opening." The principal changes were a growing pressure to win the elections, more friction with hardliners, and increasing criticism by the opposition due to a relaxation of press censorship. The altered political context and the ARP's mission to gain votes for the government party slightly influenced the subject matter of the films, yet the creation of a personality cult and the construction of an enemy in negative terms were still not permitted. Amid the petrol crisis and the end of the economic "miracle," the ARP rejected "exaggerated optimism" in favor of "reasonable optimism."[66]

The most important divergence, however, was institutional. Geisel reacted to the new political context by centralizing the communication system and bringing the ARP under tighter control. Geisel's action can be seen as more than simply a response to the circumstances. It also fit his style of governing and thus was character-bound. To avoid contradictions, all government campaigns had to be countersigned by the ARP. Whereas Costa, as AERP leader, had suffered from Médici's disinterest, the opposite applied to the ARP, which operated under strict presidential control.

Another significant difference was the larger volume of propaganda generated under Geisel. The AERP produced 308 units between 1970 and 1973, representing a yearly production rate of slightly more than 100 items of propaganda.[67] In contrast, the ARP produced 466 pieces between 1976 and 1978. Thus the average rate of production amounted to 155 units per year. While censorship decreased, the propaganda output increased under President Geisel. To summarize, the ARP operated under a more centralized institutional structure and produced more propaganda than the AERP.

Important similarities include the use of everyday themes, the high aesthetic quality of the material, and the denial of a personality cult and blatant political propaganda. Therefore it can be concluded that, overall, the AERP and ARP worked in a broadly similar way. In 1978, Camargo left the ARP, and for a brief period it was led by his friend General Rubem Ludwig. In May 1979, under the new military president João Figueiredo (1979–1985), a much larger propaganda institution, the Special System of Communication (SECOM), was created to succeed the ARP. According to Costa, the SECOM had significantly greater financial resources than the AERP and ARP, but it proved to be short-lived, as it only remained in existence until December 1980. Its leader, Said Farhat, was forced to leave office following conflict with the SNI.[68]

※

The seemingly sharp distinction between democratic and authoritarian, as well as between private and state propaganda, dissolves under closer examination. An institutional history of Brazilian propaganda reveals that the AERP and ARP were deliberately small in structure, kept personnel and financial resources to a minimum, and produced propaganda in an indirect manner by hiring private media agencies. The distinction also dissolves when looking at the content and aesthetics; propaganda may seem apolitical and center on everyday topics. Its campaigns featured slogans such as "Don't drink and drive"—slogans that are not characteristic of a dictatorship and could be broadcast in many of today's democracies as easily as they were back then. Even seemingly "democratic propaganda" may be more politically manipulative than we would expect.

2

Stars Appearing in the Sky

Unconventional Propaganda Films

In 1976, Brazilians who went to the movies or watched the evening news could see a short animated film that presented a whimsical, progressivist fantasy of the trajectory of Brazilian history. The territorial past, personified as a beautiful, bare-skinned indigenous woman, transitions to happy emblematizations of European arrival, colonialism, and Brazilian nationhood including figural allusions to cultural tradition and social concord. All scenes are cast in vibrant tropical colors and punctuated by icons of harmonious nature and nation: sunrise, sunset, rainbows, stars, flowers, birds, the Brazilian flag, people at work, light and dark children at play. The narration beneath these images ends with the statement: "This is a country that advances." This seemingly apolitical film would not look out of place today. In fact, it is one of the hundreds of propaganda short films that were produced during the military regime in Brazil, and it is certainly one of the most beautiful.

With their aesthetically appealing, entertaining, and seemingly apolitical productions, the AERP and ARP revolutionized official propaganda in Brazil. In contrast to traditional state propaganda, such as newsreels that depicted politicians or the military, the AERP and ARP films took on everyday topics as their subject matter. Film was a new and convenient propaganda channel that symbolized the virtues that the regime aimed to embody: modernity and progress. While the advertising sector was coming of age and producers were still experimenting with this new medium, the AERP and ARP cleverly used aesthetic innovations and became trendsetters, even in the eyes of professional filmmakers. The combination of having a modern cinematic quality and using noncontroversial themes concealed their official origin, and they were tailored to appeal to their audiences. This strategy was more likely to capture viewers' attention and imagination than traditional, staid, unexciting propaganda. Most *filmetes* can be classified as subliminal propaganda, and some could be broadcast as civic education films today.

A closer inspection, however, reveals that the broadcasts supported traditional values, which had been used by the regime to justify its power from 1964 onward. These included economic progress, social mobility, a strong work ethic, order, duty, and a paradoxical appeal to "void" participation, nationalism, national integration, racial democracy, and peace. Perhaps more importantly, they excluded crucial issues that can be freely debated in a democracy, such as human-rights violations, arbitrary repression, and freedom of thought. Aldous Huxley persuasively argued that what has been censored ("negative propaganda") plays a more decisive role than what is actually being said ("positive propaganda").[1] As was the case with commercial propaganda, social problems were ignored, and the overall tone was optimistic. Through their mostly white, middle-class, and male protagonists, the films denied that poverty and race and class problems existed. Many propaganda topics were related to the miracle myth, which celebrated Brazil's economic growth and suggested that it was to the benefit of all Brazilians. It was never acknowledged that under democratic regimes, such as that of President Juscelino Kubitschek (1956–1961), Brazil had witnessed similar economic growth, and the fact that inequality and debt increased under military rule was likewise concealed.[2]

What is needed is a systematic, comprehensive analysis of the 106 AERP and ARP films held by the National Archives in Rio, based on the broadcast material itself. The films are emblematic of the campaigns in general, since their themes and slogans recurred in all the other forms of propaganda as well. The film analysis focuses specifically on the production volume, the degree of political content, their aesthetical appeal, constructions of nationalism, the audience they were addressing, and those series that were aesthetically outstanding. The still images taken from the original archive films were generated from digitized film material and retouched by a graphic designer. Shooting film stills from 1960s low-resolution, non-digital film did not always produce high-quality reproductions. The images in this chapter are reproduced at the best quality possible, given these circumstances.

Production Volume

The volume of film production can most easily be deduced from the annual catalogues. Contrary to my expectations, the AERP produced fewer propaganda films overall than the ARP. Taking into account all forms of propaganda, including radio, during Médici's presidency (1969–1974), the output amounted

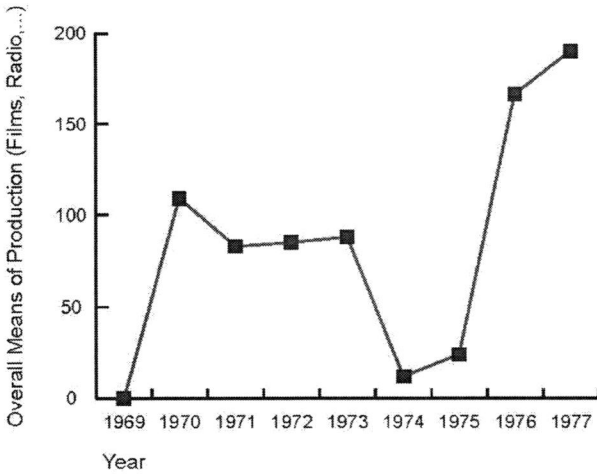

Figure 2.1. Annual total propaganda production, 1970–1977. "Overall Means of Production" refers to the sum of annual units produced between 1969 and 1973 under Médici (365) and between 1974 and 1977 under Geisel (396).

to 365 units, whereas under Geisel (1974–1979), 396 units were produced.[3] However, considering that the AERP was closed in 1974 and that the ARP only functioned fully from 1976 onward, the yearly output under Geisel was nearly double the annual output under Médici, as illustrated in figure 2.1.

In 1976/77, the annual average number of films was 178, whereas the yearly AERP average (1970–1974) amounted to just 91 units. Regarding the volume of films, during Médici's presidency (1969–1974), 170 *filmetes* were produced, whereas under Geisel (1974–1977) the number totaled approximately 205. Again, the yearly film output of the ARP (1976/77) nearly doubled during this period.

Focusing specifically on the years of high propaganda output, it can be seen that under Médici most films (fifty-one) were produced in 1973. In the election year of 1974, when the government party performed poorly, film production was minimal, following the closure of the AERP. In 1976, which was also an election year, Geisel's government produced seventy-four films, while this figure rose even higher in 1977 (ninety-five). Despite the fact that the ARP generated a higher volume of propaganda, the AERP campaigns were apparently more clearly remembered.[4] If we compare the numbers of censored topics with those of propaganda material that was actually produced, it becomes clear that the volume of propaganda increased sharply with the end of press censorship in 1975/76.[5] It is highly likely that Geisel increased

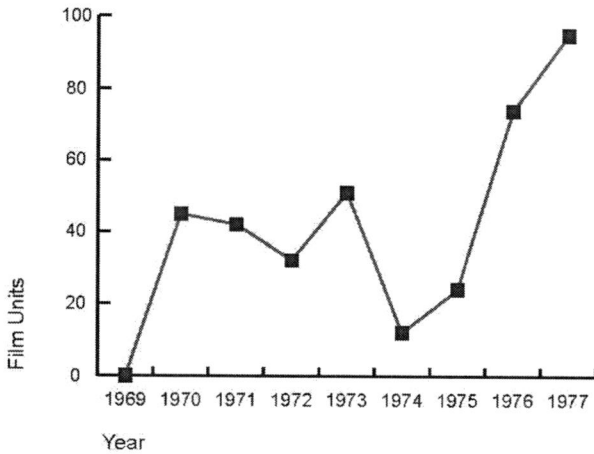

Figure 2.2. Annual film production, 1970–1977.

the propaganda output in order to counterbalance greater press criticism and win the elections. His project of "slow and gradual decompression" needed to be bolstered by more propaganda.

It is noteworthy that the production catalogues also show that some films were produced but never exhibited, and the interesting question is why. What is particularly striking is that most films that were not shown dealt with the elections.[6] It appears to be the case that the AERP had produced *filmetes* asking Brazilians to cast their votes during the 1970 elections, which were broadcast at the time, while films produced by the ARP for the 1976 election were never broadcast. A DEOPS report from October 1970 quotes a newspaper article that announced an AERP campaign calling for Brazilians to exercise their right to vote during the upcoming elections.[7] Public-opinion polls in the most populated urban centers had suggested that a large percentage of the population was not interested in politics. Moreover, student groups mounted a campaign to protest the authoritarian regime with empty ballot papers.[8] Hence the purpose of the AERP's voting campaigns was to avoid embarrassment for the authoritarian regime. The wording of the voice-over from one short film that was not exhibited is as follows: "On the 15th of November you will decide the men who will make our laws. Don't leave your ballot paper blank. Go and vote. Vote for the best."[9]

In contrast, in the election year of 1976 the ARP clearly intended to produce similar election broadcasts with a corresponding purpose: to avoid criticism of the regime in the form of empty ballot sheets. The ARP catalogue from 1976 lists five such short films, most of which have no picture or voice-over, but are annotated with the remark "not exhibited."[10] Since the catalogue lists the production company, the film format, and the title, it is highly likely that they were produced. At least one film (FE. 9) shows an image taken from the film. Whether they were produced in their entirety or whether their production was stopped, they were certainly never broadcast. A letter from the attorney general, Henrique Fonseca D'Araújo, to the minister of justice, Armando Falcão, dated July 27, 1976, explains why the *filmetes* had to be withdrawn.[11] D'Araújo had been assigned to examine whether those ARP films were legal according to existing voting legislation. In this letter he concludes that only political parties had the right to use electoral propaganda. Most importantly, the attorney general uses another argument for rejecting the campaigns: because the films were meant to end with the slogan "There is a Brazil which advances," resembling the AERP's former slogan "This is a country that advances," they could be construed as subliminal government propaganda. Surely, the attorney contends, the opposition party would complain to the Superior Electoral Tribunal (Tribunal Superior Eleitoral, TSE).

This changed attitude toward election broadcasts clearly illustrates the different historical contexts in which they were situated. While under Médici films about the elections could be shown, due to the popularity of the president and the regime's tighter control, the Geisel government could not afford to be accused of illegal activity. The opposition was too strong, hardliners could use the mounting opposition to attack Geisel's politics of decompression, and lastly, his political opening would become publicly discredited. This also shows that the electoral legislation was being taken seriously again.

Analysis of Short Films

The films did not resemble official propaganda. They did not show politicians or military personnel but predominantly featured everyday topics. On closer examination, however, most films supported the same values that had been exploited to justify military rule since 1964. Jacques Ellul has suggested distinguishing between political and social propaganda. Political propaganda denotes the promotion of governments, parties, and groups that intend to influence political beliefs or behaviors of wider society, while social propaganda refers to organizations that shape the "social behavior of the public."[12] The problem with this clear-cut distinction is that it does not account for propaganda that appears to be social but that conveys a subliminal political subtext. The pioneering study on Nazi feature films by Gerd Albrecht (1969) fruitfully classified films as more or less political.[13] He concluded that only a small percentage of the Nazi feature films were political in content and started a debate, which is still ongoing, about whether musicals and ostensibly apolitical feature films also qualify as propaganda.

However, "political propaganda" does not necessarily carry negative connotations, an example being contemporary election campaigns. There is nothing wrong with parties promoting their programs; how else are we to know who favors nuclear energy and who does not, or who supports higher tax expenditures for wars and who would prefer to invest the revenue in the health-care system? We are again faced with a problem that any negative connotations attached to the heuristic category "political propaganda" would constitute a form of simplification. I therefore chose the term "blunt (pro-regime) propaganda" for films that directly mention agents or programs of the regime, for example those that show or refer to Médici and his policies. Meanwhile, subliminal propaganda is considered by this study to be *filmetes* that sell values or norms for "the common good," including road safety, health issues, conserving petrol, family values, love, and unity. Subliminal propaganda is thus similar to Ellul's term "social propaganda." In addition to the distinction between blunt and subliminal propaganda, this book employs the classifications "indirect propaganda" and "economic propaganda."[14] Whereas the term "blunt propaganda" is reserved for films that explicitly mention and praise the government or its programs, "indirect propaganda" films make reference to or discuss programs or members of the regime without explicitly mentioning them in the voice-over or showing them on-screen. "Indirect propaganda" films thus range between blunt and subliminal pro-regime propaganda. Although they appear under the guise of information about programs rather than blunt propaganda, the viewer associates them with either the government or its policies. Lastly, "economic propaganda" films exclusively sell development and progress, whereby they focus on topics such as export and inflation. We will now attempt to visualize these categories using specific examples.

❋

The majority of films did not resemble government propaganda, and most (70.5 percent of the sample) can be classified as subliminal propaganda.[15] The second-largest group, containing eighteen films (19 percent), were "indirect propaganda," while only 10.6 percent of films constituted "blunt" and "economic" propaganda.[16] Their "apoliticalness" and aesthetic appeal were part of

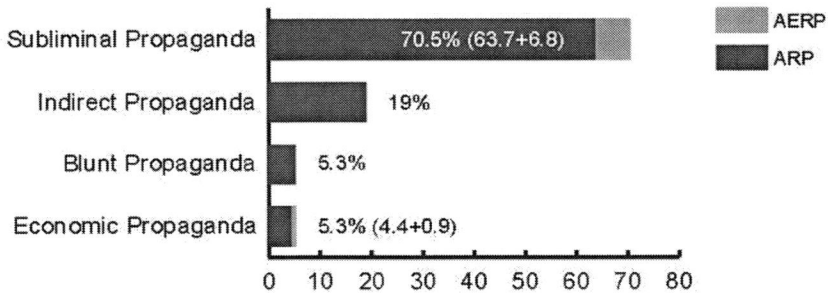

Figure 2.3. Political content of propaganda.

the strategy used to give the films a democratic appearance, in that they did not attempt to promote leading political figures. This sample has analyzed 4.1 percent of the total AERP film production and 43 percent of the total ARP film production.

To illustrate some "apolitical" films, one particularly aesthetically appealing subliminal propaganda film shows a little white boy running with his German shepherd dog in a park along a river.[17] The scenery is pleasant and dappled with sunlight, and the boy and the dog make a cute pair. The two of them play together, to the accompaniment of upbeat background music. The boy then cups his hands to give the dog water from the river to drink.

Only at the end does the voice-over chime in: "Childhood. In the naive soul of childhood lies the human soul." The film appeals to the audience with cute characters, beautiful images and music, vivacity created through constant movement, and amusing narrative elements, including a dog that is often disobedient. It depicts an idyllic, peaceful childhood that was far removed from reality for most Brazilians. The boy is white and from an apparently middle-class background. In a very subtle way the film conveys a sense of happiness, tranquility, order, security, and peace. Silently, it suggests that the regime is securing these values and creating the conditions for an idyllic childhood. Although this film is unrealistic and romantic in contrast to a reality of harsh political repression that included the use of torture and murder, it certainly does not explicitly condone violence in the way that aggressive propaganda did. The prime contrasting example would once again be the Love It or Leave It campaign.

❋

Figure 2.4a–c. *Shepherd boy*, 1970. (Still from the film F. 35, BR AN RIO EH.0.FIL.FIT.127 ANO 1970, EH.-Fil. 934.) By permission of the National Archives, Rio de Janeiro.

Another subliminal-propaganda film shows a group of young people climbing up the Gávea Rock in Rio.[18] Accompanied by dramatic music, they hold each other's hands while hoisting themselves up using ropes. When they reach the summit, a helicopter shot shows them standing on the rock looking at the beautiful Carioca landscape. A voice-over announces: "Time for action—time of the young. Time of a young country, now."

The music and images convey a sense of danger and adventure, and the breathtaking shots of the landscape suggest that Brazilians should be proud to live in a country of such natural beauty. The film imparts a sense of freedom and solidarity. It promotes both teamwork and collectivism, along with the idea that hard work and making a group effort will enable people to reach their goals, which in this case are symbolized by the mountain summit and the marvelous view. The film not only targets students, who were an important opposition group, but the slogan, "Time of a young country, now," also takes youth as a metaphor for a developing Brazil. Although the film appears apolitical, it nonetheless transmits confidence in Brazil's potential, praises participation, and promotes optimism and hard work. Without specifically mentioning government programs, it conveys a feel-good atmosphere.[19]

A good example of "indirect propaganda" is a film that praises the improved housing conditions in Brazil without directly referring to the government.[20] The film is also one of the rare examples that shows nonwhite protagonists. The camera scans to a mulatto boy who is quietly doing his homework. It moves on to a portrait of his father and then to the kitchen, where the presence of a fridge indicates prosperity and where his mother is cooking. Meanwhile, the voice-over explains that people from humble backgrounds now have the opportunity to buy houses, due to the availability of better mortgages. The final image shows laundry hanging tranquilly outside the new houses. The film conveys order (the boy doing his homework), peace (the laundry), the idea that hard work pays off (illustrated by a photo of the absent father), social progress (the fridge), and social stability. It suggests that the economic growth achieved by the regime benefits all Brazilians. Although it does not praise the government in an explicit way, it clearly suggests that the regime delivers social prosperity, jobs, peace, and order.

In contrast, another film about housing programs can be classified as blunt propaganda.[21] The images show both completed houses and houses under construction. The rapid pace of editing suggests expansion and progress. The ideas conveyed are social mobility, progress, development, the government actively

Figure 2.5a–f (*left to right, top to bottom*). *Pedra da Gávea*, 1971. (Stills from the film F. 66, BR AN RIO EH.0.FIL.FIT.126 ANO 1971, EH.-Fil. 933.) By permission of the National Archives, Rio de Janeiro.

taking care of the population, tranquility, peace, harmony, a strong work ethic, and order. The particular intention of this film is to encourage people to sign up for the government program and buy their own houses. The text explicitly refers to, and indeed praises, the government's efforts to create better housing: "Between 1964 and 1975 the federal government has financed the construction

Figure 2.6a–b. *Pedra da Gávea*, 1971. (Still from the film F. 66, BR AN RIO EH.0.FIL.FIT.126 ANO 1971, EH.-Fil. 933.) By permission of the National Archives, Rio de Janeiro.

of more than 1,200,000 houses. Between 1975 and 1979 the goal is to finance another million." The voice-over proclaims that this program will enable all Brazilians to afford to build a house. The film ends with the slogan "This is a country that advances"—one of the core slogans of the regime.

Whereas the aforementioned "indirect propaganda" film promoted the housing program through its narrative structure and pictures, the voice-over in this film explicitly praises the government and attempts to impress its audience with statistics. Images, narrative, and a politically charged voice-over powerfully coincide in this blunt propaganda film.

Economic propaganda films exclusively focus on economic issues and conceal the blunt propaganda underneath. For example, in a film on commerce, progress, and development, an emotionless voice indirectly endorses the economic policies of the government by stating: "Brazil is developing an economic policy," instead of saying "The government is. . . ." Machines, petrol, technology—the so-called instruments for our progress—are all depicted in an aesthetically appealing way. The voice-over explains that the technology was

Figure 2.7a–c. *Pedra da Gávea*, 1971. (Stills from the film F. 66, BR AN RIO EH.0.FIL.FIT.126 ANO 1971, EH.-Fil. 933.) By permission of the National Archives, Rio de Janeiro.

bought with money earned from the export trade. To the accompaniment of classical music, we see workers involved in the production process. Rhythm and activity are cleverly used to create an impression of development and progress. The film ends with the voice-over declaring in a very serious, deadpan tone: "The rhythm of progress of Brazil cannot decrease."[22] Although the gov-

Figure 2.8a–b. *Housing*, 1976. (Still from the film FI. 15, BR AN RIO EH.0.FIL.FIT.75 ANO 1976, EH.-Fil. 771.) By permission of the National Archives, Rio de Janeiro.

ernment is never directly mentioned, the viewer associates the film with its economic policies. Thus this economic propaganda film bolsters the regime in a subtle way.

Aesthetics and Story

The most important features of many films were their aesthetic beauty and innovative, often surprising narratives. They were characterized by movement, giving them a modern appearance and translating the idea of progress and development into cinematic language. Camera angles and zoom shots, the movement of objects within a scene, and the fast pace of editing are particularly striking. Several films experimented with innovative techniques, such as screen splitting, slow motion, or rewinding images. Similar to American feature films of the 1960s and '70s, the films show that there was more room

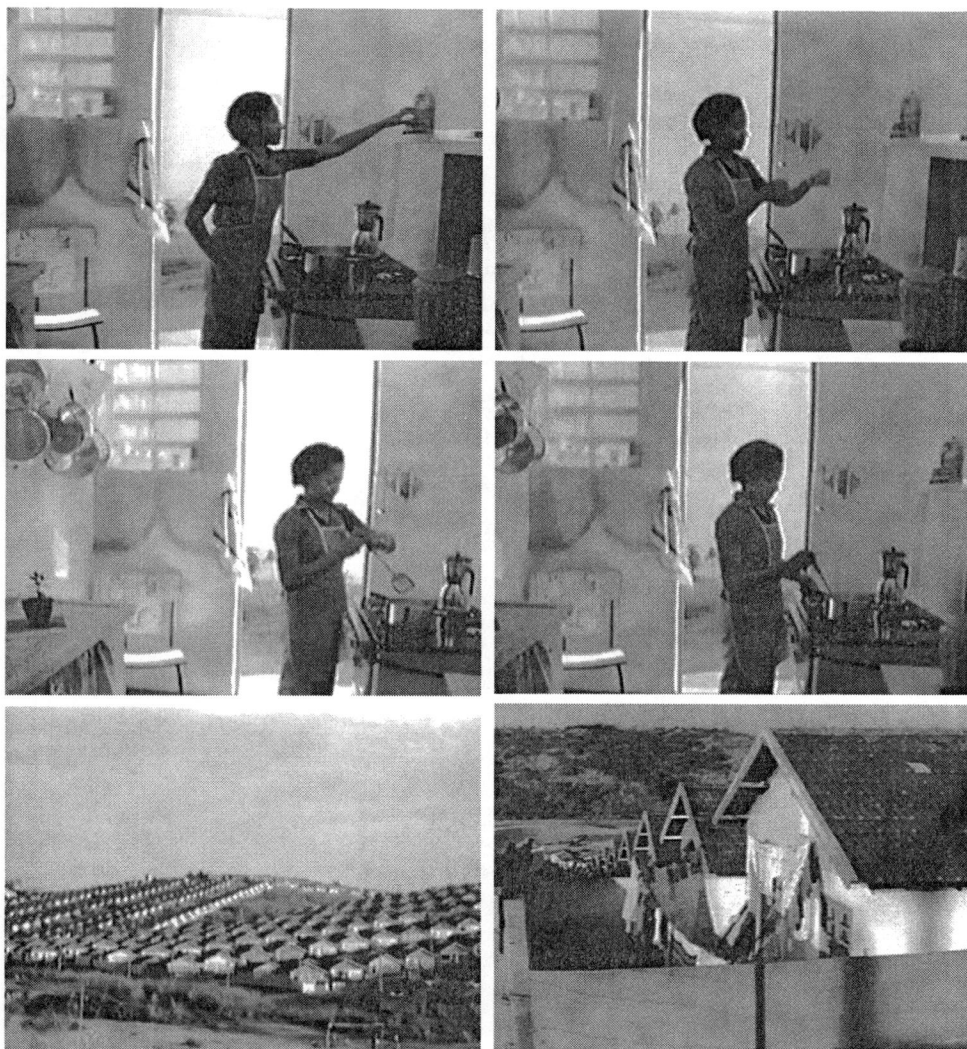

Figure 2.9a–f (*left to right, top to bottom*). *Housing*, 1976. (Stills from the film FI. 15, BR AN RIO EH.0.FIL. FIT.75 ANO 1976, EH.-Fil. 771.) By permission of the National Archives, Rio de Janeiro.

for visual experimentation. A good example of a film selling industrialization in an aesthetically modern and appealing way is one that uses the new technique of screen splitting.[23] The screen is divided into nine sections. To the accompaniment of classical music, one section after another becomes filled with a video showing a different part of the production process. Eventually, nine small videos are running simultaneously. The multiple moving screens

Figure 2.10a–c. *Housing program II*, 1976. (Stills from the film FI. 39, BR AN RIO EH.0.FIL.FIT.10 ANO 1976, EH.-Fil. 706.) By permission of the National Archives, Rio de Janeiro.

Figure 2.11. *Housing program II*, 1976. (Still from the film Fl. 39, BR AN RIO EH.0.FIL.FIT.10 ANO 1976, EH.-Fil. 706.) By permission of the National Archives, Rio de Janeiro.

convey purposeful activity, thereby supporting the ideas of "development" and "progress." The voice-over glorifies machines, petrol, and technology as instruments of "our progress," thereby suggesting that progress is for the benefit of all Brazilians. Other films of this type show the thriving alcohol industry, which was used for fuel production, the hydroelectricity complex Itaipú, and export fairs.

Another salient feature of the films was the interplay between modernity and tradition. Often a modern fabric was shown after evocative shots of the beautiful surrounding landscape. Here the regime's intention to represent both the old and the new was translated into cinematic images. Moreover, several films played with size and scale to useful effect. For example, they showed impressive helicopter shots or zoomed in on industrial sites and constructions, such as Itaipú. Clever camera angles suggested their majestic scale and symbolized progress and government efficiency in an attempt to evoke national pride.

Particularly outstanding were the technically excellent animated films, which sometimes promoted very dry and pedagogic issues in a vivid and engaging way. One particular highlight is a 1976 animated film entitled *Pindorama*, described at the beginning of this chapter. "Pindorama" is the Tupi name for the coastal region that is sometimes used as a synonym for Brazil.[24] This subliminal piece of propaganda looks like a film for children and personifies the history of Brazil in the image of a young, beautiful, naked indigenous woman, the mother of Brazil. It is accompanied by cheerful music and the following lyrics:

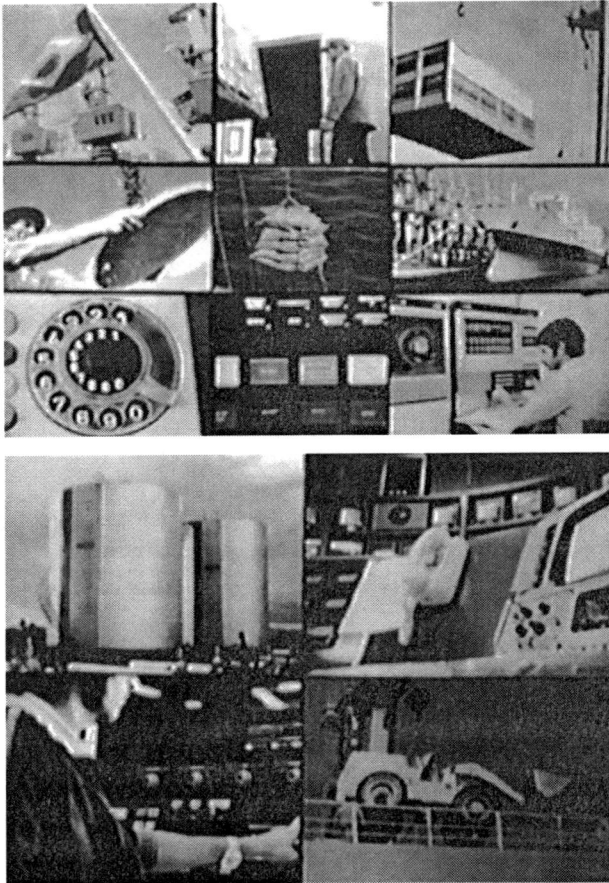

Figure 2.12a–b. Screen splitting, 1976. (Stills from the film FI. 25, BR AN RIO EH.0.FIL.FIT.76 ANO 1976, EH.-Fil. 772.) By permission of the National Archives, Rio de Janeiro.

Pindorama was the mother of this giant territory called Brazil.
United by a single language, singing and dancing, a common fate.
Native, mulatto and white, of all colors, all are for one.
The hope for a new tomorrow is already present in the smile of that people.
This is a country that advances.

Pindorama's long black hair is shown streaming in the wind under a rainbow. A tropical landscape is shown, with a hummingbird flying across it, while a Native American watches the arrival of Cabral's ships. Falling stars explode across the heavens, birds soar through the sky, and stars appear behind the clouds. The Brazilian flag flutters in the wind under a huge sun while white doves fly past, symbolizing peace. A hummingbird takes nectar from a flower, and a rainbow appears. A white girl gives her white mother a love letter. A white child and a mulatto child play ball together. Finally, birds wing their way over the ocean, and the song lyrics end on a core propaganda slogan: "This is a country that advances."

This beautifully made film sells national pride, development, Brazil's natural resources, racial democracy, a strong work ethic, scientific advancement, and peace. Song lyrics and iconic images are used to convey optimism about the future. A rainbow and smiling figures illustrate a peaceful and happy nation while the song lyrics insist: "[the] hope for a new tomorrow is already present in the smile of the [Brazilian] people." This romanticized perspective disguises poverty, inequality, and social and racial friction. The images and the lyrics, which refer to a united goal of all three races living in harmony, sell the myth of racial democracy, but on closer inspection, with the exception of the mulatto child and the native Pindorama, all the protagonists are white.

Figure 2.13a–b. *Pindorama*, 1976. (Stills from the film FE. 16, BR AN RIO EH.0.FIL.FIT.17 ANO 1976, EH.-Fil. 713.) By permission of the National Archives, Rio de Janeiro.

Figure 2.14a–c. *Pindorama*, 1976. (Stills from the film FE. 16, BR AN RIO EH.0.FIL.FIT.17 ANO 1976, EH.-Fil. 713.) By permission of the National Archives, Rio de Janeiro.

Figure 2.15. *Pindorama*, 1976. (Still from the film FE. 16, BR AN RIO EH.0.FIL.FIT.17 ANO 1976, EH.-Fil. 713.) By permission of the National Archives, Rio de Janeiro.

This film is racist, since it promotes the "whitening ideology," an ideology with roots in the nineteenth century, when the Brazilian emperor encouraged the immigration of white European settlers. In the context of the demise of slavery and the heyday of biological racism perpetuated by European theorists, the idea of this "whitening ideology" was to "improve" the genes of the Brazilian nation by eradicating the "black" elements through constant miscegenation with European blood.[25] This myth had a profound and long-lasting influence on Brazilian race relations and racial theories. The same ideology influenced the renowned Brazilian sociologist Gilberto Freyre, who developed the concept of racial democracy. His theory was revolutionary for the time, because by rejecting biological racist thought Freyre regarded the mixing of different races as a key positive feature of the Brazilian nation, but again neglected the blatant reality of racism in Brazil.[26]

The film's beauty lies in the combination of the gentle music and the charming animated images. It also uses sexuality to appeal to the audience. Arguably, in contrast to the *filmete* featuring the Gávea Rock, this short film could not be shown today without attracting criticism for its racist overtones; it was clearly produced in a very different cultural context.

✳

The AERP and ARP produced several high-quality series, out of which three on subliminal propaganda were extraordinarily entertaining: the *Sujismundo/ Dr. Prevenildo* series on hygiene and health, the series on peace, and the series about road safety. The series about the animated character Sujismundo, which gave the appearance of being unofficial, was originally shown during the time of the AERP and was so successful that a similar character, called Prevenildo, was invented.[27] This series was especially popular and perhaps the most appealing of all.[28] According to Professor Alberto Rabaça, the *Sujismundo* series was harshly criticized by the SNI, which demanded "psychological war" propaganda instead.[29] In addition to attractive animated images, the films used comical elements to entertain their audience. Sujismundo always disobeys the rules; he is lazy, violates public norms, and is so ignorant that he has to be taught by his son, Sujismundinho, and the authoritative Dr. Prevenildo, who personifies knowledge, advancement, and "civilization."[30]

Sujismundo refuses to shower or take his son to be vaccinated. He swims in the polluted river, dumps his rubbish anywhere, and takes medicine without consulting a doctor. Usually, his son warns him of the consequences of these actions, but Sujismundo does not listen, and he ends up in the hospital, where he is lectured by Dr. Prevenildo. The series promotes obedience, health, hygiene, science, education, and the ideas of "civic development" and "progress," implying that economic advancement alone is not sufficient for Brazil to qualify as a "developed" country. The short films adopt a pedagogic and patronizing tone that is, however, concealed by the comedy.

Instead of acknowledging Brazil's structural problems, the *filmetes* blame the population's ignorance. For example, Dr. Prevenildo teaches Sujismundo to visit a doctor instead of self-medicating, while failing to confront the fact that most Brazilians cannot afford to see a doctor. Nonetheless, the messages are mostly legitimate, and many of them would still make sense today—for instance, those

Figure 2.16. *Sujismundo*, 1977. (Still from the film BR AN RIO EH.0.FIL.FIT.32 ANO 1977, EH.-Fil. 728.) By permission of the National Archives, Rio de Janeiro.

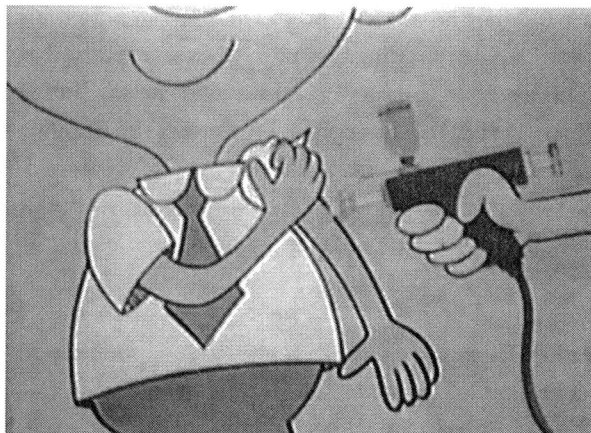

Figure 2.17a–c. *Sujismundo*, 1977. (Stills from the film BR AN RIO EH.0.FIL.FIT.32 ANO 1977, EH.-Fil. 728.) By permission of the National Archives, Rio de Janeiro.

that teach people to protect and look after the environment. Sujismundo films qualify as subliminal propaganda, because they promote behavior perceived as being for the common good. Everyone can understand these films, including the less educated and children. Again, this example demonstrates the thin line between social or "apolitical" and political propaganda. The notions of paternalism and modernization had roots going back a long time in Brazilian history, but here they coincided with the specific mentality of the regime at the time.[31]

✳

To my mind, the most aesthetically creative series was a 1978/79 production on road safety, the Respect Life campaign, which illustrates how films became increasingly professional.[32] A narratively simple yet effective film shows a traffic light turning red.[33] The viewer hears the noise of an accident happening and animated voices. While the camera zooms in on the red light, the ambulance siren gets louder. Finally, the words "Respect Life" appear on the screen, urging the audience to pay attention to the traffic lights. This road safety film is appealing because of the contrast between images and sounds. While the camera zooms in on the red light, suggesting a more profound examination of what the red light means, the story of the accident is told only via sound, and the viewer has to imagine the accident scene for him- or herself. The immediate lesson concerns appropriate behavior on the roads, but the *filmete* also conveys duty, responsibility, order, and a desire for security—again, themes used by an unelected, repressive regime to legitimize itself. But how did these road safety films compare with those shown in other countries at the same time? Did they differ, and if so, how? Did they look democratic?

Comparable in its message and appearance is another authoritarian propaganda film about the consequences of failing to use the zebra crossing properly.[34] Like the rest of this series, it plays on people's fear of death. The audience takes the viewpoint of a car driver looking at the road through the windshield. In addition to the extraordinary camera angle, the images do not flow smoothly; they freeze and jump, giving the impression of moving jerkily in a car. In contrast, the voice-over takes the perspective of a man who is crossing the street several feet before the zebra crossing. In a comforting tone, the voice-over addresses the audience directly: "You are too lazy to go to the zebra crossing, because you are in a hurry, and so you continue to believe that nothing will ever happen." The same scene is repeated—a man crosses the street, ignoring the zebra crossing. Shortly before the crash, the camera freezes, and we see, still from the driver's perspective, the man's shocked face. From this and the accompanying sounds, we deduce that this time the man has been hit. Eventually, the moral appears: "Use the zebra crossing. Respect Life."

Again, the film plays on the picture-voice contrast. At the same time that we see images from the driver's perspective and involuntarily become a perpetra-

Figure 2.18a–c. *Zebra crossing*, 1978. (Stills from the film BR AN RIO EH.0.FIL.FIT.62 ANO 1978, EH.-Fil. 758.) By permission of the National Archives, Rio de Janeiro.

Figure 2.19a–b. *Zebra crossing*, 1978. (Stills from the film BR AN RIO EH.0.FIL.FIT.62 ANO 1978, EH.-Fil. 758.) By permission of the National Archives, Rio de Janeiro.

tor, we listen to a voice-over addressing us as the pedestrian. The viewer is torn between identifying with the perpetrator and the victim. We understand that if we disobey road safety rules, one day we might get hit and possibly killed, while also identifying with the driver who now feels responsible for the death. Again, the accident is not shown directly but must be imagined by the audience.

Only the final broadcast of the series breaks the pattern and explicitly shows images of violence.[35] We see a car driving very fast. The voice-over directly addresses the audience: "If you don't have the guts to see certain things, then you should not watch this film. It shows very shocking scenes." Medical machinery and equipment in an operating room are shown. A bleeding victim is on her way there. The voice-over continues: "However, more shocking than these scenes is reality. This suffering you are watching is repeated hundreds of times in Brazilian cities. The urban traffic is wild [*selvagem*]. . . . All this suffering could be avoided."[36] The bleeding victim who is being transported can hardly breathe, and she coughs. These images are interspersed with a black-and-white photograph of a damaged car. Back in the operating room, the scissors and anesthetics are being prepared, and the victim arrives. A nurse fastens the doctor's mask. We hear the sound of an artificial respirator. The film finishes when the operation starts, leaving the viewer wondering whether the victim will survive. As a whole, the road safety series is innovative in the concise nature of its message, its creativity, and its interplay with the audience. However, the films convey the familiar values of order, security, and obedience. They were professional subliminal propaganda films, and many of them, with the exception of the racist film *Pindorama*, arguably could be shown today.

Development: The Filmic Face of the Miracle Myth

Economic development, a strong work ethic, and social mobility are values that recur in nearly all the films.[37] Key ideas in these broadcasts are the miracle myth, including the notion that everyone benefits from economic growth; the idea that Brazil is almost a "first world" nation, thanks to government efficiency; the idea (however fictitious) of a society free from conflict between different classes, races, and age groups; and the call to actively participate in raising Brazil to the status of a developed country via hard work, obedience, and the sacrifice of self-interested concerns, such as higher wages, for the "benefit" of the nation.[38] The films construct a specific type of nationalism related to the values of national integration, racial democracy, and civic and cultural development. The messages that all Brazilians benefit from economic growth and that social mobility is possible are embedded in the storylines or occasionally in the voice-over. A good example is a film on Brazilian exports (see figures 2.20a–d).[39] Images of desirable export goods and the industrial technologies and machines that produce them represent a thriving export trade. One frame announces, "With increased exports the general good grows." An accompanying voice-over that identifies the various images as they appear ends the film on the moral, "To produce steel means prosperity for all."[40] Several films about housing, the program for free school meals (Merenda Escolar), and health are suggestive of greater social mobility and increasing government assistance.[41]

The most exaggerated short film promoting social mobility for the poor and uneducated tells the story of an old man who received a grant for land in the Amazon and who made his fortune through hard work.[42] While the camera zooms out from the Transamazon Highway, a caption appears: "Transamazônica 93 km." A

Figure 2.20a–d. *Economic miracle,* 1978. (Stills from the film BR AN RIO EH.0.FIL.FIT.111 ANO 1978, EH.-Fil. 807.) By permission of the National Archives, Rio de Janeiro.

humble old man with no front teeth talks in broken Portuguese about the settlement that he has created. Images of him proudly receiving a land certificate in front of other settlers are shown. Speaking directly into the camera, the man affirms that he has worked hard for his rewards. We see images of uncultivated territory and scenes of sugar cane and coffee production. In the last image, he smiles, and a gold inlay in his teeth illustrates in an obvious manner that he has become rich.

The film's immediate intention is to inspire people to settle in the Amazon region. The moral is that, through hard work, social mobility can be achieved. Resembling a fairy tale more than reality, the notions of "development" and "progress" are promoted in a very naive and romanticized way. In addition to perpetuating the myth that unpropertied, ill-educated, and hardworking Brazilians can become rich, this film sells the success story of the Transamazon Highway and national integration.[43]

Alongside economic and scientific development, films also frequently por-

Figure 2.21a–b. *Amazon self-made man*, 1978. (Stills from the film BR AN RIO EH.0.FIL.FIT.61 ANO 1978, EH.-Fil. 757.) By permission of the National Archives, Rio de Janeiro.

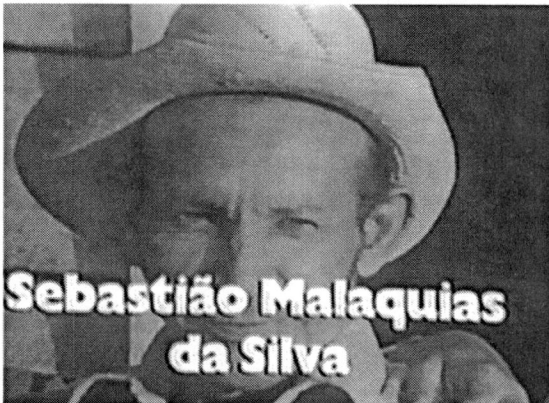

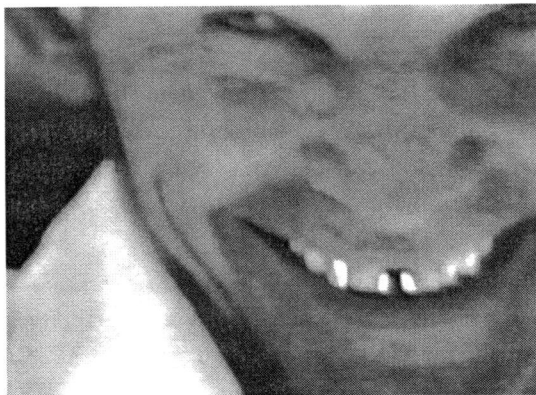

Figure 2.22a–b. *Amazon self-made man*, 1978. (Stills from the film BR AN RIO EH.0.FIL. FIT.61 ANO 1978, EH.-Fil. 757.) By permission of the National Archives, Rio de Janeiro.

tray cultural "progress" with the intention of evoking national pride. In some instances, cultural groups that have received support from government programs are depicted. Several short films suggest that obeying rules equates becoming a more "civilized" nation. Health and road-safety campaigns also belong to this category of "civilization campaigns." The famous cartoon character Sujismundo, copied from his American counterpart, Litterbug, and advertised through the usual channels (radio, television, journals, posters, and plastic disks) perpetuated the slogan "A developed country is a clean country." As Fico has shown, the notion of civilization has a long history within the discourse of Brazilian modernization.[44] The regime continually reiterated Brazil's potential to become a fully developed nation.

Films attempted to construct "Brazilianness" as a cross-class and multiracial identity. For example, one film shows members of an orchestra who all work in different professions playing in perfect harmony. The 1979 *filmete* combines cultural progress with a strong work ethic and "national integration."[45] We see a

Figure 2.23a–e (*left to right, top to bottom*). *Orchestra*, 1979. (Stills from the film BR AN RIO EH.0.FIL.FIT.70 ANO 1979, EH.-Fil. 766.) By permission of the National Archives, Rio de Janeiro.

rural scene accompanied by the caption "Aracoiaba Serra, 1979." Classical music plays while the camera pans to a village orchestra. Individual musicians are profiled together, with text listing their names and occupations (a sugar-production worker, a soldier, a student, a carpenter). Some musicians are shown making their own instruments. Finally, they appear on-screen dressed very smartly for a concert while the voice-over synthesizes the film's moral: "Independence is achieved with love, work, and unity."

The *filmete* was designed to promote the idea of independence through hard

Figure 2.24a–c. *Orchestra*, 1979. (Stills from the film BR AN RIO EH.0.FIL.FIT.70 ANO 1979, EH.-Fil. 766.) By permission of the National Archives, Rio de Janeiro.

work and national solidarity. In all, the notions of "civilization" and "progress" are constructed in a broader sense than merely economic and social. Several films about cultural productions praise the ways in which Brazil and its people have developed culturally.[46]

✳

Many films depict manual laborers from different professions whose efforts are illustrated in the form of sweat.[47] One short film promotes hard work and development through education. Upbeat modern music plays in the background. Images show men working on a railway track in the sun, a painter on a ship, a shoemaker, and a carpenter. Unusual camera angles make their stories appealing; for instance, the painter is shown from above, and the camera zooms in very close to the workers' bodies. Suddenly, the music changes to a gentler classical piece, and the workers are shown sitting in a classroom. We see their brows furrowed in concentration and their childlike handwriting. This has a comical but also thought-provoking effect, since their competence in their working environments contrasts with their difficulties in writing. The voice-over delivers the moral: "In the Brazilian man lies the biggest strength of development for this country. In his education lies our biggest challenge."[48]

The moral links together a hard-work ethos, education, and development. It pictures a diligent working class contributing to development—from the regime's point of view, the ideal worker, who does not go on strike or demand higher wages but simply obeys orders. In reality, trade unionists and laborers were repressed during the military regime, a subject currently being investigated by both the National Truth Commission and several local commissions.[49] Besides images of machines, companies, and consumer goods, contented and professional workers in action were one of the favorite motifs of the AERP and ARP films.[50]

The key terms "development" and "progress" were general enough to appeal to conflicting interest groups and unite them. In the context of the military

Figure 2.25. *Working hard*, 1971. (Still from the film F. 69, BR AN RIO EH.0.FIL. FIT.125 ANO 1971, EH.-Fil. 932.) By permission of the National Archives, Rio de Janeiro.

Figure 2.26a–c. *Working hard*, 1971. (Stills from the film F. 69, BR AN RIO EH.0.FIL.FIT.125 ANO 1971, EH.-Fil. 932.) By permission of the National Archives, Rio de Janeiro.

regime, these ideas acted as a vital force for integration, which went far beyond state propaganda from above, constituting more of a general mentality widely accepted by Brazilians at the time.[51] "Development" was part of the National Security Doctrine (NSD), which held that only through development would Brazil be protected from communism and the "internal enemy." Hence, as Maria Alves pointedly remarked, improving the social standards of the Brazilian population was a security issue rather than a social dilemma.[52]

The regime constructed a binary opposition between capitalism and communism, in which its own economic model was presented as the only capitalist option. The reform agendas of former civilian presidents Juscelino Kubitschek (1956–1961) and Goulart (1961–1964), who, incidentally, owned large estates, had in fact offered viable alternatives to the military's economic policies and had been discussed by prominent intellectuals and politicians.[53] While these debates are too complex to be examined in any depth here, it is important to recognize that the regime terminated these discussions and that its propaganda presented the anticommunist economic model as the single "capitalist" alternative.

Overall, as umbrella terms for the aspirations of all Brazilians, "development" and "progress" played a vital role, yet they cannot simply be labeled "capitalist." In the heyday of the Cold War, these values of hard work and social ascendancy were meant to undermine communist ideals. However, it would be too much of a generalization to call them "capitalist." Images of factories and workers were equally prominent in Soviet propaganda films, and it would be a mistake to read "capitalist" values into those films. The label "capitalist" furthermore requires a more thorough investigation of the regime's economic policies, which changed over the years. Although the idea of a free-market policy was perpetuated through the propaganda of the regime, in defiance of communism, it was no longer practiced under President Geisel. Moreover, military officials and civilians also diverged on economic policymaking. As Saes and Diniz have illustrated, support vanished among those businessmen who were disadvantaged by the regime's new economic policies.[54] Thus different forms of "capitalism" were practiced in Brazil between 1964 and 1985.

Addressees

The innovative look of the *filmetes*, one of the main characteristics of the AERP films, was clearly intentional. Costa wanted to produce films that were tailored to the audience. Compared to other official films, which tended to be dry and uninspiring, the overall tone of the AERP was informal and easy to grasp. Formerly, most productions were not aimed at one single audience. However, between 1971 and 1973, the AERP targeted one specific group with each campaign. In 1971, the AERP focused, in particular, on "youth," which was defined as the "urban population between fifteen and twenty-five years [old] and literate."[55] This group was furthermore split into "students" and "workers." The decision to focus on youth can be explained by the fact that the younger generations were more critical of the regime. The relevant AERP document states that the youth should be "confronted with the big national challenges" ahead and be "stimulated" for "democracy" and "development." The 1971 plan, as well as those of 1972 and 1973, also targeted other groups, thus covering the whole spectrum: the rural and urban marginalized, businessmen, religious communities, the middle class, and workers.[56] Not all campaigns had a specified target audience; many were simply addressed to the general public. In 1972 and 1973 most productions were intended for the so-called common people.

Most films portrayed white, young, middle-class men. Mulattoes with a light skin tone appeared in only a fifth of all films analyzed.[57] Colored Brazilians only appear as lower-strata protagonists in films about housing and food programs. Not a single film shows a black Brazilian. This phenomenon, however, was not invented by the regime. Many scholars, such as Muniz Sodré, have illustrated that "media racism" still persists in Brazil today.[58] Likewise, the notion of racial equality was propagated by Vargas.[59] In the context of the 1960s and 1970s the racial democracy myth entailed the regime trying to overcome racial, social, and geographic barriers in the name of the miracle myth and national integration.

Women were shown in 50 percent of the films.[60] However, they only appeared in specific roles: as mothers who took care of their children's vaccinations, in domestic roles, as lovers, as students, and occasionally as workers. They never appeared in leading roles or doing white-collar jobs. There were nurses, domestic workers, or laborers working in manufacturing.[61] This discrimination is not surprising given that, during the 1970s, emancipation was just starting to make significant headway, not only in Brazil but in other countries as well.

Regarding class, according to Camargo, the AERP and ARP did not focus on any one specific class. However, judging by the *filmetes'* protagonists, it seems that most were designed to appeal to the middle classes. One-fifth (20.5 percent) of the films addressed the middle class, and 13.5 percent were aimed at the lower-middle/upper-working class.[62] Meanwhile, 7.5 percent show and appeal to the working class and only 4 percent to the Brazilian upper class.[63] Most films, however, were not targeted at any specific class.[64] If class and racial divisions had become too obvious, it would have raised issues, such as inequality and workers' rights, and led to criticism of the regime and perhaps even capitalism itself.

Film Topics

Until now this book has focused on selected propaganda films and looked at the degree of political content that they contained. However, another question remains: what were the most common themes of propaganda films in authoritarian Brazil, and did they change over time? Are there any clues to suggest that new topics were introduced and, if so, why? If we count the number of times the most prominent film topics appeared, we discover that those of the AERP and ARP films differed significantly.[65] On average the main topics of the propaganda short films between 1970 and 1973 were nationalism/national pride (27.7 percent), work/hard work ethos (25.3 percent), youth (24.7 percent), and development (15.3 percent). The armed forces figured in 4.7 percent of the films.

In 1970, the three most frequently covered subjects were youth (60 percent), nationalism/national pride (40 percent), and work/hard work ethos (24.4 percent).[66] Other important themes were civic participation (20 percent), education, professions and order/security (15.6 percent), development (13.3 percent), and family (13.3 percent). In 1971, the principal issues were work/hard-work ethos (47.7 percent), and development and youth (33.3 percent each). Short films focusing on work/hard work ethos and development increased, whereas those concerned with youth declined. In 1972, the year of the Sesquicentenario, the most frequently covered topic was nationalism/national pride, with 34.4 percent of films covering it, followed by work/hard work ethos, which fell from 47.7 percent in 1971 to 25 percent. Other recurring themes were Brazil's historical roots (20.6 percent), education, and hygiene, at 18.75 percent each. In 1973, nationalism/national pride (34.4 percent) continued to be the most prominent issue, followed by the new themes of road safety (19.6 percent) and tourism (15.7 percent). Films about work/hard-work ethos decreased further, but there were still four occurrences of this type (7.8 percent). Development (1.9 percent) and youth (0 percent) had been removed from the agenda by this time. Costa left the AERP at the beginning of Geisel's presidency, in July 1974.

On average, the most important ARP topic between 1974 and 1977 was government programs (19.5 percent), closely followed by nationalism (17.2 percent) and development (17.2 percent). Other recurrent topics were health (10.7 percent), racial democracy (9.8 percent), petrol (9.8 percent), order and security (8.3 percent), road safety, work/hard-work ethos, youth, social integration, and energy, with 7.9 percent each, and the armed forces and national integration, both of which accounted for 6.5 percent of the films.[67]

In 1974, 33.3 percent of the twelve films dealt with development, 25 percent with nationalism/national pride, and 16.7 percent of the films centered on work/hard-work ethos. In 1975, 45.8 percent of films focused on nationalism/national pride. The second most important issue, featured in 25 percent of films, was development, followed by government programs (20.8 percent). The key issue in the election year of 1976 was government programs (40.5 percent). Further important themes were racial democracy (28.4 percent), development (18.9 percent), social integration, and nationalism/national pride (17.6 percent). In 1977, reflecting the oil crisis, the major topics were petrol (17.9 percent), road safety (15.8 percent), and energy (14.7 percent), all of which were growing in importance. Films about government programs had been reduced to a quarter of the figure seen the previous year (8.4 percent) and those on social integration had fallen to a sixth of the total (2.1 percent), while films highlighting hard work dropped by half (5.2 percent).

Whereas on average the most frequent topics featured in the AERP films from 1970 to 1973 (figure 2.27) were nationalism (27.7 percent), work/hard work ethos (25.3 percent), and youth (24.7 percent), the main ARP topic from 1974 to 1977 (figure 2.28) was government programs (19.5 percent), followed by development and nationalism (both at 17.2 percent).

All in all, the topics that appeared most consistently in propaganda films

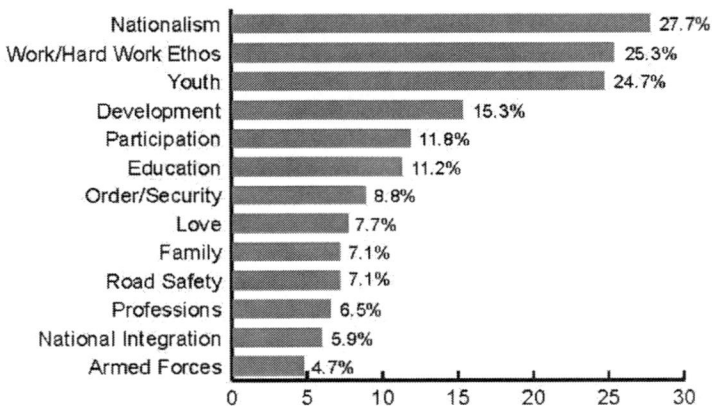

Figure 2.27. AERP film topics between 1970 and 1973.

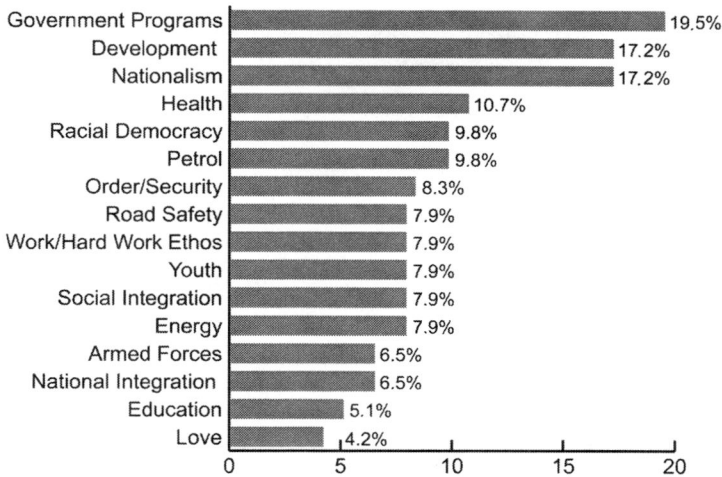

Figure 2.28. ARP film topics between 1974 and 1977.

between 1970 and 1977 were nationalism/national pride, development, and work/hard work ethos. These were followed by the topics of youth, government programs, order/security, education, and road safety, all of which were featured frequently (see figure 2.29). Although the AERP did not close down until March 1974, all of its films were produced in 1973. Therefore, all the numbers that relate to films from 1974 onward are counted as ARP productions, because although the ARP was formally reestablished in February 1976, it was Camargo who produced the small number of *filmetes* in 1974 and 1975.

Overall, this quantitative content analysis revealed that the topics of government programs and realizations dominated during Geisel's presidency, while they had been absent under Médici. This finding is in accordance with the higher percentage of directly political films produced during this period and supports the theory that a significant difference between the two eras was that the ARP films can be more readily categorized as blunt propaganda than those of the AERP. The finding corresponds to that of Galletti, who agrees that the subject of government programs was featured more frequently under Geisel's government and peaked in the election year of 1976.[68]

Ultimately, what do these results tell us? Firstly, they demonstrate that Geisel tried to legitimize his government through social issues. Arguably, this topic was appropriate given the pressure he was under to win the 1976 and 1978 elections. Confronted with increasing pressure from hardliners, who were dissatisfied with the electoral defeat in 1974, the relaxation of press censorship, and growing media criticism, Geisel needed to enhance his reputation with

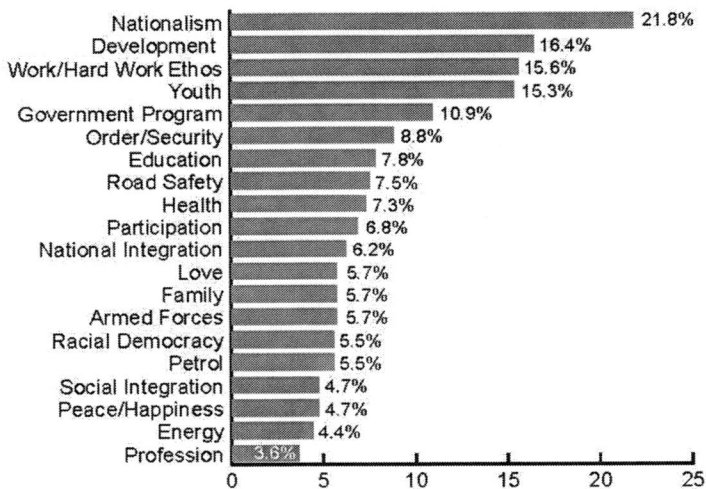

Figure 2.29. All film topics between 1970 and 1977.

the public. The "Brazilian miracle" was no longer convincing, especially in the face of the petrol crisis. Thus, Geisel's strategy switched to praising the regime's social programs. Yet it is significant that the individuals controlling the production of propaganda also changed. Whereas Costa had usually decided on the AERP's choice of topics, it was now Geisel who had editorial control, and he preferred pragmatic campaigns. However, apart from government programs, other important themes were used by both the propaganda organs, but with differing frequencies. The most consistently covered topics between 1969 and 1977 were nationalism/national pride, development, work/hard work ethos, and youth. Following those were the themes of government programs, order and security, and education.

✳

Upon examining the selection of Brazilian films covered in this chapter, it has become clear that authoritarian propaganda need not look obviously political, but may purvey specific values, like order and security, obedience, or hard work. The miracle myth was a core motif for trying to justify military rule; this notion was translated into cinematic language by the use of a rapid montage, zoom shots, and screen-splitting techniques, which were innovative for the time. However, the military regime in Brazil has surely not been the only government to highlight economic growth rates while concealing growing social injustice.

3

Beware!

More Propaganda

Many propaganda elements of the military regime—and the miracle myth, in particular—were not exclusively perpetuated by the government. Businessmen and the advertising and media sectors eagerly promoted ideas in accordance with the regime. Without this consensus the authoritarian system might not have succeeded for as long as it did and might have faced more serious opposition. This kind of broader consensus—the willing support of collaborating allies—contributes to the stability of a regime, for authoritarian rule rarely relies on the dictatorial state alone. As commercial enterprises, the advertising and media sectors can influence society more broadly, because they tend to own the financial resources and media channels necessary to reach a wider audience, and thus they deserve special scrutiny. Blunt propaganda was not broadcast by the AERP and ARP but primarily by regime-friendly media, again raising the crucial question of civilian collaboration and revealing a series of public and private organs that used media to stabilize, legitimize, and support the authoritarian regime.

State Agents

Agência Nacional and Radiobrás

While informing the public about the government's work is a necessary and democratic accountability procedure in every country—politicians (at least in theory) represent the people and thus have to justify their actions to the electorate—these bodies do not always perform their job neutrally. In Brazil, yet another official propaganda institution was the National Press Agency (Agência Nacional), which differed significantly from the AERP and ARP because of its longer history, larger number of personnel, and blunt or even aggressive propaganda style.[1] This institution was created as a successor to the Department of Press and Propaganda (DIP), the notorious propaganda apparatus under Vargas, and thus preceded the coup.

In 1971, the Agência Nacional became responsible for covering federal administrative acts and government institutions, and it produced news synopses for leading politicians. As of July 29, 1970, it was obligatory for radio stations to broadcast "educational programs," each of which lasted more than an hour and the most important of which was known as the *Voice of Brazil*. In 1975, the official radio station, Radiobrás, was founded, and it has produced the program ever since then. By 1978, the Agência Nacional employed 440 people (nine times as many as the AERP), who were dispersed among most of Brazil's major cities. One hundred were based in Brasília and were responsible for the daily edition of the *Voice of Brazil*.[2] The Agência Nacional mainly produced press briefings, newsreels, and radio programs.

Given that the Agência Nacional preceded the coup, did it experience any institutional or editorial changes under military rule? According to the documentation available, there is no suggestion that major transformations directly followed the regime change.[3] In a letter written three weeks after the coup, the director of the Agência Nacional, Octávio Alves Velho, called for the urgent creation of a National Service of Public Relations (Serviço Nacional de Relações Públicas, SENARP); however, this organ never materialized.[4] The coup did not cause institutional changes, except in the case of certain journalists who had to defend themselves during military police inquiries.[5]

An analysis of newsreels and the radio program the *Voice of Brazil* clearly suggests, based on content and tone, that coverage was highly favorable toward the regime and that the Agência Nacional was not an impartial news agency. The radio programs of 1968–69, far from presenting "neutral" governmental information, uncritically celebrated government politics. Unlike the AERP, which did not construct enemies and which simply silenced violence, the Agência Nacional exposed the tense political climate in speeches and ordinary news coverage. It openly reported military action taken against "subversives" and withdrawals of political rights (*cassações*), and created enemies instead of keeping its coverage impartial.[6] That the Agência Nacional was biased is confirmed by a corruption case uncovered by the newsweekly publication *ISTO É* in 1978. It denounced the press synopsis of a political candidate favored by the government, claiming that it had been falsified.[7]

The language of the radio program was characterized by superlatives and by statistics intended to demonstrate progress. The Ministry of Education emphasized the amount of money invested in universities and the numbers of newly built schools and of meals distributed to students. Meanwhile, the Ministry of Transport and Communication celebrated each kilometer of newly constructed road. Propaganda *topoi*, such as "development," "nation," or "national integration," appeared in half of all announcements. Specific words and expressions "which represented some sort of ideological threat to the regime" were censored; for example, the verb "denounce" was prohibited.[8]

The radio program was unpopular. In the late 1970s and early 1980s the audience declined drastically, as Brazilians rejected the program as a relic of authoritarianism. Interviews suggest that many Brazilians considered the program ridiculous and turned the radio off when it started.[9] The *Voice of Brazil* was official in content, old-fashioned in style, lacking in entertainment value, and limited in its portrayal of Brazilians (only the military elite were featured); its content consisted of mainly blunt, occasionally slightly aggressive propaganda. However, as the Agência Nacional was economically dependent on the state, its style of reporting had always been favorable toward the government, even prior to the military regime.[10]

The Agência Nacional also produced newsreels that differed significantly from the AERP and ARP films for various reasons. Most importantly, the newsreels were characterized by a personality cult; they constantly depicted the military presidents.[11] They also explicitly praised government programs and thus clearly qualify as blunt propaganda. Contrary to the *filmetes*, they were thematically and aesthetically unattractive, and so it is fair to say that the AERP and ARP revolutionized state propaganda in Brazil. The only similarity between these two forms of official propaganda was that both propagated "development," "progress," and "order." Another difference was the production process. While the Agência Nacional enjoyed far greater resources and used its own staff to produce the films, the AERP and ARP hired film production companies to execute their ideas.

Secretaries of State

Evidence suggests that the federal ministries produced their own propaganda campaigns, but these were only on a minor scale and were unprofessional. Apparently, the ministries did not have their own PR organs but mostly employed private advertising agencies to work on specific projects and produced little propaganda overall.[12] Theoretically, the official organs responsible for the wider coordination and centralization of PR were the AERP and ARP. However, in practice the communication system was not centralized during the era of the Médici government, and even during Geisel's presidency the work of ARP leader Camargo was occasionally overruled. Federal ministries violated the propaganda principles set by the AERP in several ways. Government money subsidized panegyric programs, such as *Amaral Netto Reporter* on TV Globo.[13] Camargo disliked the program, because he considered it propaganda for the election: "[its aim was] to show the beauty and riches of Brazil . . . as well as the paternalistic actions of the government."[14]

Secondly, while the AERP deliberately rejected "special supplements" in the national and international press, refusing to "buy" pro-regime propaganda, these supplements were nonetheless produced by other federal ministries. Camargo even sent memoranda to the PR units, prohibiting them from buying newspaper propaganda.[15] Despite this, Minister Delfim Netto gave exclusive interviews about economic issues to the newspapers *Estado de São Paulo* and *Jornal do Brasil*.[16] Under Geisel the communication system became more centralized, as the ARP's task to supervise the PR units of all the federal ministries was more rigorously enforced. In Camargo's opinion, the staff working in the PR units of the ministries was unprofessional, and, like Costa, he tried to address this shortcoming. Camargo was "shocked by the quantity" and "bad quality" of the majority of publications and consequently reduced their expenditure by 30 percent.[17] Big national campaigns were organized by the ARP and the PR units of the federal ministries, as they collaborated to secure ARP control.

Education

To what extent university lecturers and academic writing effectively justified the military regime is an under-researched question.[18] In fact, in 2012 several universities (the University of Brasília [UNB] and the University of São Paulo [USP], for example) instated truth commissions to investigate their institutions' authoritarian past and publish a report. What is clear, however, is that the military regime attempted to exploit the education system to manipulate Brazilians.[19] Since 1964 numerous university directors, lecturers, and students had been dismissed or expelled, and the government systematically sent out spies (gorillas) to observe the education sector and denounce potential opposition.[20] The most important measure, however, was the (re)introduction of a new subject called Moral and Citizenship Education (Educação Moral e Cívica [EMC]), which became compulsory in schools and universities as of September 12, 1969 (Decree No. 869). Similar subjects designed to teach moral and civic values had existed during the era of the New State (1937–1945), and the Federal Education Council unsuccessfully tried to resist its restoration.[21]

The implementation of Moral and Citizenship Education was another way of attempting to influence Brazilians in favor of the regime. This type of propaganda was ufanistic (boastfully nationalist) and attempted to enforce patriotism by constructing a "Great Brazil," creating national pride and promoting national symbols. It sold the ideas of "progress," "development," and "work" and was explicitly pro-capitalist and anticommunist. Furthermore, it adopted the "revolutionary" rhetoric based on the National Security Doctrine and, absurd as it seems, emphasized democracy. Although specific topics, such as national pride, "progress," "development," the miracle myth and the exclusion of social problems, obedience, and duty were also conveyed by the AERP, the type of glorifying propaganda used in EMC and encapsulated in the "Great Brazil" idea was rejected by the AERP. Furthermore, in pursuit of its stated goal to "create harmony," the AERP did not construct enemies but instead produced "positive" propaganda. Costa and Camargo both considered EMC ridiculous, since it used an obvious form of propaganda, which the AERP rejected.[22]

During the regime, Selva Guimarães Fonseca argues, the subject of EMC was transformed into an instrument of the National Security Doctrine (NSD).[23] Arguably its main purpose was to spread anticommunism.[24] However, EMC was coordinated by the Ministry of Education and Culture (MEC) and not the AERP and ARP. The guidelines and content of EMC were determined by two official organizations: the Federal Council of Education (*Conselho Federal de Educação* [CFE]) and the National Commission for Morals and Civic Education (*Comissão Nacional de Moral e Civismo* [CNMC]). The CNMC was led by a military general and included a professor who had previously written a book on education for the earlier authoritarian regime in Brazil, the Estado Novo.[25]

J. L. Werneck da Silva describes the values propagated by the EMC as socially immobilizing and politically conservative. Its stated goals were "to defend the democratic principle by preserving the religious spirit, human dignity and the love of freedom with responsibility to and the inspiration of God . . . to worship the fatherland, its symbols, traditions, institutions and important historical figures . . . the preparation of the citizen for his civic duties, a moral basis, patriotism and constructive behavior keeping in mind the common good."[26] Silva unmasks the hollowness of this intention by commenting that messages such as "human dignity" and "love" did not appear to reach the principal repressive organ, the CODI-DOI.[27]

In addition to coercive, as opposed to voluntary, patriotism, the most important values propagated by EMC were obedience, work, and community integration.[28] Instead of acknowledging the dictatorship, EMC pretended to defend the "democratic-spiritualist-Christian" cause and to combat communism.[29] Through the construction of a historical continuity, students were encouraged to believe that the military regime was simply building on Brazil's historical roots.[30] The idea was that useful citizens would be created to lead Brazil into the prestigious club of developed countries.[31] A secondary-school text states: "This is my country; I am proud to call myself Brazilian. The security of every Brazilian and the safety of every Brazilian institution is guarded by the nation's armed forces. There are two missions: defense against foreign aggression and vigilance against internal subversives. . . . There are further enemies within our midst: terrorists, subversives, and militants with communist ideologies. The armed forces combat this menace, and remind us of our obligation to hierarchy and discipline."[32]

The EMC reinforced various propaganda slogans: the importance of the "revolution," the regime's "democratic appearance," which was constructed in dichotomous contrast with undemocratic "communist" systems, the industrial potency of Brazil, the miracle myth, and civic duties. Obedience to the law was so heavily emphasized that students were even asked to denounce subversives.[33] Suzeley Kalil Mathias interprets the content of EMC books as largely informed by the values of the Superior War School and composed of a mixture of "the national security doctrine with pinches of Catholic conservatism."[34]

It is difficult to assess to what degree this new educational subject strengthened the regime or, contrarily, opened it to ridicule. Three factors potentially undermined the power of EMC propaganda: its values were vague; it depended on the interpretation of the teaching staff; and it was contingent on the students' acceptance of it. Due to the general nature of the values propagated, EMC did not turn into an ostentatious propaganda lecture exalting the regime and brainwashing students, as in the case of Nazi Germany or Soviet Russia. The few military advisers involved in the EMC curriculum seem not to have belonged to the aggressive hardliner faction. Nonetheless, it was a clear attempt to manipulate Brazilians into supporting the military regime, and in addition to blunt propaganda, aggressive elements were occasionally employed, including the construction of enemies and the use of an intimidating tone. Moreover, the outcome depended on how the teachers conveyed the content of EMC textbooks. AERP member Cavalieri, who was a schoolteacher at the time, disliked EMC, and whenever he had to teach it, he selected topics for the curriculum that raised broader philosophical questions. It is likely that other teachers did the same and thereby served as a filter. Several SNI reports in the Ernesto Geisel Archive denounce teachers for criticizing the regime.[35]

Lastly, it is questionable whether the students really accepted the content of EMC or not. Although the subject was mandatory, informal interviews with former students suggest that the obvious elements of propaganda were mocked or ridiculed.[36] Thus, the mixture of blunt and aggressive propaganda contained in EMC might even have had the opposite effect of that which was intended, fostering doubt rather than support. Nonetheless, EMC was not abolished from the school curriculum until 1993, under President Itamar Franco. Possibly it served to consolidate positive myths about the military regime in general and to naturalize euphemistic words such as "revolution," as well as promoting positive connotations of capitalism and negative connotations of communism.

Demands for Aggressive Propaganda: "Psychological War"

The term "psychological warfare," which is prevalent in military and intelligence documents produced during the military regime's reign in Brazil, was first used in a 1941 text on Nazi propaganda. Since 1945, the U.S. military and NATO have defined "psychological warfare" as involving varying tactics, including "propaganda, covert operations, guerrilla warfare, and . . . public diplomacy."[37] Thus, importantly, "psychological war" propaganda is not limited to words alone but also covers psychological and physical violence. A 1948 U.S. military manual uses the term to refer to "*any* weapon" that is used to commit violence.[38] The idea of "psychological war" propaganda is thus rooted in U.S. military strategies and was probably exported via the training of Brazilian military personnel in U.S. military schools, such as the School of the Americas (SOA) in Panama, which also trained Hugo Banzer's and Pinochet's officials. It is difficult to find evidence of psychological war propaganda in the documents available. In all probability these operations were deliberately not documented, and, even if they had been, they would be filed by the military intelligence organs (CIE, CISA, and Cenimar), whose archives are still missing.

According to a 1976 SNI report, hardliners demanded a stricter and more centralized system of censorship and suggested that this be implemented by the ARP. The circular criticized the lack of a single body responsible for censorship, as various institutions were involved in this process. The author demanded that the ARP fulfill this coordinating role and thus directly interfere in the regime's media output.[39] Another SNI document, dated November 18, 1974, analyzed the electoral defeat of the government party, ARENA, and criticized the government's PR. The document listed several reasons for the poor results, including a "lack of official propaganda," which had the effect of preparing the people psychologically for the "messages of the opposition." It criticized the "brusque transformation from a euphoric mood acquired by the anterior government to a feeling of frustration given the distorted reality that had been shown to them [the people]."[40] The same document talked of the "necessity to reorganize the official propaganda." Yet it must be remembered that between April 1974 and February 1976 very few campaigns were launched, since the ARP was only reinstated in early 1976.

Private Agents

Cultural Production

The regime constrained cultural production politically through censorship and economically through the threat of withdrawal of state subsidies. Song lyrics, literature, plays, and films had been systematically censored since 1968. Overall, Zuenir Ventura estimates that between 1968 and 1978 more than five hundred songs, around five hundred films, 450 plays, two hundred books, one hundred newspapers and magazines, and a dozen soap operas (*telenovelas*) were censored.[41] Under the National Security Laws, artists could be tried in court and lose their political rights. Some artists went into exile or fell victim to organs of repression, including the notorious Command to Hunt Communists (CCC) or the CODI-DOI.

The basic structure of cultural production, however, remained largely intact. Unlike under the Nazi system, artists were not forced to register in corporations or threatened with the confiscation of their work permits. Instead the state created several institutions with the intention of investing in aspects of the arts that were supportive of the regime and exerting indirect and financial control over the sector. Thus, despite significant political constraints, cultural production grew in the 1960s and 1970s and continued to be dominated by left-wing artists.[42] In his classic study on culture in the 1960s, Roberto Schwarz summarizes the situation as follows: "the cultural presence of the left was not liquidated at that date [1964], and . . . did not stop growing. Despite the right-wing dictatorship there existed a relative cultural hegemony of the left."[43]

✳

The regime's attitude toward the arts changed over time. Initially, censorship was not systematically employed, and according to Schwarz, the basic strategy of the regime was to allow cultural production but annihilate "its contact with the working and rural classes."[44] In 1968, artists who were critical of the regime increasingly faced intimidation. With the general decline of repression under

Geisel, violence against artists decreased but did not disappear altogether. The primary form of control under Geisel was state investment.

Several art forms functioned as means of resistance to the regime. Many artists adapted to the conditions of constraint by creatively exploring more symbolic and hidden expressions of criticism. Paradoxically, the most repressive years often produced the greatest creative output.[45] In 1967–68, the Tropicália movement emerged, which was associated primarily with music but also influenced theater, cinema, poetry, and visual art. The movement represented an aesthetic and ideological "rupture," sometimes called a "counterculture."[46] Scholars offer various interpretations of the movement, but they agree that its defining characteristic was the use of allegory, as was first observed by Schwarz.[47] While left-wing nationalists criticized tropicalists for entering the mass-culture sector, and others accused the movement of not being directly political, Dunn interprets tropicalism as less "conventional[ly] political," arguing that it criticized the military regime in more subtle ways.[48] Several musicians from the Tropicália movement participated in public protests and demonstrations against the regime or temporarily went into exile, the most prominent of whom were Chico Buarque, Caetano Veloso, and Gilberto Gil. Some were even tortured.

Cinema and the Regime—A Pragmatic Rearrangement

Parts of the heterogeneous film sector collaborated with the state. Although Vargas had already imposed restrictions by introducing a quota for domestic film production, it was only during the military regime that the government directly interfered in the Brazilian film industry by creating a subsidy system in the form of the National Film Institute (Instituto Nacional do Cinema, INC) in 1966, and EMBRAFILME in 1969. Via the INC, the state invested in cinema and distributed awards with the aim of strengthening the nation's film output.[49] The second cinema institution, EMBRAFILME, increasingly functioned as a state-controlled cinema monopoly. First, it distributed films internationally. From 1975 onward, it also produced films and showed them in Brazil.[50] In the 1970s, EMBRAFILME distributed 30 percent of all Brazilian films and controlled between 25 and 50 percent of film production.[51] Between 1974 and 1980, the Brazilian cinema audience doubled.[52] Given that both production and distribution now depended on the state, filmmakers had to cooperate with the military regime to a certain extent. Thus the INC and EMBRAFILME had an ambivalent role. They functioned as both the "most important single factor" in the development of Brazilian cinema and as efficient instruments of state control.[53] The subsidy system was highly competitive and led to favoritism and deterioration in the artistic quality of films.[54] However, the production of Brazilian films was secured.

While they acknowledge the disadvantages of state control, Johnson and Stam emphasize that subsidies constituted an important precondition for the formation of a highly creative Brazilian cinema industry.[55] Although filmmakers were constrained by the newly created coercive system and operated within "state-defined limits," cinema production nonetheless grew with the help of subsidies.[56] When EMBRAFILME was closed in 1990 by the first democratically elected president after the military regime, Collor de Mello, the Brazilian film industry's output decreased dramatically.[57] The subsequent presidents, Itamar Franco and Fernando Henrique Cardoso, reintroduced state funding, but most of the money came from private companies, which received tax breaks in return for film investment. In general, Brazilian cinema is still overshadowed by Hollywood films, as is cinema in the rest of Latin America as well.[58]

Between the 1960s and 1980s, Brazilian cinema was dominated by the aesthetic style and philosophy of the Cinema Novo movement (New Cinema), a heterogeneous movement that demanded social change, rejected the "neocolonial cultural system," and aimed for independent Brazilian art.[59] An alternative movement, which engaged in dialogue with the Cinema Novo, was the so-called Rubbish Cinema (Cinema do Lixo) or Marginal Cinema (Cinema Marginal). Not only was this one of the most radical cultural movements but it also diametrically opposed the ideas promoted by the AERP. In the context of political radicalization, this movement rejected the commercialization of cinema and demanded the acceptance of Brazil's underdevelopment, poverty, and "rubbish." Like the mainstream Cinema Novo movement, it was nationalist and anticolonialist. While the AERP and ARP promoted the idea of progress, development, and "economic miracle," and constructed a positive concept of modernization, Marginal Cinema drew attention to Brazil's underdevelopment, exposed poverty, and regarded modernity and industrialization as a threat. The movement highlighted Brazilian poverty in two senses: the actual poverty experienced by many of its citizens and the dearth of production facilities, which prevented the creation of a genuine Brazilian cinema industry.[60] Although Marginal Cinema did not cause major repercussions, it diametrically opposed official state propaganda.

Overall, the cultural sector grew and, dominated by left-wing artists and producers, remained critical of the regime. After 1968, censorship, violence, and state subsidies constrained artists politically and economically. Since the 1970s, various state institutions had given incentives to Brazilian artists, leading to what Ridenti called a "pragmatic rearrangement."[61]

Mass Media: Collaboration and Resistance

Between 1964 and 1979 the regime had an ambivalent relationship with the Brazilian mass media; the media companies, as is the case in most Latin American countries, are privately owned. Media reactions differed depending on their owners, the type of media, and the time period. On the one hand, the media were under the economic and political control of the government; on the other hand, the sector as a whole benefited from modernization and growth.[62] The government employed various mechanisms to pressure the media into reporting favorably on their activities, of which censorship was the most important and obvious.

Censorship

There has never been complete freedom of the press in Brazil, and episodic political censorship has occurred at other times in history as well. As early as the 1820s, royal censors confiscated the *Correio Brasiliense*, which was published in the United Kingdom. Even the liberal President Juscelino Kubitschek seized the *Tribuna da Imprensa* in the 1950s. However, apart from the military dictatorship's, the only other era during which a systematic form of political censorship had been installed was under the Estado Novo (1937–1945).[63] Under military rule, two kinds of censorship existed: "moral" censorship by the Division for Censorship and Public Entertainment (DCDP), and what scholars call "press censorship" or "political censorship," which focused on political issues. The DCDP censored television, radio, film and theater productions, and song lyrics according to "moral" criteria. Censors mainly prohibited allusions to sexuality and mockery of religious values. This form of censorship had formally existed since January 24, 1946, and reached its peak at the end of the 1970s.[64] Press censorship, on the other hand, only became routine after the AI 5 law, which legalized censorship, was passed in December 1968. Although it was given legal standing through norms and decrees, it was "revolutionary," since it was not legalized by a democratically elected Congress.[65] The peak time for press censorship was between 1968 and 1975.

The field of political or press censorship has been studied extensively.[66] Besides censorship, however, there were further forms of coercion. Economically, the most powerful weapon used by the government was the threat to withdraw its advertisements, as the state was the single most important advertiser.

When the *Jornal do Brasil* criticized the nuclear pact on March 11, 1977, the regime withdrew all advertisements, which were then transferred to the pages of the journal's main competitor, *O Globo*. In addition to official advertising, the government ran or supervised most banks and thus controlled loans. The *Estado de São Paulo* was refused a bank loan for equipment and had to borrow money from a U.S. bank. Branches of the media that supported the government also benefited from subsidies and tax privileges. The military regime's policies contributed to a monopolization of mass media, which still shapes Brazilian politics today and can be seen in the dominance of Globo.[67] The intelligence service, SNI, observed the media and accused them of "communist infiltration."[68] Radio and television were also controlled by a licensing system, and many stations had their licenses revoked under the regime.[69] Lastly, the regime controlled the media through legislation. The key laws were the Press Law, the National Security Law, the National Code of Telecommunications (in which government supervision of mass media was enshrined), the Institutional Acts, and several laws that established institutions designed to control the media.[70] The most important of these laws was the AI 5.

✳

Despite these pressures, the media sector benefited from the post-1964 governments and their policies in various ways: the rapid industrialization; the regime's investment in media infrastructure and a national communications system; and modernization through laws, loans, and subsidies. Although some journals disappeared, and control mechanisms such as censorship caused difficulties for the publishing industry, between 1966 and 1975 the total number of daily newspapers and weekly magazines increased.[71] The improved media network system, which was able to reach a wider area, and the growing numbers of people who owned or had access to television and radio sets increased the size of the audience. The development of an internal consumer market, as well as the regime's openness toward foreign investment, generated more advertising revenue. The multinational corporations (MNCs) contributed between 60 and 95 percent of television advertising expenditure—the most important advertising medium at the time—and thus played an important role in financing Brazilian mass media.[72] Considering that the Brazilian media were privately owned and profit-oriented, media owners must have welcomed the regime's investment in infrastructure. However, business interests could also cause friction with the government. Since the state was not the only advertiser, the media also had to negotiate and work with private businesses. A SNI report from 1972 accuses press owners of being more concerned about their own financial gain than their loyalty to the government.[73]

The press maintained a relatively high level of independence in spite of the propaganda apparatus, the DIP, under Vargas. The DIP distributed texts praising the regime, which the press was forced to print. A similar procedure had been employed by the Nazis, whereby the newspaper editors were dictated to via a daily press conference in Berlin.[74] This was never the case during the military regime in Brazil, as such a measure would have discredited the regime's claim to defend democracy against communism. Neither did the regime directly seize the property of media companies as had occurred with the liberal daily newspaper *O Estado de São Paulo* during the New State era.[75] In the context of the Cold War and to justify its position as a means of safeguarding the capitalist system against communism, the military regime had to find a more discreet way of exerting pressure on print media. Although the Brazilian press had a small readership, and the illiteracy rate was still high—36 percent of the population in 1974—the press was disproportionately influential among the upper levels of society.[76]

✳

Scholars agree that it is necessary to distinguish between different degrees of collaboration. In general, journalists had little choice; if the press refused to comply with prohibitions, censorship was quickly introduced by the state. Most newspapers "opted" for "self-censorship," among them the *Jornal do Brasil*, *O Globo*, and the *Folha de São Paulo*. The only alternatives to "self-censorship" were either the closure of the newspaper or the installation of the second form of censorship, known as prior censorship.[77] Even journalists working for the same newspaper varied in the extent of their collaboration.[78]

At one end of the scale, the journals and newsweeklies that were most relentlessly targeted and offered the greatest resistance were the satirical magazine *O Pasquim*, the center-left weekly *Opinião*, the militant-left magazine *Movimento*, the liberal-conservative *O Estado de São Paulo*, the weekly publication of the Paulista Archdiocese, *O São Paulo*, and the center-right leading weekly magazine *Veja*. *O Estado de São Paulo* was one of the three major and most widely read dailies at that time and had the biggest impact on the elite. The entire staff of *Pasquim* was once jailed but later released.[79] Some journals closed down altogether, including the *Correio da Manhã*, which had initially called for Goulart to be replaced in 1964. Its owner, Niomar Moniz Sodré, was temporarily imprisoned.[80] All newspapers, including those that supported the regime, regarded censorship as illegal and denounced it. Thus, ironically, one of the most censored subjects was criticism of censorship itself.[81]

Press resistance took many forms: symbolic refusals of censorship by highlighting the censored space in the journal; defending their actions in court; and the emergence of an alternative journalism pioneered by *O Pasquim*, established in 1968.[82] Some journals creatively and courageously tried to fool the censors with ambiguous weather forecasts (*Jornal do Brasil*), quotations from the Portuguese epic poem *Lusiadas* containing repeated or disordered stanzas (*O Estado de São Paulo*), or little pictures of angels and devils to alert the readers to which parts were censored (*Veja* magazine).[83] Smith concludes that the majority of the press "went along" with censorship, neither actively supporting it nor resisting it.[84] Most newspapers preferred "self-censorship," because the only alternative was a permanent censor appointed by the state, which would have meant an even more severe curtailment of their freedom.

However, at the other end of the spectrum were some newspapers that voluntarily praised the regime and tried to justify its repressive systems. The most important of these were *O Globo* and *Folha da Tarde*, which published blunt and even aggressive pro-regime propaganda. In the 1970s, *Folha da Tarde* was known as the "official diary of the OBAN," the journal of the police.[85] *O Globo* also parroted regime slogans through the use of headlines like "Médici: 'Nobody can stop this country'" (June 22, 1970), "Médici: 'There won't be a spiral of repression'" (April 1, 1970), and "Médici to the people: 'Revolution resurrected Brasil'" (April 1, 1970, 15). In a supplement published to commemorate the Sesquicentenario, the 150th anniversary of Brazil's independence, *O Globo* paid tribute to the regime with the headline "Rhythm of progress surpasses forecasts."[86]

Television Channels and Radio

At the advent of Brazilian television, in the 1950s, it was only affordable for the elite minority. During the 1960s, television became cheaper and of higher quality, and programs were mostly imported from the United States (canned television). In the late 1960s, audience research was introduced, and programs were increasingly planned according to viewers' tastes.[87] During the third phase, in the 1970s, the domestic telecommunications system improved markedly; more houses had television sets, television broadcasting extended to the whole of Brazil, and the number of imported programs declined. From 1974 onward the output became "nationalized," which means that the same programs were broadcast in all regions of Brazil.[88] In the early 1970s, less than 50 percent of Brazilian households were equipped with electricity, and less than 25 percent had a television, but many people still managed to gain access to television, either in public spaces or at friends' houses.[89]

Television was a new and exciting phenomenon and symbolized modernity. The first color-television pictures, which showed President Médici in 1972, must have impressed the privileged few who had access to a color-television set. The television industry was characterized by technological advancement but was simultaneously prohibited from broadcasting any important political news.[90]

Joseph D. Straubhaar argues that the majority of television broadcasters voluntarily cooperated with the regime until the moment when public opinion rejected military rule and they became afraid of losing advertisers. Although Straubhaar acknowledges conflicting interests among different branches of the media, he argues that in general most broadcasting institutions supported the military regime.[91] A 1975 report from the Ministry of Communication shows that the state regarded television as the most influential and "dangerous" medium, as it "concentrate[d] a terrible power to manipulate wills, to mentally mobilize, to conduct and form a whole generation."[92] In the 1950s and 1960s there were four channels: TV Globo, TV Excelsior, TV Tupi, and TV Record Rio.[93] The most important channel and the one that gained the most from collaborating with the regime was TV Globo.

The Rise of a Media Empire: Rede Globo

Britto and Bolaña call Globo a "legitimizing agent," and Wilkin regards Globo as the "mouthpiece for the military regime."[94] Scholars have unanimously criticized the way in which the Globo Association rose to prominence under state protection in exchange for broadcasting conspicuous pro-regime propaganda.[95] They disapprovingly point out how the Globo television company benefited from a gentleman's agreement with the military regime in 1962 that allowed it to bypass a Brazilian law prohibiting foreigners from becoming co-owners of national media. The first military president, Castelo Branco, personally sanctioned the deal with the firm Time-Life. Thus U.S. capital was directly invested in Globo's new technology, knowledge, and experience. Herz notes that Time-Life wanted to build an anticommunist base in Brazil, and Wilkin claims that Time-Life cooperated with the CIA.[96]

In terms of content, Globo rode the wave of ufanism in the 1960s and glorified the Transamazon Highway. Yet, unlike many other media companies, Globo also praised the instruments of repression. It showed extensive coverage of the so-called repenting terrorists, a form of aggressive propaganda rejected by AERP leader Costa.[97] Thus, contrary to other media companies, Globo produced a mixture of blunt and aggressive pro-regime propaganda.

Globo's relationship with the regime changed over time. By the 1970s there was friction, although that did not affect Globo's support of the regime.[98] SNI files illustrate the main causes of conflict: censorship; allegations against Globo's journalists; and the regime's fears that Globo would become too powerful and monopolize public opinion. Arguably, the longest-running and most important point of disagreement was censorship. Tufte claims that soap operas (*telenovelas*) were largely forbidden and only started to be widely shown in the 1980s.[99] Documentation from the late 1970s reveals the government's increasing ambivalence toward Globo. The government was concerned about Globo's dominance and tried to strengthen its competitors.[100] This antagonism illustrates that the free-market ideology advocated by the early military regime later became a nuisance to the government, once a company became the market leader and had the potential to threaten the government.

Although Globo's power increased during the 1970s and the company became less dependent on the regime's tutelage, it continued collaborating with the regime. The editors of the book on the daily news program *Jornal Nacional* admit that Globo only changed its favorable policy toward the regime when the movement calling for direct presidential elections (*diretas-já*) became a mass movement.[101] Today the Globo network is one of the largest private television producers in the world, running a television network comprising 113 stations, reaching 99.9 percent of Brazilian homes and directly affecting Brazilian politics. Media professionals call Globo the "Brazilian Citizen Kane" or even "beyond Citizen Kane."[102] According to Bernardo Kucinski, Globo's concentration of media concessions is illegal. When historic mass protests erupted in Brazil in the summer of 2013, Globo became a key target of discontent. Dissatisfied with Globo's media dominance and pro-elite news coverage, hundreds of protesters called for "the grand action against media monopoly." They stormed Globo's São Paulo offices and even hurled excrement onto the building's walls. The next day, on August 27, 2013, Globo's Saturday newspaper responded with a surprise apology. It recognized that "Globo supported the dictatorship," and yet claimed that Globo owner Roberto Marinho, who had struck the special deal with the dictatorship, "was always on the side of legality."[103]

Commercial Propaganda

Like the media sector, the Brazilian advertising industry went through a process of modernization, professionalization, and extraordinary growth. The late

1960s and early 1970s were the golden years of commercial propaganda.[104] The advertising sector was one of the main beneficiaries of the economic euphoria and arguably the most active propagandist of the so-called miracle. The government's economic policies of heavy state investment and encouraging foreign capital led to rapid economic growth and the formation of a limited internal consumer market. The new urban middle classes started purchasing consumer goods that had formerly been accessible only to wealthy Brazilians, such as cars and electrical equipment.[105] The number of supermarkets soared from less than one thousand in 1966 to 5,400 in 1972.[106] In 1967, the first shopping mall was built in São Paulo. Moreover, the government contributed to an expanding advertising industry by providing a modern communications system and bank loans and, above all, by being the main advertiser.[107]

Another impetus for this growth was the contribution of foreign advertisers, of which the multinational companies (MNCs) formed the largest group. Between 1930 and 1964 Brazilian advertising was dominated by multinational advertising firms. In the 1950s, domestic advertising agencies boomed, research facilities were built, and the public relations industry was modernized. Only during the military regime era (1964–1975) did domestic advertising firms regain their territory, while the importance of foreign agencies declined. The government came to prefer domestic agencies in the mid-1970s, so it is not surprising that from 1975 onward, domestic agencies dominated the market and continued to flourish.[108]

Setting aside an interest in official advertising, propaganda agencies were less constrained by the government than the media, since censorship did not apply to them.[109] Here, too, the question of collaboration is complex, and agencies reacted differently. Taking a broad perspective, the relationship between the government and propaganda agencies shifted from a predominantly supportive position in 1964 to an extremely supportive position around 1970 to an increasingly critical stance in the late 1970s. This corresponds with the changing attitude of the business sector described by Diniz and Saes.[110]

Francisco Gracioso remarked that commercial propaganda maintained its "normal course" during the dictatorship and that it was "difficult to imagine just by reading the announcements that the country experienced an exceptional situation."[111] However, I would go even further and argue that the advertising industry played a key role in propagating the notions of development, the economic miracle, and patriotism. The government, the media, foreign companies, and the advertising sector supported the triumphant miracle mentality, hoping it would generate higher levels of consumption and greater profits.

Figure 3.1. "Step firmly on this ground which is yours." Commercial made by the Conga shoe company, 1972.

Propaganda magazine commented that until 1974 the "Brazilian miracle" constituted the most frequent visual and textual image used in the communications industry, and even after that date it continued to be prominent.[112] Commercial advertisements between 1969 and 1975 illustrate this point, with the climax arguably being the celebrations of 150 years of Brazilian independence, the *Sesquicentenario*. Conga exploited the independence celebrations to market the company's shoes as "patriotic" and hail the military regime.[113] The march portrayed in this commercial looks fascist or totalitarian given that the people depicted in it are marching in a regimented fashion, are wearing uniforms, and appear to be extremely well disciplined.

Another commercial sold a brand of white rum with the tagline "the other Brazilian miracle." It won a gold award for the best new campaign of the year in 1975. A third example is a commercial made by Supercenter Superbom, which, similarly, won a silver award for the best new campaign of 1975. It alludes to the miracle myth not only in the title but also by using imagery from *Alice in Wonderland*: "Wake up! Wonderland is no longer just a dream."[114]

This emphasis on development and the overlooking of repression were elements that the AERP and ARP shared with publicists. In that sense commercial propaganda can be viewed as an amplifying agent for the AERP and ARP. However, while the AERP and ARP produced largely subliminal propaganda, and collaborative media companies like Globo produced blunt propaganda, much of the commercial advertising industry was arguably situated somewhere in between; while it hailed the "Great Brazil" in a conspicuous way, it rarely directly praised the government. Overall, while political opposition was systematically repressed, the military regime and its allies in the commercial advertising sector diverted attention "to the rise of a consumer society."[115]

Yet in two respects the publicity sector disagreed with the government. Leading figures and associations within the industry rejected censorship and frequently appealed for greater social justice. In the inaugural speech at the Second Brazilian Publicity Congress in 1969, a leading public relations event attracting 804 visitors, Mauro Salles sharply criticized censorship. In the foremost publicity magazine, *Propaganda*, Salles defended the rival magazine *O Pasquim*, which was critical of the regime, and alerted people to the fact that publicists could support the magazine through their own publicity channels.[116]

Moreover, representatives from the advertising sector frequently demanded a fairer distribution of wealth in order to help create a bigger internal consumer market. When Mauro Salles gave a speech at the Superior War School in 1971, he not only praised the economic growth achieved by the "revolution" in co-operation with publicists, but he finished by emphasizing the "ridiculously" low number of consumers in Brazil (thirty-five million out of one hundred million).[117] Fearful that the middle classes could shrink again, he appealed to people to defend the existing consumer market.

However, by the end of the 1970s, the publicity sector increasingly sided with the opposition, which had come to dominate public opinion.[118] During the 1970s, the terms "development" and "progress" became less prominent in the publicity industry discourse. Economic growth rates had fallen due to the petrol crisis, and the military regime changed its attitude toward foreign investors with the intention of strengthening Brazilian companies. Representatives of the advertising industry criticized censorship and human-rights abuses. Their policy of distancing themselves from the regime was also mirrored in announcements. The electronics company Sharp featured drawings by the caricaturist Ziraldo, who was mildly critical of the regime, in its advertising,[119] while a 1977 advertisement imaginatively used colors to allude to the political opening of the regime.

The AERP only had limited contact with major commercial advertising companies, because of its tight budget, and so firms did not make large profits.[120] In addition, the films were directly produced by film production companies chosen through an open artistic competition and not favoritism—a method disliked by commercial propaganda agencies, according to Costa. Publicity companies were employed by other government sectors, in particular the Ministry of Transport, which initiated projects itself, ignoring the coordinating role of the AERP.[121] Although there was no institutional connection between them, the AERP still observed commercial propaganda.[122] Costa mentions that he personally visited publicity agencies to convince them not to broadcast aggressive slogans such as "Be cruel" and "Down with the dictatorship of prices." His mission appears to have been successful.[123]

Another connection involved the publicity sector praising the aesthetic style of the AERP and ARP films, and apparently reproducing it. Costa asserts in an interview that businessmen asked publicity agencies to copy the style of the AERP. Cavalieri, who was an adviser to the AERP, also states that several companies, including the state petrol company Petrobrás, created similar campaigns. A leading representative of the commercial advertising sector, Ney Peixoto do Vale, even praised the AERP by applauding the government's "serious and professionalized communication structure, that produced high level campaigns directed towards making each Brazilian conscious of his responsibility" and assuring people that it was not "glamorizing" the government.[124]

✳

To sum up, the military regime in Brazil was not only legitimized by the official propaganda organs but amplified by other agents that used the media to stabilize, legitimize, and support the dictatorship. Authoritarian rule relied on this willing support and assistance of collaborators to maintain its stability over its twenty-one-year existence. Yet critical questions about the role of the advertising and media sectors can be raised in democracies, too. Commercial advertising and mass media in a democratic system might support other kinds of power structures, including a financial system that depletes the world's resources or that is prone to financial crises with consequences for millions of ordinary citizens. It might also support asymmetric global power structures, which exploit less developed countries. Highly monopolized private media ownership has become a global fact, as illustrated by Globo. We have seen this in Italy, where Berlusconi owns the major television channels, and in Great Britain, where Rupert Murdoch has exercised great influence by controlling parts of the media. Like any place where power is concentrated, media monopolies have the potential to endanger critical thought.

4

Getting Into Their Heads

Propagandists' Intentions

Trying to determine the intentions of the propagandists of authoritarian Brazil is a difficult task, because supporting evidence is often lacking. We have considerable insight into how Hitler conceived of propaganda, because he dedicated sections of his notorious book *Mein Kampf* to the subject. His chief propagandist—Joseph Goebbels—gave a series of speeches and wrote about propaganda in his diaries. However, even when such sources are available, they may not accurately and honestly reveal the propagandists' true intentions. Another way to try to discover the propagandists' intentions is to interview them. Fortunately, in addition to AERP leader Octávio Costa, I was able to interview the other four core members of the official propaganda organ (José Camargo, who later became the leader of successor organ ARP, João Baena Soares, Alberto Rabaça, and José Cavalieri), which shed some light on their intentions. Whenever they contradicted each other, I had to think that someone was hiding or distorting the truth. Surprisingly, however, this rarely happened.

Nonetheless, reconstructing the intention of a propagandist is a challenge in democratic and authoritarian regimes alike. When studying authoritarian regimes we are inclined to condemn propaganda agents from the outset. Fico, for example, raises the vital question: "How can we not previously condemn a political regime which suppressed the most elementary liberties? . . . How can we not presume a concealing intention in that propaganda?" Approaching the task with a "naively neutral attitude" is impossible, but Fico believes that it is possible to avoid "the simplicity induced by superficial condemnations."[1] This illustrates the classic dilemma that any scholar working with oral history faces: on the one hand, we do not want to succumb to the error of being biased from the start, because we are dealing with someone who worked for an authoritarian regime. We have to listen to their words open-mindedly, because it will not be very illuminating if we select only those quotations that support our preconceived ideas. On the other hand, we cannot sacrifice our critical distance.

The best technique available for keeping oneself as objective as possible is to locate and compare various sources, a method also called triangulation. I was fortunate in this respect, because Costa published books and newspaper articles dating from the 1960s to the present day, many of his oral history interviews were published, and I was able to interview him directly on four occasions.[2] Apart from cross-checking them against each other, I compared all my interviews with manuals or reports produced by the propaganda organizations and personal and published writings by the propagandists. Researching the intentions that lay behind propaganda is therefore true detective work in the Ginzburgian sense of the term, which requires an alertness and sensitivity to clues.[3]

The Sacked Ghostwriter

On October 30, 1969, a new military president assumed power, under whose auspices Brazil would experience one of its darkest moments in history, the "years of lead," as they came to be called. At the inauguration ceremony, Emilio Garrastazú Médici gave a speech that was broadcast on both television and radio, reproduced in the newspapers, and even published in a book.[4] This speech, like all of Médici's early speeches, was authored by the AERP leader Costa, who deliberately imbued it with moderation. On the one hand, it was addressed to the Brazilian people, and therefore Costa tried to emphasize themes that would "bring hope to the nation." On the other hand, Costa aspired to send a message to Médici himself. "Disarmament of the spirits, union, national pacification. . . . All that I tried to put into his mouth . . . to make him read it. But I wanted it to penetrate his heart and his head," Costa says. Although Médici apparently enjoyed the success of his inaugural speech, Costa comments dejectedly that his effort was "in vain," because repression and subversion continued to escalate.[5]

Reactions to Costa's speech varied, and they serve to illuminate how Costa was misperceived all along. While a columnist from the *Jornal do Brasil*, Carlos Castello Branco, a leading journalist and intellectual at the time, congratulated Costa for having managed to put his own words into the president's mouth, others, including both opponents of the regime and hardliners, criticized him sharply. Don Evaristo Arns, a clergyman and principal opponent of the regime, denounced it as a "misleading talk." Others misunderstood his "strategy" and accused Costa of being "insincere." Hardliners, on the other hand, mocked him and sarcastically asked whether he was trying to secure Médici's place in the

Brazilian Academy of Literature. Soon his career as the president's ghostwriter was over. He was dismissed. Subsequent speeches were written by the hardliner Hugo de Abreu.[6]

As Costa could no longer influence the government as a speechwriter, he attempted to use the AERP instead but was significantly hampered by the minor role that the institution played within the government.[7] In the interviews conducted with Costa and his staff, as well as those edited by the CPDOC, Costa repeatedly insists that Médici had no interest in his work and that he felt ostracized and unsupported. The narrative of suffering, through misunderstanding from all sides—as with the inauguration speech—and his position as an outsider, is a key element of Costa's self-portrayal. He mentions that, on one occasion, he felt so miserable that he stayed in bed for several days. He claims that he was a "nobody in the Planalto" and describes his AERP years as follows:

> I would say to you that they were the worst years of my life. Not because of the AERP, but because I felt like a pariah. . . . I was totally lost in the Planalto. Without, without any support. Without support. I didn't have the total support of my boss, it was only a formal support. . . . I was taking a risk doing what I thought I should be doing, all right?! . . . and I was met with huge incomprehension, the biggest incomprehension. Incomprehension from within and from outside. Incomprehension from my comrades and incomprehension from outside the military. The people thought that I was Machiavellian, that I was a Dr. Goebbels, and I was none of that. I have had to swallow incomprehension right up to the present day, like that of Professor Carlos Fico who did not know how to do justice to me."[8]

The interviews are filled with the vocabulary of suffering; for example, he uses expressions like "I suffered," "incomprehension from all sides," and "like a fish out of water" and says, "I was precisely the most marginalized person within the Palace of the Planalto. I was the culprit who took all the blame, the disloyal person who spoke to all the journalists, the one who always told the truth."[9] A prime and often quoted example is the "Brazil: Love It or Leave It" campaign (Brasil: Ame-o ou deixe-o), which was actually directed against Costa's philosophy and wrongly attributed to him. As mentioned previously, this hardliner campaign was launched during Operation Bandeirantes in June 1969, which marked the formation of a systematic repressive system that was later institutionalized in the form of the CODI-DOI. Stickers bearing this slogan were initially distributed freely, on a wide scale, and later sold. The AERP rejected this sort of overt propaganda that created a specific enemy and sought to radicalize society. Camargo ironically commented on the AERP's impotent position by stating that those behind that campaign "did not recall that there existed a government organ capable of centralizing this type of work [campaigns]."[10]

Costa's Relationship with Dictator Médici

In several interviews Costa says that he admires Médici and that he was a "good man." However, I noticed that his disappointment with Médici dominates his narrative. Costa implies that Médici was neither a hardworking nor powerful president.[11] In addition to Médici's lack of interest in the AERP, the two men diverged in their worldviews. Costa critically observes that Médici's ultimate intention was to crush "subversives," by violent means if necessary. Eventually Médici succeeded, "with a terrible result." Costa rejected this strategy of institutional violence.[12] In another interview, he characterizes Médici once again as a "good man," "personally," but also says that he was not "a man of great vision" and that he conceived of himself more as a soldier whose personal strategy was to combat subversives.[13] This is interesting, because Costa conceived of himself as both citizen and soldier, and although he also wanted to defeat the subversives, he rejected the use of violence to achieve that. In Costa's view, Brazil found itself in a "terrible situation," marked by the imminence of more violence and attacks on the "constitutional state": "the duel between subversives and repression caused a big national discomfort." The AERP leader's stated intention was to change the national climate and contribute to a "disarmament of spirits" and a "harmonization of positions." Costa says: "[I thought that] if I succeeded in making the propaganda promote values of union, harmony, hope, trust, instead of values of violence, I would change it all."[14]

However, his strategy failed. President Médici did not actively support his philosophy, and several hardliners openly attacked it, meaning that the role played by the AERP was ultimately minor. Costa's story, as well as those of other AERP members, is that of an outsider constantly struggling with a balancing act. "In order to create a positive atmosphere . . . hoping that the creation of such an atmosphere would lead to better days. . . . That was my strategy," he says. "And it was within this strategy that I lived and suffered intensively for four years. With incomprehension from all sides . . . and with the incomprehension even of the beneficiaries. The president never, never valued what I did for him, never."[15]

He seems to have been much more open-minded than Médici. From his own and others' interviews, I know that Costa tried to persuade Médici to make the system more open at the end of his term of governance.[16] When I asked Costa directly, he said that he tried to talk to him but that he was considered too unimportant to be able to convince Médici. Several other interviewees confirmed that Costa tried to impress upon the dictator the need to hand power over to civilians. According to Costa's account, he was unable to influence Médici: "And I did not succeed in modifying his point of view. I think that essentially he proceeded as a military officer. To his mind, a military officer had to win the war."[17]

Cavalieri believes that Costa became disenchanted with Médici and that the hardliner Hugo de Abreu tried to bar Costa from gaining access to the president. Leitão de Abreu was the chief of staff (chefe da casa civil) under Médici. Cavalieri believes that Médici's power was limited and that the Planalto was largely ruled by Abreu. This view is shared by another AERP member, João Baena Soares, who believes that Médici was so powerless that effectively he could not be in any camp—neither that of the hardliners nor the moderates.[18] Costa believes that the president would have been in favor of normalization at the end of his term of governance but feared the radical military, which wanted to remain in power.[19]

"I Balanced Myself on a Rope"

According to the AERP official Baena, the hardliners accepted neither Octávio Costa nor the AERP's slogans, which were often harshly criticized.[20] These problems were rooted in a philosophy contrary to that of the hardliners.[21] Costa's passion for poetry and his lyrical writing style contributed further to his sidelining, as these were at odds with notions of what a good or masculine soldier should be, and he was dismissed as a "dreamer or non-realist."[22] The AERP regularly organized film screenings in the Planalto, and hardliners always criticized the films personally. This also explains why I could not find any documents criticizing the short films. Apparently, even the famous animated character Sujismundo drew criticism from hardliners.[23]

Nonetheless, Costa managed to resist two forms of propaganda: the blunt propaganda of his predecessor, D'Aguiar, propaganda à la "Brasil grande," and aggressive propaganda promoting the so-called psychological war. As mentioned earlier, propaganda à la "Great Brazil" emphasized Brazil's natural resources and encouraged patriotism.[24] In contrast, aggressive or "psychological war" propaganda was based on a radical form of anticommunism. Camargo, Baena, and Rabaça criticize both types of propaganda and admire Costa's ability to resist them. Rabaça recalls that the hardliners demanded the use of "tough language in the media" and campaign slogans like "whoever does not walk on the right had better leave Brazil."[25] Costa feared that the government or hardliners would try to make the AERP into an instrument of psychological war, thus strengthening repression. To Costa, this would have been the point at which he would no longer have been able to combine his roles as citizen and soldier: "I would have left everything, if they had wanted to make my communication organ [AERP] promote psychological warfare, all right?! Use it for the benefit of repression, the benefit of repression, all right?! Then I would not have been able to reconcile the soldier and the citizen. This was not the case either. They preferred to make *guerra psicológica* inside the organs of repression themselves."[26]

During the late 1960s, Costa was clearly already critical of repression and aggressive anticommunism. For example, on October 30, 1968, he wrote in the *Jornal do Brasil*: "It is the hand of the 'shoot the scoundrel' who orders the hunt for communists. . . . I feel pity for this hand which nourishes ideological terrorism, deepens the rift, and degenerates into an attitude of 'an eye for an eye.' And the man who this hand belongs to is convinced that he defends democracy, freedom, and Christian civilization."[27]

In another article, Costa criticizes military paranoia about the "revolutionary war" and places communists, fascists, and paranoids on the same level, saying, "It's time to realize that this chaotic freedom caused by the lack of a philosophy of democratic education has brought us a harvest of so many people teaching communism and fascism . . . and several militaries to exaggerate the threats of revolutionary war as an exclusive priority."[28]

On the other hand, what Costa, hardliners, and the Brazilian right-wing camp in general have in common is their rejection of a communist society. Between 1961 and 1963 the armed forces adopted the theories of a "war of insurrection." Almost 80 percent of the texts that they read propagated these theories and more or less brainwashed the key military personnel of the time.[29] However, Costa wanted a debate about communism and to allow communists to express themselves openly, rather than discarding their views, let alone by force: "I have never accepted a complete rejection of communism, never."[30] According to Costa, extreme anticommunism was not part of the military tradition, since famous communists of the past had also been military officials (the prime example being Luís Carlos Prestes). What he demanded instead was "education for development, freedom and democracy," which he contrasted with communist systems that completely politicized institutions.

Addressing communists and the right-wing camp within the armed forces, he called for an "authentic democracy" via education. His concept of democracy, he explained in his interview, is one "where all opinions are heard."[31]

Divided Between Teaching and Giving Orders

For several years prior to the coup, Costa taught at a military school. Balancing roles as a teacher and a soldier resulted in inner conflict: "With a whole life divided between teaching and giving orders, with a conscience of having always defended the armed forces, to the brink of our powers, the bad habit/mistake of dishonorable militarism, . . . arbitrariness and contempt."[32] When I asked him whether the AERP and ARP films constituted propaganda, Costa denied it. He said that he conceived of them as a form of civic education, and he defined propaganda as "an act of social communication in which you sell a product," whereby the product of political propaganda is the elections. To his mind, slogans like "This is a country that advances" [Este é um país que vai pra frente] or "Nobody can stop Brazil" [Ninguém segura o Brasil] do not constitute political propaganda but are "messages of ambition, construction, and civic energy." Following Costa's strategy, the AERP tried never to glorify anybody. Asked whether this emphasis on the fatherland did not indirectly promote the government, he denied it, arguing that he intended to stoke up feelings of love for the fatherland because these were in short supply at the time.[33] At this point, it is difficult to understand Costa's reasoning, since his work nonetheless sells Brazil as a product. In Costa's view, selling a specific government was not the same as selling patriotic feelings.

Similarly, the other AERP members complained whenever I used the term "propaganda" during interviews and insisted on the neutral expression "social communication" (communição social) or "social education" (educação social) instead. Cavalieri, who was trained not only in psychology but also philosophy, constantly emphasized the AERP's task of providing moral and civic education. He linked this idea with Brazil as a developing country and patronizingly talked about Brazil's "moral inferiority" compared with Europe. Baena also emphasized that the AERP tried to "awaken love and affection for Brazilian things."[34] Baena argued that the AERP did not create propaganda but carried out "civic education, or . . . citizenship training . . . via nationalist messages to give an incentive to the development of society and the participation of the citizen."[35] In sum, all AERP members thought of themselves as educators or teachers promoting "civilian education" and not as propagandists.[36] Yet the question remains whether, under dictatorships, the championing of civil society may in fact mask that dictatorship's true intentions. According to the AERP members, they did not intend it to function that way.

✳

Costa used his personal relationships with former classmates to free the renowned journalist and intellectual Alberto Dines, who was imprisoned by a wholehearted "revolutionary" and good friend of Costa.[37] Costa maintains that he did not have any connection to the circles of repression but simply used his friendship with this individual to convince him that Dines was a friend and that it would demonstrate a "lack of intelligence" to keep a man with such an enormous national reputation as a political prisoner. This is interesting, because it demonstrates on a micro level how personal relations often bridged ideologically opposed camps.

Personal relations also bound the different military camps together. Carlos Alberto Cabral Ribeiro, whom Costa describes as "one of the harshest hardliners that you can imagine," and who later became minister of the Military Supreme Court, was his teaching colleague at the General Staff School, a military school that provides training for future military leaders. They shared one common interest—poetry. Cabral Ribeiro showed Costa his poems, and although Costa described them as "terrible," he diplomatically found nice words for them. This "terribly harsh hardliner" helped Costa a few times because of their shared love of poetry. Another radical hardliner and a key figure in the repression was General Umberto Melo, Commander of the Second Army, who "immensely liked" Costa. "A few times he helped me as well," he says. "But albeit very cautiously. Very cautiously, because these things, these things—you can imagine what the atmosphere was like at that time."[38]

These episodes illustrating how Costa helped people (and vice versa) not only highlight a certain open-mindedness but also demonstrate how personal relations between individuals from different ideological camps held the military regime together for twenty-one years despite the many internal conflicts that existed.

Costa's propaganda philosophy, however, presented a major obstacle for certain hardliners, particularly the National Security Service (SNI). In a talk given at a conference held at the Superior War School (ESG) in 1970, Costa argued that lying to the public is counterproductive and that, instead, the government should change its policies; in other words, stop the repression and publish the truth. After this speech, he was challenged by an SNI official from the psychological warfare department, who disagreed with his pronouncement that "truth is the essence of communication."[39]

When I asked the AERP staff whether it was their intention to confront the hardliners, they replied that it was not. Yet, although it was not a *deliberate* strategy, many argued that they wanted to put the AERP's moderate philosophy into action and that the confrontation with the *linha dura* was merely a consequence of the AERP's work rather than a stated intention.[40] Baena holds that provoking the *linha dura* was not an explicit objective, as they could have closed down the AERP: "Also, because what we have done to diminish the impact of the hardliners was more efficient than arguing with the hardliners. [*laughs*] . . . Our work was more subtle. . . . This result was more intelligent than 'Let's finish off the hardliners . . . '—then we would have caused a reaction, of course."[41]

Camargo uses a similar argument when justifying the AERP's choice of seemingly apolitical topics:

[W]e were living in a dictatorship. There was almost no dialogue between the government and the people. . . . Thus, we felt obliged to bridge this gap. . . . We chose ways that allowed us to communicate with the people. Therefore we used topics for the public good. For example, "love for your work." . . . As we could not talk about democracy and dictatorship, which would have been the big topic at that moment, because it would have been censored, we chose a sector which to us seemed useful."[42]

Despite the constant friction that the AERP experienced with hardliners and its relative lack of power, it nonetheless managed to act surprisingly independently. Although, as Rabaça states, "Octávio balanced himself with caution," the AERP members were never afraid of losing their political rights (*cassações*). Secondly, they were never censored, as has been common practice in other authoritarian regimes, including the Nazi and Vargas regimes.[43] The hardliners could have sent a so-called *gorilla* into the AERP but refrained from doing so. Baena also believes that Costa was hugely respected, even by those with opposing views.[44] These are important points that suggest either a certain weakness in the hardliner camp or a specific disinterest among hardliners on the issue of official governmental PR. It also illustrates that moderate or more liberal-minded and hardliner elements came into conflict to a limited extent without daring to interfere too much in each other's work. Consequently, although the uniformly liberal-minded AERP team constantly faced acts of sabotage, it was nonetheless exempt from censorship and direct threats by the intelligence services. The precise reasons remain unclear, but comments from AERP officials suggest that personal bonds and the respect with which Costa was regarded played a significant role, rather than pursuit of the same ends.

Credibility of Costa

Ex-AERP member Baena emphasized that there was no link whatsoever between the AERP and organs of repression and that the AERP was clearly against military extremism. He insists that the messages should be viewed within their historical context, rather than uncritically judging what happened outside of this frame of reference: "In no way were we allies of the repression. . . . If you stimulate feelings of patriotism, . . . self-confidence among the population, if you prime the population to receive educational messages—then you are a counterpart . . . to extremism. The AERP was never extremist. In no way."[45]

In Baena's view, the value of the AERP lay precisely in this "counterpart" role [contrapartida] and, in his book, he confirms that Costa and Camargo criticized repression, saying "neither Octávio nor Camargo were happy with the situation. On the contrary, they always tried to modify it. Today it is very easy to talk about the past, but at the time one didn't know the extent to which things were happening or could happen."[46]

While this sounds like an easy excuse offered by members of regimes that are responsible for human-rights abuses, it is striking that all AERP members fervently affirm the AERP's rejection of repressive politics. Similarly, Rabaça argues that "at no time was the AERP's intention to distract from repression": "We didn't agree with that form of repression. The group was led by Octávio Costa and he himself didn't agree with that form of repression. Thus we weren't auxiliary instruments—absolutely not, on the contrary. We were an instrument that believed that the country needed social cohesion. Needed integration between the antagonists. Needed to bring them all together."[47]

Cavalieri argues that, since the AERP was "very disconnected from the core of hardliners in the government," it faced many conflicts.[48] Contrary to Fico's implication that the AERP intended to strengthen the regime by concealing repression, Cavalieri says: "The AERP tried to achieve a certain tranquility, a certain peacefulness, a certain balance. I would not say that this distracted the people—no. This was not the intention. The intention was precisely to create an atmosphere conducive to moral and civic education."[49]

Camargo also refutes Fico:

I believe that in no way can our work be considered to have been helping the repression. The contrary was true, we opposed the repression, and tried to enter into communication with the people via noble subjects. I don't believe that this could have influenced the repression. This is something I would never have done, and I don't agree. [laughs] . . . My position is radically against this accusation. This is not based on the slightest evidence that we helped the repression, nor the contrary. We tried to search for a new space of communication. . . . And succeeded. Small, but those were absurd times, and thus he who achieved a little had already earned a victory. And we managed a lot of things. We also made mistakes. . . . If this was the case [that the AERP supported the repression] that would have been a complete failure of our work, to help the repression. The "Brazil: Love It or Leave It" campaign would have been exactly that type which we have never accepted.[50]

Along with the AERP members who attest to Costa's position, the most important evidence is Costa's own writing from the time. In an article published on June 21, 1964, Costa justifies the coup as an anticommunist intervention largely supported by the public.[51] However, even at this stage, he warned that the "revolution" should not lead to military tyranny and a lack of civilian power: "That they [military personnel] don't become arrogant as infallible arbitrators in all questions, that they contribute with all their energy to the quickest strengthening of civilian power."[52] Hence, while Costa rejected communism as a social system, he also rejected the paranoid anticommunism practiced within the armed forces, particularly among the radicals. Costa surely desired a specific kind of civilian power, namely one that defended a moderate form of anticommunism while rejecting an aggressive anticommunist stance. My reading of Costa is that, ideally, he wanted civilian forces to be in power rather than the military, yet he had an interest in defying communism in a general sense, too. What this passage effectively illustrates is that, at that time, he was already appealing for "comprehension and mutual understanding among Brazilians without hatred and irreconcilable passions."[53]

❋

In 1968 and 1969, Costa regularly published articles in the leading daily newspaper, *Jornal do Brasil*.[54] In order to set his articles in their political context, it is important to keep in mind how politically tense this period was in Brazil. In 1968, students, workers, and the progressive clergy stepped up their acts of protest against the regime in the form of demonstrations, strikes, and public criticism. An important incident was the Protest March of the One Hundred Thousand (Passeata dos Cem Mil) on June 26, 1968, which led the National Security Council (CSN) to prohibit further protest in the streets. Throughout the year, police officers and right-wing terrorist groups launched several attacks on civilians. In March, policemen killed the student Edson Luís; in April the headquarters of the liberal daily newspaper *O Estado de São Paulo* were bombed; and in October the notorious Command to Hunt Down Communists (Comando de Caça aos Comunistas [CCC]) assassinated the student José Guimarães. At the same time, several armed guerrilla groups consolidated themselves or were founded, among them the Popular Revolutionary Vanguard (Vanguarda Popular Revolucionária [VPR]) and the National Liberation Command (Comando de Libertação Nacional [COLINA]), founded in 1966 and 1967, respectively. On October 12, 1968, guerrilla fighters shot a member of the CIA, Captain Chandler.

The regime's response to the political friction was the Institutional Act No. 5 (AI 5), issued on December 13, 1968. This law—the most notorious in the dictatorship's history—abolished basic political rights and legalized systematic political censorship. On July 1, 1969, the repressive operation OBAN was created in São Paulo, which eventually led to the establishment of a repressive system throughout Brazil. Most of the victims came from the urban middle class and were between fourteen and twenty-five years old. Furthermore, the armed forces faced huge internal schisms over the succession of Costa e Silva, who had a stroke in August and died on December 17, 1969. A military junta assumed power, but struggles within the military continued for months.[55]

Costa's articles at the time prove that even during those politically tense years he adopted a moderate view and appealed for reconciliation. For example, one week after the notorious Institutional Act No. 5, he pleaded for negotiation and diplomacy in his article "The Hour and Moment for Diplomacy."[56] On the one hand, he justified the regime's actions by arguing that those who criticized the regime were doing nothing to improve the country's situation. He condemned a member of the opposition party, Moreira Alves, who, in an act of antidictatorial resistance, had appealed to all Brazilian women to refuse to give their love to any military official.[57] Costa criticized Alves' behavior as a "provocation of very bad taste" and argued that it could only lead to "the reopening of the revolutionary process in all its possible forms." In other words, Costa believed that Alves' "provocation"—which alternatively might be regarded as a courageous act of resistance against the regime—would strengthen the hardliners and fuel repression. But equally, he harshly criticized the AI 5, calling it an "answer in terms of a revolutionary reality that is not legitimate for anyone with common sense." He hoped that the AI 5 would not lead to future turmoil, saying, "We trust in God that this moment is short and fruitful, so that the revolution of our dreams, the true change, occurs in favor of our people, in the name of our future."[58] The phrase "revolution of our dreams" implies that what was happening at the time was not the "revolution" that Costa desired.

In September 1969, Costa commented on another politically tense event. On September 4, 1969, a guerrilla group had kidnapped the United States ambassador Charles Elbrick and demanded the release of a group of guerrilla fighters from Brazilian prisons in exchange for Elbrick.[59] It should be noted that this occurred shortly after the implementation of the OBAN, on July 1, 1969, which institutionalized a repressive system in Brazil. When the Brazilian government eventually decided to release the guerrilla fighters, a significant number of military officials strongly disagreed with this policy. On September 6, 1969, a manifesto was issued, and twenty radical officials stormed the National Radio building to read it on air to the Brazilian people.[60] The hardliner manifesto vehemently attacked the military junta, who had been in power since August 31, 1969, following President Costa e Silva's stroke. Radical officials also distributed pamphlets together with the manifesto in the barracks. One radical group even tried unsuccessfully to prevent the prisoner exchange—guerrilla fighters in return for the U.S. ambassador—from taking place at the airport. The rebellion by military hardliners was eventually defeated, and the thirty officials involved were imprisoned. This illustrates just how politically tense the situation became.

In his article, Costa wrote: "My fatherland was born peacefully, adding, understanding, uniting, freeing. . . . My fatherland is unity. My fatherland is not the country of the revolutionary war, but the vocation of peace, of understanding and agreement. It's the wisdom of greater solutions without convulsions and without blood."[61] He appealed for reconciliation by portraying Brazil as a peaceful nation and demanding calm from both the left and right. He indirectly criticized the current system as undemocratic and violent: "My fatherland is neither a fascist dictatorship, nor a communist dictatorship. . . . My fatherland is this democracy planted in the heart of the people rather than among politicians. . . . My fatherland is not radicalism . . . is not irreconcilable hatred. . . . My fatherland is not repression and retaliation . . . is not arbitrariness. . . . My fatherland is brotherhood among the people."[62]

It goes without saying that this was wishful thinking. This article nonetheless demonstrates that, even in politically tense situations, Costa tried to adopt the role of arbitrator or diplomat, who appealed to peace and unity. His articles already foreshadowed the propaganda philosophy that would later characterize the short films made by the AERP. The problem is that both peace and unity are abstract concepts, and one wonders on whose terms he visualized them.

Yet, if Costa opposed radical hardliners and disapproved of the AI 5, we need to ask what role he played in the coup itself. In an interview, Costa says, "I did not have any revolutionary concept. I did not launch any revolution. I was at a [military] school." Although in hindsight these remarks may sound like a self-serving justification, I found confirmation that he was not a staunch defender of the coup in his personal file at the military headquarters in Brasília. A section entitled "participation in the revolution" revealed a check in the "no" box. However, Costa provided passive support to his "revolutionary" comrades: "Meanwhile showing solidarity with my companions, I was not an activist. . . . I stayed very happy in my position as a spectator."[63]

Costa obviously shared some values with the military regime. If his experience with the AERP caused him so much suffering, why did he not leave?[64] In 1964, Costa justified the coup as an anticommunist intervention. Even in a recent interview, in 2007, he defended that view. In a press article published in June 1964, he writes that the coup was an act "of the democratic revolution."[65] However, in the same article he is disparaging about the Vargas dictatorship, warning of arbitrariness and a military schism and calling for more power to be given to civilian forces. Another aspect that Costa shares with coup supporters is his striving for "development"—a key element in his propaganda philosophy. However, it remains unclear precisely what he envisioned when he used the term. Hardliners also called for "development," but in their view it meant a society without either political representation or a labor movement. In all likelihood, Costa conceived of development in its literal sense—the industrialization and transformation of Brazil into a developed country. It is striking that he also used typical propaganda expressions related to modernization, like "fixing the country."[66]

Yet a key difference between Costa and hardliners was his open-mindedness and willingness to consider different perspectives. Costa wanted an open debate rather than the suppression of opposing viewpoints, and he was surrounded by liberal intellectuals, like students and journalists. Moreover, although Costa justified the coup as a defense against communism, he was not a radical anticommunist either. Lastly, and most importantly, Costa rejected violence as a political weapon.

Ultimately, then, in which camp did Costa belong? Although he respected Castello Branco and harshly criticized the "ideologically intoxicated . . . radicalized" part of the armed forces and intelligence services, he claims not to have belonged to any specific camp, including the so-called moderates.[67] But despite his tolerant and pacific attitude, Costa had friends who were clearly involved in the repression. I have already mentioned Camara Senna, Carlos Alberto Cabral Ribeiro, and Umberto Melo, who secretly helped him to secure the release of political prisoners.

However, given Costa's aversion to repression, his friendship with Orlando Geisel is strikingly paradoxical. Until approximately 1967–68, Costa worked as a personal assistant to Orlando Geisel, as well as his ghostwriter, when Geisel held the top military position of the Military General Staff (ECEME).[68] Every day, Geisel gave Costa a ride to work. They became such good friends that Geisel was asked to be the godfather at the wedding of Costa's eldest daughter. "He was an extraordinary man, a privileged head; I wished him well," Costa says. "He was particularly caring with me. He called me pal."[69] Orlando Geisel also employed Costa's sister, Aniger, as a dressmaker for his sister-in-law—Ernesto Geisel's wife. Later, when the Geisel brothers were in dispute, Ernesto used Costa to inquire about the health of his brother.[70] So what does this tell us? On the one hand, Costa displayed a strong and consistent aversion to repression, and on the other, he clearly liked Orlando Geisel, who, as the Army minister, was extremely powerful and ultimately responsible for the repression—a fact that Costa openly admitted, saying "He . . . held all the military power, acted in the area of repression."[71] Nonetheless, Costa visited him until his death. Clearly, ideological divides were overcome by friendships that to us seem paradoxical, if we accept Costa's proclamations that he saw himself as outside of the regime.

Besides feeling a certain amount of solidarity with the coup, another reason why Costa did not leave his job was his strong identification with the armed forces. Although he describes himself as an atypical soldier, because he did not come from a military family and because of his passion for poetry, his dedication to the military is consistent.[72] The armed forces are based on discipline and comradeship, and this bond was strengthened by Costa's participation in the Brazilian Expeditionary Force (FEB) during the Second World War. The FEB fought in Italy against the fascists, and this experience inspired antitotalitarian beliefs among many military officials. Moreover, his identification with the military institution was fortified by his role as a teacher within the armed forces. Most significantly, when Costa was a boy he dreamed of his father, a lawyer who had died before he was born. His father appeared to him and said: "Why don't you join the army? Go, and everything will turn out fine."[73] In 1969, *Veja* magazine wrote that Costa was "considered to be one of the most cultured and discreet army officials."[74]

In his later interviews, Costa argues that despite the "militarism"—a form of state power dominated by the "radicalized" parts of the army—a significant part of the armed forces was still characterized by military professionalism. What he most clearly criticizes is the later military regime, which he also refers to as the "criptogoverno"—a state ruled by the intelligence services.[75] A press article from 1978 claims that Costa was regarded as the possible future leader of the SNI, and quotes his reaction to this suggestion: "In no way. I am not a man of the intelligence sector."[76] While concrete proof that Costa's propaganda aimed to support violent repression is lacking, there is enough evidence to cast serious doubt on this allegation, including the consistent views of the entire AERP staff, Costa's articles at the time, and his critical interviews during the 1990s.

José Maria Toledo de Camargo

In a similar fashion, Camargo's narrative centers around his experience of suffering, on his "balancing act," and his aversion to repression.[77] Between 1977 and 1978 he fulfilled a double function as leader of the ARP and spokesman for President Geisel. Camargo hated this post. "I seriously thought of leaving my profession," he says. He describes the years he spent doing this job as the worst time of his life: "I ended up counting the days and I imagined that I would not make it to the end." Camargo believes that he was unsuited to the post, since he distanced himself from censorship and the extreme [political] right. Furthermore, he says he lacked "talent, preparation and principally pleasure," as well as "political flexibility."[78]

One of the main problems Camargo encountered, yet again, was tension with the SNI and other powerful hardliners, including Hugo de Abreu.[79] On one occasion SNI officials prohibited a performance by a Russian ballet troupe, because they feared that the artists were communists in disguise. Camargo anticipated criticism and protested against the order, but to no avail. Later this prohibition was publicly attacked, and Camargo was blamed for having failed to protect Geisel's reputation. Like Costa, he recounts how the SNI regarded him and his staff as "a gang of inexperienced men" and exerted constant pressure on him. He also says that he wanted to "open new paths," whereas the SNI wanted to "shut paths down." Hugo de Abreu also often undermined his position by publishing material that contradicted Camargo. Hardliners continually sabotaged Camargo's public relations work.

In addition to friction with hardliners and the SNI, justifying Geisel's authoritarian policies presented another challenge. In one instance Geisel was strongly criticized for having publicly referred to the MDB party as an enemy. Camargo had to rectify this pronouncement and try to restore Geisel's tarnished image. "I tried, with any means, to explain to the attendant journalists that this was not a radicalization but a professional deformation," he says. "I tried to handle the balancing pole like an acrobat trying to adjust, but I noticed that things increasingly deteriorated. . . . I was relieved when I left."[80]

Camargo's View on Propaganda

Camargo was in broad agreement with Costa's propaganda principles; however, he was not always powerful enough to bring them to fruition. Unlike Costa, he acknowledged that the AERP was somewhat propagandistic. He admitted that they exploited the Brazilian football team's World Cup victory to pass a law that promoted the use of national symbols and that they used a football slogan of Médici's for a campaign ("Nobody can stop this country anymore" [Ninguém segura mais este país]). In addition, he acknowledged that the AERP produced propaganda in favor of the Transamazon Highway. Nonetheless, to Camargo's mind, the ARP campaigns were more "propagandistic" than the AERP's, because the ARP reported on government policies and national industries positively: "Some things were a little bit of propaganda . . . 'the government did that.' . . . In the times of the AERP it would have been 'the people did that,' 'the nation did that.'"[81] This accords with the content analysis of the ARP films, which—as we have seen—dealt largely with government programs.

During the election campaigns, Camargo found himself in a double bind; on the one hand, he wanted to win the elections, as this was the task demanded of him by Geisel, but on the other hand, he wanted to follow Costa's principles of "legitimacy and truth." He frequently met with leaders of the government party, ARENA, and their strategy entailed focusing on "[government] measures with examples and statistics."[82] Although the ARENA party undoubtedly benefited from this matter-of-fact type of propaganda, he determinedly refused a more euphemistic and blunt (and maybe even false) propaganda style. Camargo complained that during the campaign he felt "surrounded by premises of a definite moral." The ARP's direct involvement in the election campaign strategy is one important differentiator between it and the AERP. However, the ARP did not directly produce the election campaigns.

The Propagandist's View on Torture

In his biography, Camargo writes: "A single act of torture is already malignant enough to compromise the whole [system]."[83] Identifying with the military institution, Camargo explicitly states that he feels some measure of guilt by association, even though he was never actually linked to its most repressive elements. He regrets the death of the student Edson Luis and argues that it was not only unnecessary but in fact had the effect of increasing popular support for the student movement.[84] He was shocked by the AI 5 and its list of *caçados*, saying, "The way the whole AI 5 functioned was a disaster."[85] Camargo clearly disapproves of the system used by the intelligence services and the way in which they overestimated the so-called subversives: "[It was] a crude evaluation error with harmful and disastrous consequences," he says. He also denounces their violation of the law: "Nothing original; that is invariably the course that world history shows us: when legality dies, when arbitrariness prevails over the constitutional state, human rights abuses are committed, on pretexts that are always available."[86]

Camargo condemns the fact that many members of the armed forces refused to acknowledge their involvement in torture: "Some . . . vehemently deny the accusations of torture that weigh heavily on the armed forces. But all . . . know they were practiced. And the vast majority, like me, is terribly embarrassed at having to admit to them."[87]

Although Camargo did not have direct knowledge of what happened, rumors filtered through: "During this whole period . . . I have been working in different commissions; none of them was directly linked to security issues. But I heard, reflected, and meditated." He claims that, all in all, few military officials were directly involved and that torture was never institutionalized. As evidence he points to the decommissioning of General Ednardo de Mello in São Paulo. Researchers have contradicted Camargo, arguing that torture was used systematically.[88] However, to what extent ordinary military officials knew about these crimes remains unclear. Although both Camargo and Costa reject violence and were not directly involved in the organs of repression, they appear unwilling to bear any direct responsibility for the use of violence, absolving themselves of it completely. I wondered whether the idea of complicity is a peculiarly German or European notion and whether these issues became naturalized through intense debate about Nazi collaboration. Could it be that Brazilians are less aware of the issue of collaboration? However, despite his sharp condemnation of its use, Camargo also believes that fewer instances of torture actually occurred than was believed to be the case and that guerrilla fighters felt no pity either.[89]

Although Camargo rejects repression, he still feels some residual guilt about it. Referring to the cover-up of the Riocentro, he describes his "Kafkaesque feeling": "I felt guilty, excluded, responsible for the occurrence of episodes I had not committed ... with which I totally disagreed. ... This feeling of living alongside torture and the collective responsibility tortured me."[90] The Riocentro trial upset Camargo so much that he retired.[91] According to their own accounts, the two propaganda leaders, Camargo and Costa, recall their public relations work in a similar way—as a form of suffering. Perhaps this is surprising, because who would have expected the leading propagandists of authoritarian Brazil to tell such a "narrative of suffering"?[92] I had anticipated, at least, that the propagandists would be fervent supporters of the regime that it was their job to promote.

✳

In this case, even though I had access to a variety of sources, the task of establishing how it might have been remains very difficult. Much of the evidence consistently suggests that the AERP and ARP did not want to actively promote violence. However, to what degree did they collaborate with its deployment? Did that not ultimately support the system by promoting seemingly apolitical motives? We can only draw our own conclusions and hope that one day new sources are discovered that allow us to gain further insight. Still, this case has also served to illustrate that, even within a single regime, different forces fight against each other—the SNI and hardliners, on the one hand, and the AERP and ARP, on the other. To depict these internal conflicts accurately is often very difficult, due to a lack of solid evidence. What we can say for sure, however, is that although Costa and Camargo consistently defended the coup as prevention from a communist takeover and supported the military rule that followed, both wanted a regime in which violent repression played no part. When I was making a copy of a particular report from Camargo, I found the following note, handwritten by Costa: "For my friend Camargo in memory of the challenge which united we managed to overcome, a hug in gratitude, Octávio (18.3.74)."[93]

5

The End of the Story

Propaganda Reception

When I claimed at the beginning of the last chapter that the most challenging part of propaganda analysis was uncovering the propagandists' intentions, I was not being entirely truthful: propaganda reception is even harder to assess. The AERP did not systematically measure the impact of its campaigns, and unfortunately, many regard this as the most exciting part of propaganda. Although systematic research into public opinion was originally planned, as the documentation of a seminar on public relations reveals, it never became institutionalized. The same documentation also shows that originally the AERP leader was meant to work closely with the SNI and provide the organization with survey results. It was suggested that the AERP write daily and weekly summaries of major incidents that had an impact on public opinion—a job that was eventually done by the SNI itself.[1]

Many of these initial suggestions were not executed under Costa's leadership. Public-opinion research proved to be too expensive, and only one AERP survey was undertaken for the Rondon campaign in 1973.[2] The AERP measured the campaign's reception in three ways. The main barometer was the reaction of communications students from the University of Brasília (UNB), whom Costa taught regularly and to whom he showed his films in order to collect feedback. Students in Rio and São Paulo were questioned as well. Secondly, the AERP showed the films to friends and organized screenings in the Planalto.[3] A third method was to carefully observe comments in the press by Congress members and military officials.

Assessing the impact of propaganda or other forms of media is a difficult task, since not only sound evidence but also adequate theories and methodologies are lacking.[4] It is necessary to consider numerous parameters and distinguish among different kinds of effects. Media effects depend on how society is structured, on the nature and size of the media system, the importance of media as a source of information, and the audience's dependence on media information. Furthermore, the impact depends on factors other than the media, as each individual processes information according to personal needs, interests, values, and experiences.[5] Research has increasingly emphasized that our relations to and conversations with other people—so-called personal interrelations—have a more significant effect than broadcast media.[6] For example, your opinion about war is influenced more by what your mother thinks about war than by media reports about the issue. Although scholars have varying views on the impact of the media, they suspect that its power to alter beliefs and attitudes over the long term is limited. Some studies suggest that the media reinforce existing beliefs rather than change opinions, or that the media help consumers to prioritize their values.[7]

Moreover, whereas propaganda was formerly viewed as an all-powerful and dangerous tool of manipulation to be used on the malleable and passive masses, contemporary scholars agree that viewers decode texts differently, generating the "individual meaning" that can be most easily assimilated into their personal belief system. This change has become apparent in the substitution of the term "viewer" with that of "reader."[8] The Frankfurt School, which drew researchers' attention to the cultural industry, emphasized the might of media owners but paid little attention to the viewer's power to reinterpret media. In the 1940s and 1950s, questionnaire-based studies used the "stimulus-response" model to measure media effects, but this cause-and-effect model failed.[9] The relationship was in fact more complex, and the social and cultural environment was found to play a crucial role.

Although scholars still debate the extent of freedom and constraint set by the media industry, one may summarize the current consensus as follows: there exists an "original meaning," which offers a certain but limited number of meanings to the reader, who reads "against" a film-text and thus has the possibility of "resistance." The debate is related to the radical point made by Stanley Fish, who rejects any sort of "original" meaning ("no 'original' thesis"). According to this view, the text has no stable meaning but only comes into existence at the moment it is read, thus providing an infinite number of possible readings. In contrast, John Tulloch and Henry Jenkins accept the viewer's agency but rightly point to a "relative powerlessness of audiences" caused by the concentration of media ownership. Tulloch and Jenkins doubt that the "frameworks of power" created through media ownership can be "subverted merely by the act of viewing."[10]

This study assumes that media producers and potential propagandists frame the text and limit its possible readings. The reader has a restricted but significant number of choices for ascribing "meaning" to the film. Stuart Hall calls this the "relative autonomy" of the viewer.[11]

Propaganda Reception

The actual propaganda reception has never been systematically examined before.[12] Although concrete evidence of the campaigns' popularity is scarce, press coverage, interviews, and the final AERP report suggest that the films were generally well received. The AERP films won prizes, and their aesthetic style was not only praised by the press but also imitated by commercial propaganda agencies. A documentary produced for an overseas audience won a prize at an international tourism festival.[13] *Veja* magazine reported that the AERP received the "best of the year" prize in 1970 for the "quality and the success" of its films. In the same year, the leading publicity sector magazine, *Propaganda*, awarded a prize for Médici's slogan "Nobody can stop this country anymore," because it "translated the motivation of the whole nation and became a symbol of necessary trust to build a great nation."[14] In 1971, the AERP won yet another prize for its "You Construct Brazil" campaign. The justification was as follows:

> Integration Campaign of the Government—not only proving that it [the AERP] loves all of us, but also knowing the product it sells, the AERP team united Brazilians. The campaign for development and government integration has shown that today we are not only the country of Pelé, of the *jeitinho* and carnival, but also the country that is growing and that knows that it is growing. The AERP campaign has brought us near the Amazon, closer to the government and integrated us in a common effort which we have never experienced before.[15]

The prizes attest to the fact that commercial propaganda agencies fully supported the Médici government and actively promoted the miracle myth. The fact that the AERP won the most respected publicity prizes two consecutive years suggests that the campaigns were highly regarded and acclaimed by the professional public relations sector. Interestingly, *Veja* magazine mentions that Costa discouraged publicity about the prize awarded in 1970 and asked journalists to refrain from mentioning it.[16] The scarcity of press articles commenting on the AERP is striking, and most articles merely announced campaigns. This silence might have been a result of Costa's directive to the press. Given his own publications for the *Jornal do Brasil* and his cordial relations with respected journalists such as Carlos Castello Branco, it would have been easy for him to ask them to publish positive reviews. Was Costa, perhaps, trying to avoid causing more friction with hardliners?

Nonetheless, a few press articles confirm the popularity of specific campaigns—above all the one featuring the character Sujismundo, who is celebrated in all AERP interviews and some accounts by ordinary Brazilians who witnessed that period in history. The AERP official Rabaça repeatedly stated that even today Sujismundo's legacy persists, as many Brazilians remember him.[17] According to the *Jornal do Brasil*, a similar character was invented on the basis of Sujismundo's popularity. The *Jornal* also reveals that Sujismundo was voted the favorite cartoon hero among children, ahead of Zorro and Batman. *Veja* magazine and the daily publication *O Estado de São Paulo* also wrote about the huge success of the Sujismundo campaign.[18]

Another production that received a positive reaction from the press was a campaign designed to encourage people to read. Costa received a letter from a member of the public demanding that this campaign continue. The newsweekly publication *Visão* reported that the AERP received "thousands of letters from the whole of Brazil praising its films"; unfortunately, these have not been preserved.[19] In an interview, Costa gives some clues about more popular campaigns. A short film about medication was stopped, because the pharmaceutical company was unable to satisfy popular demand. A film featuring a yellow-green kite was also abandoned, because an electricity company complained about too many kites causing problems with the electricity network. Costa also remembers that a short film about a trapeze artist was admired, as well as one that depicted a child packing her school bag.[20]

In the final AERP report Costa mentions two very successful films made in 1971, one entitled *Time to Construct*, a campaign broadcast for the seventh anniversary of the coup, and a second called *Yesterday, Today, and Always Brazil*. The report's overall conclusion is that "most of the productions seem to have been highly constructive, . . . they were referred to in various sectors, won prizes, acclaim." Costa also remarks that radio campaigns achieved "extraordinary" success.[21] His judgments seem to be accurate overall, given that this was an official report, that he clearly mentions failed campaigns, and that press articles and interviews support his assessments.[22]

The new aesthetic style of the AERP was praised by *Veja* magazine as a "high level publicity campaign" and a "healthy aesthetic change."[23] It criticized former short films for being ufanistic (boastful), blatantly praising the "revolution" and the government, and stated that they had been repeated excessively and were unpopular. *Propaganda* magazine praised the AERP for making animated films much more acceptable, as apparently they had previously been rejected: "Producers of commercial advertising, and, in particular, of cartoon films, owe the AERP [a debt] for its efforts to promote campaigns of the Sujismundo kind. This type of campaign gives the producers the opportunity to show that the audience will accept cartoon films."[24] Costa reports that the AERP campaigns were even imitated by publicists.[25] The popularity of the campaigns furthermore led to Costa being asked to advise the Bolivian government about propaganda. Costa refused, but the SNI forced him to meet the Bolivian ambassador.[26]

Another, albeit indirect, way to measure the "success" of the campaigns is to consider whether their civic appeals led to measurable changes in people's behavior. In 1975, *Propaganda* magazine published an article about the success of a meningitis vaccination campaign, which led to the vaccination of eleven million people in a mere three days.[27] Although this campaign was launched by the National Propaganda Council (CNP), a former collaborator of the AERP and not the AERP itself, one may argue that the numerous AERP films from earlier years urging people to get vaccinations probably contributed to that outcome. In February 1973, the AERP produced a road-safety series, specifically aimed at preventing car accidents. According to Rabaça, the number of car accidents decreased following this campaign.[28] The other AERP members agree that the campaigns were well received. Cavalieri believes that overall the AERP improved the reputation of the government and contributed to "a better atmosphere." Camargo writes in his biography that although colleagues congratulated him, his work went unappreciated within the government itself.[29]

In October 1977, *O Estado de São Paulo* interviewed eight successful publicists about their opinions on government promotion. While they agreed that government propaganda was legitimate if it avoided creating a personality cult, they disliked the Sujismundo campaign for various reasons. While Alex Periscinoto disliked its aesthetic style, Ercílio Trajan objected to the patronizing tone used. "I think they start from the assumption that the Brazilian people are a little stupid," he said.[30] However, the publicists revealed mixed opinions about other campaigns. While Alfredo Borges disliked the slogan "Brazil is made by us," because it "sells hope" and "false euphoria," Alex Periscinoto read it as a positive manifestation of Brazilian self-esteem that countered accusations of human-rights abuses from abroad. However, the article also mentions that although Periscinoto did not invent the slogan, which came from the ARP, his company developed the campaign. While some publicists, such as Laurence Klinger, argued that the government produced too much propaganda, others, including Alex Periscinoto and Mauro Salles, found no grounds for criticism. Roberto Duabili, who praised the vaccination campaigns, argued that propaganda was acceptable as "social marketing," but not in the form of "triumphalist propaganda."[31]

Yet the campaigns also drew criticism. *O Estado de São Paulo* complained that, regardless of the new propaganda style, press censorship continued. Moreover, Cavalieri claims that some viewers, particularly intellectuals, considered the campaigns to be "silly." Former AERP members Rabaça and Baena Soares mention that hardliners often denigrated the films after screenings in the Planalto.[32] However, this criticism was only expressed verbally and thus has not been documented.

The Brazilian historian Odair Lima mentions popular jokes at the time that mock AERP and ARP propaganda slogans and provide evidence of skepticism. The phrase "Brazil made a step forward" was answered with the rejoinder "and found itself on the brink," while the slogan "Brazil is constituted by ourselves" was supplemented by "the difficulty is to get rid of us." Arguably the best example was the hardliner campaign "Brazil: Love It or Leave It," launched during Operation Bandeirantes in 1969–70. This was complemented by the phrase "The last one turns off the lights"—a slogan still vividly remembered today.[33]

According to AERP interviews, the anti-inflation campaigns, produced against Camargo's wishes, were unpopular.[34] The series blamed consumers and suggested that they take action to curb inflation. By May 1973, the campaign "Say No to Inflation," which recommended that consumers visit several shops before deciding to make a purchase, had already failed. A 1977 campaign instructed the audience to compare prices.[35] Ironically, in 1973, when the first anti-inflation campaign was launched, the government falsified the real inflation rate, reducing it from an actual figure of 22.5 percent to an official one of 15.5 percent.[36]

Authoritarian regimes often use their intelligence-gathering systems to track the reception of their propaganda and changes in public opinion. The Nazis, for example, dispatched spies to cinemas, who then reported back on how the audience reacted to the propaganda films.[37] When I researched the SNI files, I did not find anything to suggest that public opinion was investigated systematically and professionally.[38] On a more general level, evidence from opinion polls and SNI reports confirms that the regime was largely regarded positively in the early 1970s during the "miracle" period.[39] According to a Gallup survey, the general mood of Brazilians improved significantly between 1968 and 1971.[40]

However, while evidence suggests that public opinion became less favorable throughout the 1970s, scholars disagree as to when and why this change occurred. Letters addressed to President Geisel and the SNI, along with public opinion reports and recommendations by the consultant Mauro Salles, clearly point to an increasing sense of dissatisfaction with the Geisel government. The letters and Gallup reports identify 1976–77 as the breaking point, whereas the political scientist Lamounier Bolivar believes that this process had already started in 1972–73, even before the economic crisis had caused major damage.[41] Bolivar's thesis is not only plausible, given ARENA's electoral defeat in 1974; it is also confirmed by a 1974 SNI report from the Amazon region. Apparently, dissatisfaction had already reached significant levels in 1974, but it deepened significantly from 1976 onward. Abundant evidence confirms that the regime was unpopular among the younger generation.

The political scientist Youssef Cohen investigated why Médici enjoyed cross-class popularity by analyzing 1,314 interviews conducted in southeastern Brazil in 1972. He wanted to discover why poorer segments of the population approved of Médici despite decreases in the real minimum wage. Cohen argues that the majority were not politicized, nor were they particularly interested in political affairs. According to him, 86 percent of the surveyed population were unpoliticized.[42] It is usually the case that unpoliticized people will not be concerned about a regime change if their customary way of life is not affected. They will be apathetic toward new regimes or may even support them. Thus, he concludes, the survey responses in favor of Médici cannot be read as a positive attitude toward the political system or a high level of right-wing sympathy but rather as a "do not care" or a "non-attitude" position.[43] Thus, Cohen added to the debate by demanding that the apathy of large parts of the population be taken into consideration when interpreting the results of public-opinion polls. The high approval rates for the Médici government, he proposes, do not provide evidence of long-term and grounded political support but rather illustrate the volatile momentum of a largely unpoliticized and apathetic population.

Function of AERP and ARP Propaganda

The AERP and ARP were key parts of the official government and pro-military propaganda, but there was other pro-military-dictatorship political propaganda, too. Contrary to this other pro-regime propaganda, which tended to be blunt and aggressive, a key characteristic of the AERP and ARP short films was their "apolitical" nature. So how can we interpret their function and broader historical meaning? Should the AERP and ARP films be classified as disguised political propaganda or as civic education films? Do the AERP and ARP officials share responsibility for the dictatorship's crimes, because their subliminal propaganda was arguably more effective in increasing support?

✳

Scholars lack useful methodologies with which to interpret this kind of propaganda. Most definitions of propaganda are related to the selection or manipulation of information—in Eagleton's terms, "epistemological truth"—and search for lies.[44] They fail to account for propaganda that sells values through an ostensibly apolitical, entertaining story or an aesthetically pleasing image. Often films are only revealed to be propaganda when the concrete historical context becomes clear, when the "functional" falsehood becomes apparent. Let us refer to a similar case: the debate about Nazi feature films.

What may come as a surprise to some is that most of the Nazi feature films produced were musicals, tragic or romantic love stories, idyllic scenes in the Black Forest, and ordinary family dramas. This was the finding of the German sociologist Gerd Albrecht, who discovered that less than 15 percent of Nazi feature films were directly political,[45] a finding that subsequently triggered a debate about the propaganda value of seemingly apolitical films. Stephen Lowry suggested analyzing the values and patterns of behavior that underlie such films. He criticized scholars who relate manipulation to political content but neglect the form it takes.[46] However, Clemens Zimmermann highlighted several practical problems with this model. First, it is difficult to analyze values perpetuated by a film, especially, I would add, considering that the "message" is partially constructed by the reader. The same film might be interpreted in a variety of ways by different spectators. Zimmermann suggests comparing the films with the social values of the time; however, he acknowledges that the necessary sources for analyzing film reception are rarely available.[47]

Out of the Nazi film discussion two broad schools of thought emerged. The first, which includes David Stewart Hull, interprets Nazi feature films as apolitical overall.[48] The second, which includes Eric Rentschler, argues that although these films do not directly show ideological or political content, they fulfilled a political function in that their effect was to distract the population from everyday problems.[49] Applying Rentschler's argument to the AERP and ARP, the crucial difference, I propose, lies in the intention of the propagandists. During the Nazi regime, particularly as of 1942, when Germany began edging toward defeat, film producers deliberately aimed to distract the audience from violence; this was not, however, the stated intention of the AERP members, and indeed evidence, too, suggests that it was not.

The evidence presented in chapter 4 questions Fico's argument that the AERP's use of common beliefs and values was a mere strategy, ultimately designed to cover up the dictatorship and repression.[50] Fico distrusts Costa's stated intention to pacify Brazil and holds that the AERP used popular topics because they knew that overt political propaganda would have been rejected.[51] Following this line of reasoning, one could claim that the AERP, Médici, and even hardliners were working toward the same goals and ideals. In contrast, this book advocates distinguishing between different degrees of perpetration and considering the range of evidence that calls into question the idea that Costa wanted to support violence. While I agree with Fico that the concealment of violence may have been the actual consequence of the AERP propaganda, I advocate differentiating between the deliberate intent on the one hand (what the propagandists aimed to achieve) and the ultimate consequence (how the campaigns may have been interpreted) on the other.

Certainly, Costa wanted to support the military regime by stressing the normality and the positive aspects of Brazilian life, as he and other AERP members have said: "To encourage popular trust in the government team, emphasizing its honesty, austerity, comprehension of the desires of the people and spirit of renewal."[52] However, he upheld a specific version of the regime; it was certainly not the one dominated by the SNI and hardliners, who unsuccessfully tried to force him to produce aggressive and blunt propaganda and whose practice of violence he has consistently attacked in public, both in his newspaper articles in the late 1960s and in his oral history interviews in the 1990s. Different visions of the regime coexisted, and they surfaced during moments of internal conflict. Costa's propaganda was intended to strengthen the regime, but specifically its moderate, and not its violent, agenda.

While it is plausible that the political function of propaganda in terms of its consequences was distraction, I propose to differentiate between the calculated intention of the propagandist and the ultimate consequences of the films. Various sources from the 1960s and 1970s illustrated that AERP officials did not want to justify repression. I would even go further and highlight the AERP and ARP's possible role in adopting a position that was counter to this, given that the pressure from the SNI and hardliners on Costa and Camargo was significant. Evidence for this viewpoint is found in all the AERP interviews, Camargo's autobiography, and press articles dating back to the 1960s. Even documentation from the Ernesto Geisel archive shows that intelligence officials approached the

AERP and ARP to ask them to actively produce blunt pro-regime propaganda, particularly at election times, which, however, both institutions rejected. Radicals even demanded that the ARP be a central organ for censorship.[53] Costa and Camargo managed to refute blunt and aggressive propaganda. Most of their propaganda was "positive"; it defied the construction of enemies, most notably the communist threat, prevalent in the propaganda produced by other Brazilian agents and in the United States at the time. The Agência Nacional, parts of the media, and political speeches feature much more clearly as blunt pro-regime propaganda, as Martins has appropriately stressed.[54]

✳

Taking a balanced view of the function of propaganda, I conclude that despite the films' apolitical character, in the specific context of the military regime they operated as a silent form of pro-regime propaganda, as they perpetuated values that aimed to justify the regime, the most important of these being the miracle myth. This arguably functioned as the single most important justification of the regime, and it managed to unite different social groups that presumably would not have backed an authoritarian regime otherwise—businessmen or moderate military personnel, for example. Conventional definitions based on the manipulation of information fail to consider this type of propaganda, which I refer to as subliminal pro-regime propaganda. Subliminal propaganda may be described as apolitical in style yet political in consequence.

However, critics could argue that everything is political within an authoritarian regime. By the same token, I would reply, everything in a democracy can also be seen as political. A very broad definition of propaganda lays itself open to the argument that everything is political in both democratic and authoritarian systems alike. From that angle, would present-day civic education campaigns that tell people not to drop litter in the street but to throw their trash in a bin, much like the Sujismundo films, also qualify as political propaganda? And what about all the entertainment programs that lull their audience into political apathy and torpor? As Eric Rentschler, an expert on Nazi feature films, once said, Hollywood films can function as narcotics, too.[55]

Conclusion

The campaigns produced by the official authoritarian propaganda organs AERP (1968–1974) and ARP (1976–1979) reflected two distinguishing characteristics of the civilian-military regime in Brazil: its strenuous efforts to create the appearance of a democracy, and its inner conflicts, which the authoritarian propaganda skillfully disguised. The official propaganda's democratic pretense can be seen in their institutional structure, their production mechanisms, the aesthetic style of the campaigns, and their subject matter. Their minor institutional structure, with limited financial and staff resources, paid for by the state rather than the business sector, the procedure for commissioning production to private film companies while remaining in complete control over the content, the unofficial, modern aesthetic style, and the seemingly apolitical content were designed to appear democratic and thus unlike dictatorial propaganda, such as that of the DIP under the Vargas regime.

This book has also shown that the military regime was not united but characterized by internal factions that were in constant conflict. Radicals belonging to the so-called hardliner group, mostly SNI intelligence officials, demanded blunt and aggressive propaganda and wanted to turn the ARP into a central organ for censorship. Costa and Camargo managed to resist these pressures. Most of their propaganda was "positive"; it defied the construction of enemies, such as the "communist threat," which characterized the red-scare propaganda produced by other Brazilian agents and the U.S. government at the time. Despite the persistent and intense nature of these internal conflicts, they never seriously threatened the regime. Future research may explore in greater depth why this was so, but personal bonds and a strong identification with and loyalty to the military institution may have contributed to the regime's cohesion.

Moreover, this book has demonstrated that between 1968 and 1979, authoritarian propaganda was multifaceted and contradictory, and that the AERP and ARP were not the only propaganda organs, but coexisted with other state and private propaganda makers, which had varying intentions, strategies, and styles. Other state organs (Agência Nacional, Radiobrás) and private agencies (the media, commercial advertising) produced a form of propaganda that often praised the regime more obviously—through what this book has characterized as blunt (pro-regime) propaganda—or worse, tried to justify the regime's human-rights transgressions via so-called aggressive propaganda. Others supported the regime's values in subtler ways, such as by celebrating Brazil's progress and development, stirring up patriotism, or promoting order and security. This foregrounds a third, unique aspect vital to comprehending the authoritarian regime in Brazil: civilian collaboration. More studies on this topic are expected to be published during the next few years.

In terms of cultural life, the press, and the commercial propaganda sector, the civilian-military regime had a double-edged effect. While the cultural arena and the press were subject to economic and political control by the government, both sectors benefited from modernization and growth. The cultural sector expanded and, still dominated by left-wing artists and producers, remained critical of the regime. After 1968, however, censorship, violence, and state subsidies constrained artists politically and economically, and various state institutions gave incentives to Brazilian artists from the 1970s onward, leading to what Ridenti coined a "pragmatic rearrangement."[1] A national film industry was developed under the auspices of the military regime. Similarly, more newspapers emerged at the time. Like the media sector, the Brazilian advertising industry underwent a process of modernization, professionalization, and extraordinary growth. Both the media and the commercial propaganda sector benefited from the regime's strategic strengthening of Brazil's communications infrastructure, state investments, and the country's economic growth during the so-called miracle years. The miracle myth— propagated by the AERP and ARP, the media, and the commercial sector alike—arguably functioned as the single most important justification of the regime. It managed to unite different social groups, including businessmen and moderate military personnel who would have been unlikely to back an authoritarian regime otherwise.

While commercial propaganda amplified the AERP and ARP's messages, their campaigns also diverged. Publicists and the AERP and ARP both emphasized development and overlooked the regime's violent repression, as well as class and racial tensions. However, while the AERP and ARP produced largely subliminal propaganda and collaborative media companies like *Globo* produced blunt propaganda, the majority of commercial advertising was arguably situated somewhere in between. In contrast with the AERP and ARP, it hailed the "Great Brazil" in a conspicuous way; however, it rarely praised the government directly.

The AERP and ARP short films were seemingly apolitical, aesthetically appealing, and claimed to be on a mission to "enlighten" and "civilize"—to represent civic education campaigns for a country aspiring to become a developed nation. Many films were racist in their perpetuation of the whitening ideology, never portraying Brazilians with darker skin tones, and depicting mulattoes mostly as poor. Similarly, from today's vantage point, most films appear sexist, because women were mostly represented as housewives. Films from other countries at that time, however, presumably perpetuated similar gender roles. The large majority of films analyzed in this study did not resemble government propaganda; 70 percent of the sample can be classified as subliminal propaganda. While the AERP and the ARP functioned in a broadly similar way, the latter operated under a more centralized institutional structure, produced a higher volume of propaganda, and created more campaigns directly praising government programs than the AERP did. Whereas on average the most frequent topics featured in the AERP films (1970–1973) were nationalism/national pride (27.7 percent), work/hard-work ethos (25.3 percent), and youth (24.7 percent), the corresponding ARP topics (1974–1977) were government programs (19.5 percent), development (17.2 percent), and nationalism (also 17.2 percent). The increased propaganda output under Geisel coincided with the demise of censorship from 1975 onward. Although evidence of the campaigns' popularity is scarce, press coverage, interviews, and the final AERP report suggest that the films were generally well received. They won prizes, and their aesthetic style was not only praised by the press but also imitated by commercial propaganda agencies.

This book has called for a more nuanced view regarding degrees of perpetration during the military regime in Brazil. Various sources from the 1960s and 1970s have consistently suggested that the AERP and ARP did not seek to actively promote violence. I would go even further and highlight the AERP and ARP's possible role in adopting a position that was contraviolence, given that the pressure exerted by the SNI and hardliners on Costa and Camargo was significant. Evidence for this viewpoint is not only provided by all the AERP interviews and Camargo's autobiography, but most importantly by press articles authored by Costa in the 1960s. While I agree with Carlos Fico that the concealment of violence may have been the actual consequence of the AERP propaganda, I advocate differentiating between the deliberate intention (what the propagandists aimed to achieve) and the ultimate outcome (how the campaigns may have been interpreted).

The Brazilian example may also serve to heighten our sensitivity to propaganda, in its many forms and sizes, produced under democratic or authoritarian rule, by state or private agents. Propaganda has been used as a tool to constrain human liberty for centuries and still exists today. Arguably, dissecting propaganda today has become more difficult: it is often unclear where the power interests lie and who its key agents are. We are not taught how to deconstruct it.

Appendix 1

Sources and Methods

Throughout the book I use different references for each film. The "F"-number (FE. or FI.) indicates the original description used in the AERP and ARP catalogues of the 1960s and 1970s, and the "EH.-Fil."-number is the old archive description of the film. The National Archives in Rio has recently renamed its film material. While I worked with film codes starting with "EH.-Fil." followed by a number, they now have a longer name that provides detailed reference to the film series. In the captions I use the original description from the production catalogues (e.g., F. 35), the new archive code (BRAN Rio EH.0.Fil.Fit.127 ANO 1970), and the old archive designation that I used to work with (EH.-Fil. 934). Cláudio and Valeria from the National Archives in Rio kindly supplied a partial conversion list, and I compiled a table listing all three descriptions. The table's purpose is to help future researchers to allocate the films; I filled in the table to the extent that the information was available (otherwise the column for the new designation is left blank).

When I went to the National Archives I first had to find the 123 propaganda films, view them, and match them one by one with the original numbers in the AERP and ARP catalogues to find out when they were produced. During that process two problems occurred. First, numerous films were not listed in the catalogues, and I concluded that either they had not been produced between 1969 and 1977 or they had been produced by another institution. Thus if the FE. or FI. number is blank in the table, it means that these films were not listed in the production catalogues. Second, the National Archives collection only holds seven AERP films (7.4 percent of the total sample) and none for the years 1974 and 1975. The total figures are calculated from the number of AERP and ARP films found in the archive sample (106). As the catalogue does not list films from 1969, it must be deduced that production started in 1970. The remaining years included the following AERP films: 1970: EH.-Fil. 756 (F. 37) and

EH.-Fil. 934 (F. 35); 1971: EH.-Fil. 932 (F. 69) and EH.-Fil. 933 (F. 66); no films from 1972; and 1973: EH.-Fil. 749 (F. 151), EH.-Fil. 935 (F. 123), and EH.-Fil. 936 (F. 126). Most films were from 1976 (23.2 percent) and 1977 (40 percent). This sample collected from the National Archive in Rio comprises only 4.1 percent of the total AERP film production (1970–1973) and 43 percent of the total ARP film production (1974–1977).

The ARP films hosted by the National Archives are listed in the table, whereby the original production number can be provided for the years 1976 and 1977. The ARP code for film EH.-Fil. 787 (1976) remains unclear, but the ARP trailer clearly identifies it as an ARP production. The catalogue lists a similar film (FI. 3), but with a different voice-over text than that displayed in archive film EH.-Fil. 787. Perhaps the text was amended afterward and the catalogue was not updated. For 1977, three *filmetes* do not have a trailer number given by the archive, but were named arbitrarily XXXX (FI. 70), WWWW (FE. 42), and DDDD (FE. 42); so films EH.-Fil. DDDD and WWWW are the same film (FE. 42). The ARP *filmetes* finished with a logo in the shape of Brazil. Therefore, the thirty-eight unknown films (40 percent) show that this specific trailer must have been produced in 1978/1979, the years for which the ARP catalogues are missing. This is substantiated by the voice-overs of four films that confirm that they were produced in 1978/1979. One film was produced in 1978 and the other three in 1979 (1978: EH.-Fil. 759; 1979: EH.-Fil. 754, 765, and 766). EH.-Fil. 804 does not have a trailer, but it looks like an ARP film. This is the only film without a trailer that I considered to be produced by the ARP without any further evidence. In addition, errors might derive from the original production catalogues themselves.

The total number of identifiable AERP and ARP films located in the National Archives amounts to 106 films; the other films were duplicates or made by other producers. These films are EH.-Fil. 697, EH.-Fil. 698, EH.-Fil. 699, EH.-Fil. 700, and EH.-Fil. 701 (1968); films that are duplicated are EH.-Fil. DDDD (=WWWW [FE. 42, 1977]) and EH.-Fil. CCCC (=809, 1978/79?); films that were supposedly produced during the Médici government, but not by the AERP, because they are not listed in the catalogues, are EH.-Fil. 915, EH.-Fil. 901, EH.-Fil. 889, and a group of other films (EH.-Fil. 704, EH.-Fil. 705, EH.-Fil. 740, EH.-Fil. 741, EH.-Fil. 793, EH.-Fil. 722, and EH.-Fil. 804). "Others" include three films covering the "people's movement against inflation" (EH.-Fil. 740, EH.-Fil. 741, and EH.-Fil. 793), possibly created by a state department, and one film of the Fraternity Campaign (EH.-Fil. 804). The Fraternity Campaign is an annual campaign that has run since 1964 and is organized by the Brazilian National Bishops' Conference (CNBB). The three remaining films could not be identified at all (EH.-Fil. 889, EH.-Fil. 901, and EH.-Fil. 915). Those might also have been productions of the secretaries of state. Five *filmetes* were produced by Hernani D'Aguiar in 1968. They did not feature in the AERP catalogue, were shot in black and white, did not finish with the typical trailer, and, most importantly, had a different aesthetic style (EH.-Fil. 697, 698, 699, 700, and EH.-Fil. 701). They looked like obvious propaganda and repeated euphoric slogans like "Great Brazil" (see, for example, films EH.-Fil. 697 or EH.-Fil. 701).

Table 2. Propaganda film conversion list

	Producer	Year	Original production number	Old archival code	New archival code
1	AERP	1970	F. 37	EH.-Fil. 756	
2	AERP	1970	F. 35	EH.-Fil. 934	BR AN RIO EH.0.FIL. FIT.127 ANO 1970
3	AERP	1971	F. 69	EH.-Fil. 932	BR AN RIO EH.0.FIL. FIT.125 ANO 1971
4	AERP	1971	F. 66	EH.-Fil. 933	BR AN RIO EH.0.FIL. FIT.126 ANO 1971
5	AERP	1973	F. 151	EH.-Fil. 749	
6	AERP	1973	F. 123	EH.-Fil. 935	
7	AERP	1973	F. 126	EH.-Fil. 936	
8	ARP	1976	FI. 39	EH.-Fil. 706	BR AN RIO EH.0.FIL. FIT.10 ANO 1976
9	ARP	1976	FI. 47	EH.-Fil. 707	
10	ARP	1976	FI. 27	EH.-Fil. 709	
11	ARP	1976	FI. 4	EH.-Fil. 711	
12	ARP	1976	FI. 36	EH.-Fil. 712	
13	ARP	1976	FE. 16	EH.-Fil. 713	BR AN RIO EH.0.FIL. FIT.17 ANO 1976
14	ARP	1976	FE. 15	EH.-Fil. 715	
15	ARP	1976	FE. 12	EH.-Fil. 716	
16	ARP	1976	FE. 13	EH.-Fil. 717	
17	ARP	1976	FE. 10/A	EH.-Fil. 718	
18	ARP	1976	FI. 52	EH.-Fil. 719	
19	ARP	1976	FI. 33	EH.-Fil. 769	
20	ARP	1976	FI. 35	EH.-Fil. 770	
21	ARP	1976	FI. 15	EH.-Fil. 771	BR AN RIO EH.0.FIL. FIT.75 ANO 1976
22	ARP	1976	FI. 25	EH.-Fil. 772	BR AN RIO EH.0.FIL. FIT.76 ANO 1976
23	ARP	1976	FI. 38	EH.-Fil. 773	
24	ARP	1976	FI. 46	EH.-Fil. 774	
25	ARP	1976	FI. 48	EH.-Fil. 776	

	Producer	Year	Original production number	Old archival code	New archival code
26	ARP	1976	FI. 49	EH.-Fil. 777	
27	ARP	1976	FE. 14	EH.-Fil. 779	
28	ARP	1976	FI. 51	EH.-Fil. YYYY	
29	ARP	1976	? FI. 3	EH.-Fil. 787	
30	ARP	1977	FI. 65	EH.-Fil. 710	
31	ARP	1977	FI. 74	EH.-Fil. 720	
32	ARP	1977	FI. 71	EH.-Fil. 721	
33	ARP	1977	FI. 73	EH.-Fil. 723	
34	ARP	1977	FE. 20	EH.-Fil. 724	
35	ARP	1977	FE. 21	EH.-Fil. 725	
36	ARP	1977	FE. 29	EH.-Fil. 726	
37	ARP	1977	FE. 22	EH.-Fil. 727	
38	ARP	1977	FE. 26	EH.-Fil. 728	BR AN RIO EH.0.FIL. FIT.32 ANO 1977
39	ARP	1977	FE. 23A	EH.-Fil. 729	
40	ARP	1977	FE. 25	EH.-Fil. 730	
41	ARP	1977	FE. 34	EH.-Fil. 731	
42	ARP	1977	FE. 33	EH.-Fil. 732	
43	ARP	1977	FE. 24	EH.-Fil. 733	
44	ARP	1977	FE. 35	EH.-Fil. 734	
45	ARP	1977	FE. 18	EH.-Fil. 735	
46	ARP	1977	FE. 41	EH.-Fil. 736	
47	ARP	1977	FE. 38	EH.-Fil. 737	
48	ARP	1977	FI. 85	EH.-Fil. 738	
49	ARP	1977	FI. 87	EH.-Fil. 739	
50	ARP	1977	FE. 52	EH.-Fil. 742	
51	ARP	1977	FE. 55	EH.-Fil. 743	
52	ARP	1977	FI. 58	EH.-Fil. 781	
53	ARP	1977	FI. 69	EH.-Fil. 783	
54	ARP	1977	FI. 72	EH.-Fil. 784	
55	ARP	1977	FI. 60	EH.-Fil. 785	
56	ARP	1977	FI. 75	EH.-Fil. 786	
57	ARP	1977	FI. 57	EH.-Fil. 788	
58	ARP	1977	FE. 23	EH.-Fil. 789	
59	ARP	1977	FE. 32	EH.-Fil. 791	
60	ARP	1977	FE. 47	EH.-Fil. 795	
61	ARP	1977	FE. 46	EH.-Fil. 796	
62	ARP	1977	FE. 51	EH.-Fil. 797	
63	ARP	1977	FE. 44	EH.-Fil. 798	

(*continued*)

	Producer	Year	Original production number	Old archival code	New archival code
64	ARP	1977	FE. 53	EH.-Fil. 799	
65	ARP	1977	FI. 70	EH.-Fil. XXXX	
66	ARP	1977	FE. 42	EH.-Fil. WWWW	
67	ARP	1977	FE. 42	EH.-Fil. DDDD	
68	ARP	1978	?	EH.-Fil. 759	
69	ARP	1979	?	EH.-Fil. 754	
70	ARP	1979	?	EH.-Fil. 765	
71	ARP	1979	?	EH.-Fil. 766	BR AN RIO EH.0.FIL. FIT.70 ANO 1979
72	ARP	1978/1979?	?	EH.-Fil. 804	
73	ARP	1978/1979?	?	EH.-Fil. 708	
74	ARP	1978/1979?	?	EH.-Fil. 744	
75	ARP	1978/1979?	?	EH.-Fil. 745	
76	ARP	1978/1979?	?	EH.-Fil. 746	
77	ARP	1978/1979?	?	EH.-Fil. 474	
78	ARP	1978/1979?	?	EH.-Fil. 750	
79	ARP	1978/1979?	?	EH.-Fil. 752	
80	ARP	1978/1979?	?	EH.-Fil. 757	BR AN RIO EH.0.FIL. FIT.61 ANO 1978
81	ARP	1978/1979?	?	EH.-Fil. 758	BR AN RIO EH.0.FIL. FIT.62 ANO 1978
82	ARP	1978/1979?	?	EH.-Fil. 760	
83	ARP	1978/1979?	?	EH.-Fil. 761	
84	ARP	1978/1979?	?	EH.-Fil. 762	
85	ARP	1978/1979?	?	EH.-Fil. 763	
86	ARP	1978/1979?	?	EH.-Fil. 767	
87	ARP	1978/1979?	?	EH.-Fil. 768	
88	ARP	1978/1979?	?	EH.-Fil. 778	
89	ARP	1978/1979?	?	EH.-Fil. 792	
90	ARP	1978/1979?	?	EH.-Fil. 800	
91	ARP	1978/1979?	?	EH.-Fil. 801	
92	ARP	1978/1979?	?	EH.-Fil. 802	
93	ARP	1978/1979?	?	EH.-Fil. 803	
94	ARP	1978/1979?	?	EH.-Fil. 804	
95	ARP	1978/1979?	?	EH.-Fil. 805	
96	ARP	1978/1979?	?	EH.-Fil. 806	
97	ARP	1978/1979?	?	EH.-Fil. 807	BR AN RIO EH.0.FIL. FIT.111 ANO 1978

	Producer	Year	Original production number	Old archival code	New archival code
98	ARP	1978/1979?	?	EH.-Fil. 808	
99	ARP	1978/1979?	?	EH.-Fil. 809	
100	ARP	1978/1979?	?	EH.-Fil. 810	
101	ARP	1978/1979?	?	EH.-Fil. 811	
102	ARP	1978/1979?	?	EH.-Fil. 812	
103	ARP	1978/1979?	?	EH.-Fil. 813	
104	ARP	1978/1979?	?	EH.-Fil. 814	
105	ARP	1978/1979?	?	EH.-Fil. 815	
106	ARP	1978/1979?	?	EH.-Fil. ZZZZ	

Other films and duplicates

	Producer	Year	Original production number	Old archival code	New archival code
1	D'Aguiar?	1968	EH.-Fil. 697		
2	D'Aguiar?	1968	EH.-Fil. 698		
3	D'Aguiar?	1968	EH.-Fil. 699		
4	D'Aguiar?	1968	EH.-Fil. 700		
5	D'Aguiar?	1968	EH.-Fil. 701		
6	? not AERP		EH.-Fil. 915	Médici era?	
7	? not AERP		EH.-Fil. 901	Médici era?	
8	? not AERP		EH.-Fil. 889	Médici era?	
9	ARP	1977	EH.-Fil. DDDD = WWWW	FE. 42	
10	ARP	1978/79?	EH.-Fil. CCCC? = 809		
11	?		EH.-Fil. 704	?	
12	?		EH.-Fil. 705	?	
13	?		EH.-Fil. 722	?	
14	People's movement against inflation	?	EH.-Fil. 740	State department ?	
15	People's movement against inflation	?	EH.-Fil. 741	State department ?	
16	People's movement against inflation	?	EH.-Fil. 793	State department ?	
17	Brazilian National Bishops' Conference (CNBB)	?	EH.-Fil. 804	Fraternity Campaign	

Appendix 2

The Men behind Brazil's Propaganda, 1968–1979

Of the three phases of propaganda development during Brazil's military regime, phases two and three were the best organized, the most pervasive, and their impacts the most profound. During the second phase, 1968–1974, President Artur da Costa e Silva and his successor, Emilio Garrastazú Médici, institutionalized the production and dissemination of propaganda on a large scale and introduced press censorship. After a one year period without a formal propaganda organ, phase three began under President Ernesto Geisel and lasted from 1976 to 1979. During this period, the systematic production of propaganda was reinstated but press censorship relaxed significantly.

Figure A.1. General Octávio Costa, the former leader of the AERP (1969–1974), Rio de Janeiro, October 4, 2007. Photo by Nina Schneider.

Figure A.2. Military president Emilio G. Médici (1969–1974) gives a speech for the radio program *Voice of Brazil*. By permission of the Marines Archives, Rio de Janeiro. Photos Médici/No. 009570.

Figure A.3. Military president Ernesto Geisel (1974–1979), *center*, on a boat. By permission of the Marines Archives, Rio de Janeiro. Photos Geisel/No. Geisel 07764.

Notes

Introduction

1. Important earlier studies: Ianni, *O colapso do populismo*; O'Donnell, *Modernización y autoritarismo*; and Cardoso, *O modelo político brasileiro*. Other classics are Stepan, *Authoritarian Brazil*; R. Schneider, *The Political System of Brazil*; Alves, *State and Opposition*; Skidmore, *The Politics of Military Rule*. For the pioneering oral history interviews edited by the Center for Research and Documentation of Contemporary Brazilian History (CPDOC), see D'Araújo, Castro, and Soares, *Os anos do chumbo*, *Visões do golpe*, and *A volta aos quartéis*. For a more recent study on the history that introduces current debates and provides a bibliography, see Fico, *Além do golpe*. On the U.S.–Brazilian opposition movement and its creative denunciation of human-rights crimes, consult Green, *We Cannot Remain Silent*.

2. For an overview, see Mezarobba, "Brazil"; Brito, "Truth, Justice, Memory"; Pereira, *Political (In)justice*; and Abrão and Torelly, "As dimensões da Justiça de Transição no Brasil."

3. Montero, *Brazilian Politics*, 20.

4. Gaspari, *A didatura encurralada*.

5. Lamounier, *Voto de desconfiança*, 7; Alves, *State and Opposition*; "Gallup culpa reformas pela queda de prestígio de Geisel," *Jornal do Brasil*, May 26, 1977, n. p.

6. Montero, Brazilian Politics, 20.

7. Aquino, "A especifidade do regime," 275; A. Smith, *A Forced Agreement*, 22.

8. Klein and Figueiredo, *Legitimidade e coação*, 22, 24, 26.

9. Pereira, *Political (In)justice*, 22.

10. According to the report of the Comissão Especial sobre Mortos e Desaparecidos, 136 cases had been accepted by the state in 1995, out of which just one was found to be a natural cause of death. The commission investigated a further 339 cases that occurred between 1961 and 1988, thus amounting to a total of 474. Secretaria Especial dos Direitos Humanos da Presidência da República (SEDH), *Direito à memória e à verdade*, 17, 20–21, 48. The estimates for Argentina and Chile—something scholars disagree on— are taken from Pereira, *Political (In)justice*, 21.

11. The truth commission is investigating previously neglected groups of "victims," including the rural population of the Araguaia region, the indigenous population of the Amazon, and purged military officials, the so-called *militares cassados*.

12. Safatle and Teles, *O que resta da ditadura*.

13. Fico, *Como eles agiam*, 115–19, 121.

14. D'Araújo, Soares, and Castro, *Os anos do chumbo*, 17; Fico, *Como eles agiam*, 123. English-speaking scholars have furthermore translated the terms DOI-CODI and CODI-DOI in different ways. Martha Huggins, in "Legacies of Authoritarianism" (60), translates DOI-CODI as "Internal Defense and Operations Directorate," while Pereira in *Political (In)justice* (255–56) translates DOI-CODI as "Department of Internal Operations–Operational Command for Internal Defense."

15. The term "manufacturing consent" originally goes back to Walter Lippmann and has been used by Edward S. Herman and Noam Chomsky in *Manufacturing Consent: The Political Economy of the Mass Media*.

16. N. Schneider, "Impunity in Post-Authoritarian Brazil," 39–54.

17. Corte Interamericana de Derechos Humamos, Caso Gomes Lund Y Otros ("Guerrilha do Araguaia") vs. Brasil, Sentence of November 24, 2010, CORTE INTERAMERICANA DE DERECHOS HUMANOS, http://www.corteidh.or.cr/docs/casos/articulos/seriec_219_esp.pdf (accessed May 10, 2011).

18. The PNDH-3 was elaborated in a lengthy and democratic process that involved both state officials and representatives of civil society. In all, 137 federal, regional, and municipal conferences were organized, and approved suggestions from more than fifty conferences have been incorporated into this plan. The idea to create a truth commission was originally suggested by civil society representatives. See Schneider, "Truth No More?" 164–70.

19. Various scholars have presented nuanced accounts of the tensions within the regime, including J.R.M. Filho, *O pálacio e a caserna*; Fico, "Versões e controvérsias sobre," 29–60; Stepan, *Authoritarian Brazil*; Bacchus, "Development under Military Rule," 413–16, and "Long-Term Military Rulership in Brazil," 113; and Zirker, "Civilianization and Authoritarian Nationalism in Brazil," 263–76. A recent study by the French historian Maud Chirio elucidates revolts and protests within the armed forces; see Chirio, *A política*.

20. Pereira, *Political (In)justice*, 69; Fico, "Versões e controvérsias sobre," 23.

21. Stepan, *Authoritarian Brazil*, 18; Fico, "Versões e controvérsias sobre," 23.

22. Skidmore, *The Politics*, 108.

23. That this is a simplification can best be illustrated with reference to President Geisel. In an interview conducted by the CPDOC, Geisel justified torture as an occasionally necessary means. See D'Araújo and Castro, *Ernesto Geisel*, 224–55. Yet most scholars agree that Geisel tried to weaken the organs of repression under his presidency.

24. A. Smith, *A Forced Agreement*, 32.

25. According to Pereira, 44 percent of those Brazilian citizens purged immediately after the coup in 1964 were military officials (*Political (In)justice*, 67).

26. Arguably, the term "civilian-military coup," which can increasingly be found in the literature, stems from Dreifuss' account (*1964*, 361) where he calls the coup a "civilian-military movement" (movimento civil-militar). The term has been strongly advanced by Daniel Aarão Reis (*Didatura militar*) and Denise Rollemberg ("História,

memória e verdade"). Carlos Fico (*Como eles agiam*, 19–20) also points to the initial support by large parts of the urban middle class and civilian political leaders, yet clearly emphasizes that overall it was "doubtlessly" a military movement.

27. Literature discussing the reasons for the military coup abounds, and varying views coexist. Classic studies are Stepan, "Political Leadership," and Skidmore, "Politics and Economic Policy Making." Helpful edited volumes include Reis, Ridenti, and Motta, *O golpe*; Toledo, *1964*; and Soares and D'Araújo, *21 anos*. For more recent studies, I suggest Johnson, *Brazilian Party Politics*, which provides an explanation for the coup contrary to Stepan's, and Fico, *Além do golpe*, 13–69 and 139–205, which introduces the scholarly debates evolving around the coup and a helpful bibliographic guide.

28. For attitudes of the business sector and the middle classes, see Diniz, "Empresariado," 198–231; Gomes, "Classe media," 594–98; and Saes, *Classe média*; Moraes, "O colapso," 128.

29. This part is restricted to the major ideological think tanks. The history of the ESG ideology could be traced back further. Moreover, additional roots could be considered, such as the Institute of Applied Economic Research (IPEA) or ideological similarities with the Vargas regime.

30. Stepan, *Authoritarian Brazil*, 54, 57.

31. Alves, *State and Opposition*, 14.

32. Oliveira, "As forças armadas," 22.

33. Davis, "Brazil: National Security Doctrine," 442.

34. Stepan, "Political Leadership," 120; Stepan, *Authoritarian Brazil*, 50–51; Alves, *State and Opposition*, 9, 17–18.

35. Klein and Figueiredo, *Legitimidade e coação*, 47. Patrick Wilcken estimates that the number of Brazilians actively engaged in the armed struggle was minor, ranging between five hundred and one thousand men and women, and that the regime "never faced serious opposition" ("The Reckoning," 68).

36. Alves, *State and Opposition*, 31. Alves has argued that the NSD changed over time, due to its dialectic relationship with oppositional groups (9–10); Klein and Figueiredo, *Legitimidade e coação*, 47.

37. A. Smith, *A Forced Agreement*, 24. It is also well expressed by a book title of Gaspari's: "The enclosed/confined dictatorship [encurrulada]."

38. Stepan, *Authoritarian Brazil*, 54–55; Oliveira, "As forças armadas," 54.

39. Alves, *State and Opposition*, 26.

40. Wanderley, "Desenvolvimentismo: ideologia dominate," 155–92; Toledo, *ISEB*, 12–13, 31, 81, 186–89.

41. Fico, "Versões e controvérsias sobre," 34–35; Klein and Figueiredo, *Legitimidade e coação*, 51–53.

42. Oliveira, "As forças armadas," 31–33; Alves, *State and Opposition*, 6; Fico, "Versões e controvérsias sobre," 38; Fico, "A pluralidade," 78. The term first appeared in D'Araújo, Castro, and Soares, *Visões do golpe*, 9.

43. In the programmatic publication *O processo revolucionário brasileiro* (AERP, 9),

the ESG ideology is explicitly recognized as the basis of the "Revolutionary Doctrine," alongside the president's statements.

44. Here, I contradict scholars who contrast the hardliners' ideology with that of the ESG, which they attribute to the moderates. For example, Drosdoff, *Linha Dura no Brasil*, 24–25.

45. National Archives Rio, Fundo IPÊS, Caixa 61; Dreifuss, *1964*, 229, 337–38; Assis, *Propaganda e cinema*, 22–23, 67, 69.

46. Garcia, *Sadismo*, 58; Assis, *Propaganda e cinema*, 21.

47. Leacock, "JFK, Business, and Brazil," 640, 669; Dreifuss, *1964*, 102, 123.

48. Dreifuss, *1964*, 105–7, 229.

49. Dreifuss, *1964*, 232–51.

50. Fifteen of those IPÊS film productions are held by the National Archives in Rio de Janeiro. Assis, *Propaganda e cinema*, 31; Lima, Priolli, and Machado, *Televisão e Vídeo*, 22.

51. Dreifuss, *1964*, 645.

52. Assis, *Propaganda e cinema*, 53, 60. Denise Assis refers to interviews with women from the female wing of the IPÊS, the *Campanha Da Mulher pela Democracia* (CAMDE). The CAMDE supported the regime until the early 1970s. While some women later realized that they had supported censorship and violent repression and felt deceived, others still proudly claim that they defended Brazil against a communist invasion.

53. Dreifuss, *1964*, 337–38.

54. Please note that the published documentation from Camargo's private archive (CAM) and the National Library (BN) are listed in the bibliography. CAM, AERP, *Relatório*; Camargo, *A espada virgem*, 193; interview with Gen. Octávio Pereira da Costa, Rio de Janeiro, March 22, 2007; interview with Ex-Minister Jarbas Passarinho, Brasília, May 9, 2007.

55. CAM, AERP, *Manual*, Item 7.1, 9.1, and appendix model 14.

56. Garcia, *Sadismo*, 60; Caparelli, *Televisão*, 157.

57. Capelato, *Multidões em cena*, 51. The DIP was divided into five divisions: "divulgation," which was responsible for culture, conferences, and pamphlets; "radio"; "theater and cinema"; "press"; and, finally, a division for "tourism," which was also responsible for propaganda abroad.

58. Jowett, "Propaganda and Communication," 97.

59. Taylor, *Film Propaganda*, 7; Driencourt, *La propaganda*, 112, 236, 241.

60. I borrow this poignant term from Eagleton, *Ideology*, 7.

61. Qualter, *Propaganda*, 15, 20–21; Ellul, *Propaganda*, 26, 62; Christenson and McWilliams, *Voice of the People*, 321.

62. Epistemology studies the nature of knowledge, its presuppositions, and its validity.

63. Eagleton, *Ideology*, 24–25.

64. When I use the term "reality," I do not wish to be construed as what is often wrongly referred to as a Rankean historian, establishing "how it really was." However,

similarly to Eagleton and in contrast to much postmodern historical writing, I believe that it is possible to judge to a certain degree if incidents were true or false. I do not claim to know how "reality" actually was, but I can search for information that shows how it was *not*.

65. Eagleton, *Ideology*, 11, 221–22.

66. I am aware that the AERP and ARP films were not apolitical in a literal sense. They supported values like order and discipline. Yet I argue that this support was much more indirect in nature than the work of other agents. It also depends on the definition of *political*. Using a broad definition, the word "apolitical" does not make sense, since everything is political.

67. Several propaganda scholars have pointed out that a common function of political propaganda is to enhance the nation's self-esteem: Ellul, *Propaganda*, 62; Eagleton, *Ideology*, 27; Qualter, *Propaganda*, 38, 52; Huxley, "Notes on Propaganda," 331.

68. As Fico points out ("Versões e controvérsias sobre," 30, 40–41), between 1971 and 2000, 241 MA and PhD theses examined the military dictatorship; most focused on urban social movements, the economy, left-wing opposition groups, and arts and culture, particularly music. For a concise overview of archive material in Brazil, consult Ludmila da Silva Catela, "Do segredo à verdade," 451–55. Also see the final chapter of Fico, *Além do golpe*. While documents belonging to the repressive organs the State Department of Political and Social Order (Departamento Estadual de Ordem Política e Social, DEOPS) and the Department of Political and Social Order (Departamento de Ordem Política e Social, DOPS) have already been made accessible in several state archives, including São Paulo and Rio, as of December 2005 documentation from the former intelligence organization, the National Intelligence Service (Serviço Nacional de Informação), the National Security Service (Conselho Nacional de Segurança), and the General Investigation Commission (*Comissão Geral de Investigações*) can be researched in the National Archives in Brasília. The DEOPS was the police force "for political and social order" in São Paulo, while the DOPS, the police force for "social order," operated in Rio. For both state archives, catalogues and guidance literature are available: For São Paulo, see Aquino, Mattos, and Swensson, *No coração das trevas*. For Rio, consult Arquivo Público do Estado do Rio de Janeiro, *Os arquivos das polícias políticas* and *DOPS lógica da desconfiança*. Another vital archive is the Brasil Nunca Mais Project, which contains the secretly copied documentation of the Military Supreme Court. The project compiled the first major report on torture, published in 1985 by the archdiocese of São Paulo. While the original files are hosted by the Edgar Leuenroth Archive in Campinas, since July 2013 the documentation has been made available online at http://bnmdigital.mpf.mp.br/#!/.

69. The four studies of official propaganda in dictatorial Brazil are Garcia, *Sadismo, sedução e silêncio*; Fico, *Reinventando o otimismo*; Weber, *Comunicação e espetáculos*; and Assis, *Propaganda e cinema*. Dreifuss' account in *1964* does not focus specifically on propaganda but covers the prime propaganda organ during the coup. For dissertations, consult Carrilho, "A legitimação da ditadura"; Martins, "Ditadura militar"; O. Lima,

"A tentação do consenso"; Matos, "Modos de olhar"; and Galletti, "Propaganda e legitimação." Other works that briefly consider the AERP are Oberlaender's *História de propaganda no Brasil* and Caparelli's *Televisão e capitalismo no Brasil*.

70. Altogether I conducted twenty-seven oral history interviews. I recorded fifteen hours of material with the five most important AERP officials, which forms the basis of my fourth chapter, and I undertook four interviews with the key propaganda strategist, Octávio Costa (interviews with Gen. Octávio Pereira da Costa, Rio de Janeiro, March 2, 2007, March 22, 07, October 23, 2007, June 5, 2009; interview with Gen. José Maria Toledo Camargo, Rio de Janeiro, March 7, 2007; interview with Professor João Clemente Baena Soares, Rio de Janeiro, March 20, 2007; interview with Professor Alberto Rabaça, Rio de Janeiro, March 14, 2007; interview with Professor José Cavalieri, Rio de Janeiro, March 27, 2007).

In addition, I conducted eleven qualitative oral history interviews on the reception of the propaganda produced by the military regime (interview with Clovis, Rio de Janeiro, September 17, 2007; interview with Ricardo Corrêa, Rio de Janeiro, September 8, 2007; interview with Dona Dalva, Rio de Janeiro, August 31, 2007; interview with Jane, Rio de Janeiro, October 8, 2007; interview with Seu João, Rio de Janeiro, July 18, 2007; interview with Seu José Pinto, Rio de Janeiro, July 19, 2007; interview with Seu Fridinan Caitano, Rio de Janeiro, July 19, 2007; interview with Clarino Santos, Rio de Janeiro, September 7, 2007; interview with Regina Souza, Rio de Janeiro, October 3, 2007; interview with Dona Tereza, Rio de Janeiro, July 23, 2007; interview with anonymous local politician, Rio de Janeiro, October 10, 2007). In addition, I interviewed the former journalist and prominent intellectual Alberto Dines and Jarbas Passarinho, the widely known former minister and unofficial spokesman of the armed forces (interview with Professor Alberto Dines, São Paulo, August 2, 2007; interview with ex-Minister Jarbas Passarinho, Brasília, May 9, 2007). Passarinho served as minister of labor under President Costa e Silva and Figueiredo, as minister of education and culture under President Médici, and as justice minister under President Collor. Lastly, I conducted interviews with Brazilian archivists and victims of the regime (interview with Vivien Ishaq, Coordinator of the National Archives in Brasília, May 2, 2007; interviews with Captain Corrêa, Coordinator of Centre of Documentation of the Armed Forces [CDOCex], Rio de Janeiro, July 10, 2007, and June 5, 2009; interviews with Brigadier Rui Moreira Lima, Rio de Janeiro, June 9, 2009, and June 11, 2009; interview with Professor Gustavo Barbosa, Rio de Janeiro, March 14, 2007, and July 30, 2007). Moreover, I consulted various edited oral history interviews, most notably the series produced by the CPDOC and the fifteen-volume edition made by the editing company of the armed forces, Biblioteca do Exército (hereafter Bibliex Edition).

Chapter 1. Small and "Democratic"?

1. Garcia applies a fairly similar periodization; see *Sadismo*, 58. He locates the third phase in the years 1973–80, whereas I suggest 1975/76–1980, because between 1973 and

1975 almost no propaganda was produced. Alternatively, one could describe these few years as another phase.

2. National Library (BN), AERP, *1° Seminário*, 41–42.

3. BN, AERP, *1° Seminário*; D'Araújo, Castro, and Soares, *Os anos do chumbo*, 267; Fico, *Reinventando*, 90.

4. Decree Law No. 62.119. BN, AERP, *1° Seminário*, 3, 8, 27–28.

5. Oberlaender, *História de propaganda*, 32–33; D'Araújo, Castro, and Soares, *Os anos do chumbo*, 267; Fico, "A pluralidade das censuras," 77. A few articles previously mentioned the early AERP under D'Aguiar; see "O show dos três minutos," *Veja* 12, November 27, 1968, 6969. However, with the appointment of Costa and Camargo, they became more frequent.

6. The first entry on the AERP appeared in Abreu and Paulo, *Dicionário histórico-biográfico*, 30–31. The only other entry on the ARP, in the *Historical Dictionary of Brazil* (Levine, 18), is flawed, as it holds that the ARP was created in 1964.

7. Fico, *Reinventando*, 92, 146. In fact, the AERP had already been founded in March 1968, while the 1968 opposition movement reached its climax on June 26, 1968, with the Passeata dos Cem Mil in Rio de Janeiro. Nonetheless, protests had already started in 1967.

8. Caparelli, *Televisão*, 156.

9. CAM, AERP, *Relatório*, 5. See also Costa's statement in D'Araújo, Castro, and Soares, *Os anos do chumbo*, 267.

10. O. Lima, "A tentação do consenso," 21–22, 36.

11. Arguably, some traces of this kind of propaganda can still be observed in Brazil today. As explained in Fico (*Reinventando*, 30), the word *ufanism* goes back to Affonso Celso de Assis Figueiredo, who, in 1901, published the book *Porque me ufano do meu paiz* [Why I have patriotic feelings about my country].

12. Interview with Gen. Octávio Pereira da Costa, Rio de Janeiro, March 2, 2007; Fico, *Reinventando*, 113.

13. Interview with Gen. Octávio Pereira da Costa, March 2, 2007.

14. See the principles and objectives mentioned in the basic documentation: CAM, AERP, *Relatório*; CAM, AERP, *Manual*; CAM, AERP, *Documentos*. See also numerous newspaper articles, including: "Governo deseja esforço geral," *O Estado de São Paulo*, April 24, 1970, 5; "Octávio Costa prega o entendimento," *Jornal do Brasil*, October 16, 1970, 3; "Otávio Costa diz que a AERP obteve entendimento entre o pôvo e o Govêrno," *Jornal do Brasil*, July 7, 1971, 4.

15. CAM, AERP, *Manual*, appendix C.

16. CAM, AERP, *Relatório*, 6–7.

17. "Otávio Costa diz que ARP não pretende ser o antigo DIP e nem mudar opinões," *Jornal do Brasil*, April 24, 1970, 3; "A propaganda sútil que cobre o País," *O Estado de São Paulo*, August 3, 1973, 14.

18. CAM, AERP, *Manual*, Item 7.1 and appendix model 14; "A grande campanha," *Veja*, May 19, 1976, 29.

19. CAM, AERP, *Documentos*, Item 5, 4; CAM, AERP, *Relatório*, 34.

20. See Fico, *Reinventando*, 130. As Pereira shows, ruling groups had attempted to socially and politically demobilize Brazilian society prior to the military regime ("An Ugly Democracy?" 217–35).

21. "Sistema de Comunicação." CAM, AERP, *Documentos*.

22. CAM, AERP, *Relatório*, 40.

23. CAM, AERP, *Relatório*, 31–32.

24. Gabinete do Ministro da Marinha, Serviço de Relações Públicas, Ofícios 207 a 441, 1973, No. 20,216, "Of. No. 21,782, November 8, 1973."

25. Interviews with Gen. Octávio Pereira da Costa, March 2, 2007, March 22, 2007, October 23, 2007; interview with Gen. Camargo, March 7, 2007. See also Camargo's autobiography, *A espada virgem*, 144, 184, 216. Fico, *Reinventando*.

26. D'Araújo, Castro, and Soares, *Os anos do chumbo*, 268; interviews with Gen. Octávio Pereira da Costa, March 2, 2007, March 22, 2007, October 23, 2007.

27. Camargo, *A espada virgem*, 230–33; interview with Gen. Octávio Pereira da Costa, March 2, 2007.

28. CAM, AERP, *Relatório*, 32.

29. Interview with Gen. Octávio Pereira da Costa, March 2, 2007.

30. According to Filho, the OBAN was a kind of trial phase. Once the military were convinced that it worked, the system of repression was institutionalized (*O palácio*, 164).

31. Parts of the armed forces seemed to have a special interest in this case, as many articles could be found in the CDOCex at the military headquarters in Brasília; for example, "O assassinato de Biolensen," *Ombro a ombro*, January 1995, n.p. According to a military expert, the CDOCex archive, however, was closed down on December 30, 2011.

32. Gorender, for instance, makes this argument in *Combate nas trevas*, 156–57. Gaspari (*A didatura escancarada*, 380) links it to the CIE, led by Tavares.

33. Since 2005, the National Archives in Brasília have allowed access to the documentation of the former SNI. The procedure involves providing a keyword or a name (since the enactment of a new archive law in November 2011, personal authorization is no longer required), and the archivist checks whether the system retrieves any documents filed under the term. Surprisingly, the system retrieved neither files related to the AERP and ARP nor to Costa during his time as AERP leader. However, the State Archive of São Paulo holds a few SNI reports that mention the AERP and Costa; see State Archive São Paulo, DEOPS, OP1115; SNI Boletim Agência de São Paulo, No. 247, 1; State Archive São Paulo, DEOPS, OP1115; SNI Boletim Agência de São Paulo, No. 238, 3, and No. 240, 1. Although these were regional SNI reports, they should have been sent to the central agency headquartered in Brasília. This finding at least proves that the AERP and Costa appeared in SNI reports at the time. It remains unclear whether these reports were deliberately filtered before the documentation arrived at the Archives,

whether further documentation exists but cannot be retrieved under the current problematic keyword system, or whether it was destroyed in a routine process to get rid of unnecessary data. The Manual of the SNI, held in the National Archives in Brasília, shows that the SNI regularly discarded documentation that was no longer regarded as useful.

34. "Silêncio da melhor," *Veja* 122, January 6, 1971, 60.

35. AERP, *Documentos*; see the various yearly plans.

36. CAM, AERP, *Relatório*, 6.

37. CAM, AERP, *Manual*, Item 7.1 and appendix model 14, Item 9.1.

38. Interview with Carlos Alberto Rabaça, March 14, 2007.

39. CAM, AERP, *Manual*, Item 5.1, and CAM, AERP, *Relatório*, 49.

40. CAM, AERP, *Relatório*, 23–24; "Otávio Costa diz que AERP obteve entendimento entre o pôvo e o Govêrno," *Jornal do Brasil*, July 7, 1971, 3; "Otávio Costa fala sôbre ação da AERP," *Jornal do Brasil*, July 1, 1970, 14; State Archive São Paulo, DEOPS, OP1115, No. 238, 3.

41. "Otávio Costa diz que AERP obteve entendimento entre o pôvo e o Govêrno," *Jornal do Brasil*, July 7, 1971, 3; "Otávio Costa fala sôbre ação da AERP," *Jornal do Brasil*, July 1, 1970, 14; State Archive São Paulo, DEOPS, OP1115, No. 238, 3; CAM, AERP, *Relatório*, 24.

42. Interview with Gen. Octávio Pereira da Costa, March 2, 2007; interview with Professor Cavalieri, March 27, 2007; interview with Professor Soares, Rio de Janeiro, March 20, 2007.

43. CAM, AERP, *Catálogo de peças produzidas—out. 69/Mar 74*; CAM, AERP, *Relatório*, 14–15; "Otávio Costa diz que AERP obteve entendimento entre o pôvo e o Govêrno," *Jornal do Brasil*, July 7, 1971, 3.

44. Camargo, *A espada virgem*, 152; interview with Gen. Octávio Pereira da Costa, March 22, 2007; CAM, AERP, *Relatório*, 44.

45. Costa, "Governo e comunicação social," 9; Garcia, *Sadismo*, 78; CAM, AERP, *Relatório*, 36; interview with Rabaça, March 14, 2007.

46. Pinto, "The Brazilian Media Scene," 65.

47. "The Brazilian Communications Media," 31; Pinto, "The Brazilian Media Scene," 67.

48. Pinto, "The Brazilian Media Scene," 64–68.

49. Pinto, "The Brazilian Media Scene," 66; "The Brazilian Communications Media" calculates that, in 1974, 24 percent of the Brazilian population had access to a television set (31).

50. Many Brazilians watched television at friends' houses, which suggests that the actual number of viewers was even higher. See Bechtos, "Não existe falta de veículos de propaganda no Brasil"; Garcia, *Sadismo*, 76.

51. "The Brazilian Communications Media," *Propaganda* 214, May 1971, 34.

52. Wickerhauser, "O cinema como veículo publicitário," 14–16.

53. Interview with Gen. Octávio Pereira da Costa, March 2, 2007. Regarding outdoor propaganda, there were no reliable outreach figures at the time. Pinto, "The Brazilian Media Scene," 67; CAM, AERP, *Relatório*, 31; Camargo, *A espada virgem*, 150.

54. Interview with Pinto, July 18, 2007; Fico, *Reinventando*, 103–4; CAM, AERP, *Catálogo de peças produzidas—Out. 69/Mar 74.*

55. Camargo, *A espada virgem*, 150; "A propaganda sútil que cobre o País," *O Estado de São Paulo*, August 3, 1973, 14; "A imagem oficial, retocada para o consumo," *O Estado de São Paulo*, October 16, 1977, 8; Fico, *Reinventando*, 113; Garcia, *Sadismo*, 77.

56. CAM, AERP, *Manual*, Item 8.3, Item 8.8, Item 8.12, appendix E, Decree Law No. 483, March 3, 1969, Art. 5 § 1, 2; Camargo, *A espada virgem*, 150; interview with Rabaça, March 14, 2007.

57. CAM, AERP, *Manual*, Item 8.13; interview with Gen. Octávio Pereira da Costa, March 2, 2007.

58. Camargo, *A espada virgem*, 153, 193; interview with Gen. Octávio Pereira da Costa, March 22, 2007; interview with ex-Minister Passarinho, May 9, 2007.

59. Garcia, *Sadismo*, 78.

60. Katz and Wedell, *Broadcasting in the Third World*, 5.

61. Schramm, *Mass Media and National Development*. Schramm's name appears in the bibliographies of Costa's texts; see Costa, "Governo e comunicação social," 10; "A imagem oficial, retocada para o consumo," *O Estado de São Paulo*, October 16, 1977, 8.

62. "Três livros sôbre a função da comunicação nos PMD (países menos desenvolvidos)," *Propaganda* 181 (June 1971): 13–16.

63. Fico, *Reinventando*, 104, 106.

64. "A AERP vai acabar em março," *O Estado de São Paulo*, August 29, 1973, 4.

65. Galletti, "Propaganda," 44–45.

66. "Governo vai dar mais informação," *O Estado de São Paulo*, November 27, 1974, 4; "Governo lança em maio campanha publicitária," *O Estado de São Paulo*, March 17, 1976, 5.

67. CAM, AERP, *Catálogo de peças produzidas-Out. 69/Mar 74*; CAM, AERP, *Catálogo de peças produzidas 1974/1975*; CAM, ARP, *Catálogo de peças produzidas 1976*; CAM, ARP, *Catálogo de peças produzidas 1977*.

68. Information on the SECOM is generally scarce. Abreu and Paulo, *Dicionário histórico-biográfico*, 30–31; Costa, "General-de-Divisão," 85; "O General na educação," *Veja* 639, December 3, 1980, 27.

Chapter 2. Stars Appearing in the Sky

1. Huxley, "Notes on Propaganda," 331.

2. According to the Brazilian Central Bank and the Getúlio Vargas Foundation, the annual growth rate in 1960 was 9.7 percent, and in 1961 it was 10.3 percent. In 1968 it was 11.2 percent, in 1970 8.8 percent, in 1972 11.7 percent, and the growth record year was in 1973, when the annual growth rate amounted to 13.9 percent. See Mattos, "Domestic and Foreign Advertising," 68.

3. The figures from the annual catalogues seem relatively reliable. Occasionally, two films were counted under one number (for example, 23 and 23a), and the catalogues might not have listed all the productions. Numbers were added whenever two films were listed under one number. In my copy of the catalogue some numbers are missing, but as they probably existed in the original and were not copied properly, missing numbers have also been added. This might be another reason why my figures differ slightly from Galletti's. Galletti's study found an even larger difference in production quantities. For Médici's presidency (1970–1973), she counted 308 units, whereas for Geisel's presidency (1974–1978) she calculated 507. The higher ARP output can be explained by the production figures from 1978, which are missing from my calculation, as I lacked the relevant copy of the catalogue ("Propaganda," 59).

4. Caparelli, Televisão, 160.

5. Based on Galletti's AERP and ARP production figures (as she provides the figures for 1978 as well), and on Soares' censorship figures, we can see that the peak period of censorship occurred in late 1973/early 1974. In 1975, censorship sharply declined, and the propaganda volume visibly rose in 1975. Soares' analysis is based on censorship orders of the Jornal do Brasil (edited in the so-called Blackbook) and on figures provided by Marconi. Soares, "A censura," 29, 41; Galletti, "Propaganda," 59.

6. CAM, AERP, Catálogo de peças produzidas—Out. 69/Mar; CAM, AERP, Catálogo de peças produzidas 1974/1975; CAM, ARP, Catálogo de peças produzidas 1976; CAM, ARP, Catálogo de peças produzidas 1977. As mentioned previously, these catalogues are not held in an archive, but I was kindly allowed to copy them from General Camargo.

7. The newspaper was Jornal da Tarde. São Paulo State Archive, DEOPS, OP1115, No. 240, 1.

8. São Paulo State Archive, DEOPS, OP1115, No. 240, 1–2; No. 246, 2.

9. CAM, AERP, Catálogo de peças produzidas-out. 69/Mar 74, films number 40 and 41.

10. CAM, ARP, Catálogo de peças produzidas-1976, FE. 8, FE. 7, FE. 9, FE. 10, FE. 11.

11. FGV, CPDOC, EG Pr.1974.11.25 (microfilm 18), Of. No 6/232, 27.06.1976.

12. Cole, International Encyclopedia, 622.

13. Albrecht, Nationalsozialistische Filmpolitik.

14. Some films could have been classified under more than one category, in which case I chose the most appropriate one.

15. Subliminal propaganda films between 1970 and 1973 were EH.-Fil. 934 (F. 35), EH.-Fil. 756 (F. 37), EH.-Fil. 932 (F. 69), EH.-Fil. 933 (F. 66), EH.-Fil. 933 (F. 66), EH.-Fil. 935 (F. 123), and EH.-Fil. 936 (F. 126). In 1976, EH.-Fil. 715 (FE. 15), EH.-Fil. 713 (FE. 16), and EH.-Fil. 787 (unknown original number, but about SENAC). In 1977, EH.-Fil. 781 (FI. 58), EH.-Fil. 783 (FI. 69), EH.-Fil. XXX (FI. 70), EH.-Fil. 721 (FI. 71), EH.-Fil. 784 (FI. 72), EH.-Fil. 723 (FI. 73), EH.-Fil. 720 (FI. 74), EH.-Fil. 786 (FI. 75), EH.-Fil. 739 (FI. 87), EH.-Fil. 735 (FE. 18), EH.-Fil. 724 (FE. 20), EH.-Fil. 725 (FE. 21), EH.-Fil. 727 (FE. 22), EH.-Fil. 789 (FE. 23), EH.-Fil. 729 (FE. 23A), EH.-Fil. 733 (FE. 24), EH.-Fil. 730 (FE. 25), EH.-Fil. 728 (FE. 26), EH.-Fil. 726 (FE. 29), EH.-Fil. 791 (FE. 32), EH.-Fil. 732 (FE. 33), EH.-Fil. 731 (FE. 34), EH.-Fil. 734 (FE. 35), EH.-Fil. 737 (FE. 38),

EH.-Fil. 736 (FE. 41), EH.-Fil. 798 (FE. 44), EH.-Fil. 795 (FE. 47), EH.-Fil. 791 (FE. 51), EH.-Fil. 742 (FE. 52), EH.-Fil. 799 (FE. 53), and EH.-Fil. 743 (FE. 55). In 1978/79, EH.-Fil. 765, 766, 800, 801, 803, 748, 751, 763, 792, 812, 815, 750, 758, 760, 762, 813, ZZZZ, 744, 745, 747, 746, 752, 761, 767, 768, 778, 802, 804, 805, 810, and 811.

16. Blunt-propaganda broadcasts were, in 1976, films FI. 39 (EH.-Fil. 706) and FI. 46 (EH.-Fil. 774); in 1977, FI. 57 (EH.-Fil. 788); in 1978/79, EH.-Fil. 754 and EH.-Fil. 708. Economic-propaganda films were: in 1973, F. 151 (EH.-Fil. 749); in 1976, FI. 25 (EH.-Fil. 772); in 1977, FE. 46 (EH.-Fil. 796); in 1978/79 EH.-Fil. 759 and EH.-Fil. 807.

17. 1970 F. 35 (EH.-Fil. 934).

18. 1971 F. 66 (EH.-Fil. 933).

19. Another example of subliminal propaganda is a film about New Year's Eve, which shows Brazilians of different age groups and professions and evokes a feeling of peace and togetherness (see 1976 FE. 10A [EH.-Fil. 718] and 1978/79 EH.-Fil. 761), and a film that promotes domestic tourism by showing the beauty of Brazil's beaches (see the 1973 production F. 123 [EH.-Fil. 935]).

20. 1976 FI. 15 (EH.-Fil. 771).

21. 1976 FI. 39 (EH.-Fil. 706).

22. 1976 FI. 25 (EH.-Fil. 722).

23. 1976 FI. 25 (EH.-Fil. 772).

24. 1976 FE. 16 (EH.-Fil. 713). The Tupi were the Native American tribe who lived on the coast of Brazil and who were exterminated by the Portuguese after the arrival of Cabral in 1500. "Pindorama" is a Tupi name for Brazil. The short film may have been inspired by a 1970/71 feature film with the same title and shot by the Cinema Novo director Arnaldo Jabor.

25. For a description of the whitening ideology in Brazil and its development, consult Skidmore, *Black into White*.

26. Freyre, *The Masters and the Slaves*; Skidmore, "Raízes," 1–20.

27. "Boneco vai ajudar a manter cidade limpa," *O Estado de São Paulo*, September 16, 1972, 60; "Ceará forma a turma Sujismundo," *Jornal do Brasil*, December 1, 1972, 19. As for the name Sujismundo, "sujo" means "dirty," and "-mundo" is a typical ending for names (for example, Raimundo, Edmundo) but can also come from "mundo," meaning "world." Dr. Prevenildo is derived from "prevenir," which means "to prevent." "'Prevenildo,' o irmão de 'Sujismundo,' vai liderar campanha contra acidente," *Jornal do Brasil*, November 21, 1972, 14.

28. Interview with Professor Rabaça, March 14, 2007; interview with Pinto, July 18, 2007.

29. According to Professor Rabaça, they tried to exert pressure on Costa to produce slogans like "Those who don't walk on the right had better leave Brazil" (interview with Professor Rabaça, March 14, 2007).

30. For Sujismundo/Dr. Prevenildo films, see 1977 FE. 24 (EH.-Fil. 733), FE. 25 (EH.-Fil. 730), FE. 26 (EH.-Fil. 728), 1978/79 [?] (according to the National Archive's new coding, the film was produced in 1977 [BR AN RIO EH.0.FIL.FIT.32 ANO 1977];

however, the ARP production catalogue of 1977 fails to list this film. I suspect that this film was wrongly associated with the year 1977), EH.-Fil.748, and EH.-Fil. 751.

31. See Fico, *Reinventando*.

32. See 1978/79 [?] EH.-Fil. 750, 758, 760, 762, 813, and ZZZZ (arbitrary name, as no archive code exists).

33. See 1978/79 [?] EH.-Fil. 750.

34. See 1978 EH.-Fil. 758 (BR AN RIO EH.0.FIL.FIT.62 ANO 1978).

35. 1978/79 EH.-Fil. ZZZZ.

36. The text continues: "And we cannot allow scenes like these to be repeated so many times a day. Too much speed. Lack of respect for the traffic lights. Lack of respect for pedestrians. Death and maiming in the traffic."

37. 1976 FE. 4 (EH.-Fil. 711), 1977 FI. 57 (EH.-Fil. 788), 1978 EH.-Fil. 759, 1978/79 EH.-Fil. 809, EH.-Fil. 708, and EH.-Fil. 744.

38. Films arguing that everyone benefits from economic growth are, for example, 1973 F. 151 (EH.-Fil. 749), 1976 FI. 27 (EH.-Fil. 709), FI. 38 (EH.-Fil. 773), FI. 48 (EH.-Fil. 776), 1977 FI. 60 (EH.-Fil. 785), FI. 85 (EH.-Fil. 738), FE. 21 (EH.-Fil. 725), FE. 35 (EH.-Fil. 734), FE. 55 (EH.-Fil. 743), 1978/79 EH.-Fil. 807, and EH.-Fil. 757.

39. 1978/79 EH.-Fil. 807.

40. 1976 FI. 38 (EH.-Fil. 773).

41. Housing 1976 FI. 15 (EH.-Fil. 771), FI. 39 (EH.-Fil. 706), and FI. 36 (EH.-Fil. 712). For Merenda Escolar see 1976 FI. 48 (EH.-Fil. 776) and 1977 FI. 85 (EH.-Fil. 738). Merenda Escolar was a program providing school meals for children. It was launched before the military coup.

42. 1978/79 EH.-Fil. 757.

43. Another film that praises the government programs is 1976 FI. 27 (EH.-Fil. 709). It also promises to distribute the fruits of economic progress to all.

44. Fico, *Reinventando*, 135. In various parts of his book, Fico describes the meaning of the word "civilization" in Brazil.

45. 1979 EH.-Fil. 766.

46. For example, 1979 EH.-Fil. 766 and EH.-Fil. 810. In another film an orchestra is being instructed while we listen to classical music (1977 FI. 87 [EH.-Fil. 739]).

47. See 1971 F. 69 (EH.-Fil. 932), 1976 FI. 27 (EH.-Fil. 709) and FI. 38 (EH.-Fil. 773), 1977 FI. 60 (EH.-Fil. 785) and FE. 51 (EH.-Fil. 797), and 1978/79 EH.-Fil. 747.

48. 1971 F. 69 (EH.-Fil. 932).

49. The National Truth Commission instated a working group called Dictatorship and the Repression of Workers and the Trade Union Movement (Ditadura e repressão aos trabalhadores e ao movimento sindical); see http://www.cnv.gov.br/index.php/2012-05-22-18-30-05/veja-todos-os-grupos-de-trabalho, accessed October 30, 2012.

50. Another film depicts a family working hard but joyfully together harvesting fruit, laughing, and smiling; see 1977 FE. 51 (EH.-Fil. 797). A little boy stops, wipes the sweat from his forehead, and continues working. In this case, development is symbolized by

the harvest. Another film shows students working in a laboratory, concentrating hard on their studies; see 1978/79 EH.-Fil. 747.

51. Lucia Klein argues that on the whole "national security" and "development" were the prime elements of legitimization, yet under Médici, the latter was even more important. See Klein and Figueiredo, *Legitimidade e coação*, 58, 61–62.

52. Alves, *State and Opposition*, 9, 17, 26.

53. See, for instance, Furtado, *Formação econômica do Brasil*.

54. Saes, *Classe média*, 136, 125–219; Diniz, "Empresariado," 202–3. See also the articles by Singer and Oliveira in Toledo, *1964*, 15, 17–19, 26–27; or Skidmore, "Politics and Economic Policy Making," 4.

55. Costa, "Discurso de abertura," 397, quoted in Moura Silva, "Segurança e desenvolvimento," 47; CAM, AERP, *Documentos fundamentais*; see the various yearly plans, here yearly plan of 1971, 2.

56. CAM, AERP, *Documentos fundamentais*, yearly plan of 1971, 8, and yearly plans of 1972 and 1973.

57. Censuses have shown and researchers have admitted that it is impossible to precisely define race criteria or skin tones in Brazil. I refer to "mulatto with a light skin tone" here to emphasize that they looked almost white and to emphasize that the racism was reflected in these campaigns. See 1976: FI. 15 (EH.-Fil. 771), FI. 27 (EH.-Fil. 709), FI. 36 (EH.-Fil. 712), FI. 46 (EH.-Fil. 774), FI. 48, FI. 49 (EH.-Fil. 777), FE. 13 (EH.-Fil. 717), FE. 14 (EH.-Fil. 779), and FE. 16 (EH.-Fil. 713); in 1977, FI. 57 (EH.-Fil. 788), FI. 70 (EH.-Fil. XXX), FI. 72 (EH.-Fil. 784), FI. 85 (EH.-Fil. 738), FI. 87 (EH.-Fil. 739), FE. 32 (EH.-Fil. 791), FE. 38 (EH.-Fil. 737), and FE. 41 (EH.-Fil. 736); in 1978, EH.-Fil. 759; in 1978/79, EH.-Fil. 800, EH.-Fil. 803, EH.-Fil. 805, and EH.-Fil. 757.

58. For literature on racism and media, see Sodré, *Claros e escuros* and "O negro." For more empirical studies, consult Leslie, "The Representation of Blacks," 94–107, and "Representation of Blacks on Prime Time Television," 1–9.

59. See Garcia, *O Estado Novo*, 93: Vargas even called his labor legislation the "true abolition."

60. I counted fifty-eight films showing women; however, mostly they played minor roles. 1971: F. 66 (EH.-Fil. 933); 1973: F. 123 (EH.-Fil. 935); 1976: FI. 15 (EH.-Fil. 771), FI. 36 (EH.-Fil. 712), FI. 39 (EH.-Fil. 706), FI. 46 (EH.-Fil. 774), FI. 48 (EH.-Fil. 776), FI. 49 (EH.-Fil. 777), FI. 52 (719), FE. 10/A (EH.-Fil. 718), FE. 12 (EH.-Fil. 716), FE. 13 (EH.-Fil. 717), FE. 14 (EH.-Fil. 779), FE. 15 (EH.-Fil. 715), and FE. 16 (EH.-Fil. 713); 1977: FI. 69 (EH.-Fil. 783), FI. 72 (EH.-Fil. 784), FI. 73 (EH.-Fil. 723), FI. 74 (EH.-Fil. 720), FI. 85 (EH.-Fil. 738), FI. 87 (EH.-Fil. 739), FE. 18 (EH.-Fil. 735), FE. 21 (EH.-Fil. 725), FE. 22 (EH.-Fil. 727), FE. 23A (EH.-Fil. 729), FE. 32 (EH.-Fil. 732), FE. 35 (EH.-Fil. 734), FE. 41 (EH.-Fil. 736), FE. 51 (EH.-Fil. 797), and FE. 55 (EH.-Fil. 743); 1979: EH.-Fil. 766; 1978/79: EH.-Fil. 800, EH.-Fil. 801, EH.-Fil. 803, EH.-Fil. 763, EH.-Fil. 762, EH.-Fil. ZZZZ, EH.-Fil. 744, EH.-Fil. 747, EH.-Fil. 746, EH.-Fil. 752, EH.-Fil. 761, EH.-Fil. 763, EH.-Fil. 768, EH.-Fil. 804, EH.-Fil. 807, EH.-Fil. 806, and EH.-Fil. 810.

61. As mothers, see, for example, 1976: FI. 39 (EH.-Fil. 706); in domestic roles, 1976:

FI. 15 (EH.-Fil. 771) and 1978/79: EH.-Fil. 763; as lovers, FE. 14 (EH.-Fil. 779); as students, see 1976: FI. 52 (EH.-Fil. 719) or 1978/79: EH.-Fil. 747 and FE. 15 (EH.-Fil. 715); as nurses, see 1976: FI. 46 (EH.-Fil. 774) and 1977: FE. 18 (EH.-Fil. 735); as domestic workers, see 1976: FI. 48 (EH.-Fil. 776) and 1977: FI. 85 (EH.-Fil. 738).

62. Middle-class characteristics in this analysis are respectable, well-kept houses, good quality clothing, or an expensive car. For middle class, consult 1970: F. 35 (EH.-Fil. 934) and F. 37 (EH.-Fil. 756); 1971: F. 66 (EH.-Fil. 933); 1973: F. 151 (EH.-Fil. 749); 1976: FI. 52 (EH.-Fil. 719), FE. 4 (EH.-Fil. 711), FE. 12 (EH.-Fil. 716), FE. 15 (EH.-Fil. 715), FI. 39 (EH.-Fil. 706); 1977: FE. 29 (EH.-Fil. 726), FE. 23A (EH.-Fil. 729), FE. 34 (EH.-Fil. 731), FI. 71 (EH.-Fil. 721), FI. 58 (EH.-Fil. 781), FI. 69 (EH.-Fil. 783), FI. 72 (EH.-Fil. 784), FI. 73 (EH.-Fil. 723), FI. 74 (EH.-Fil. 720), FI. 75 (EH.-Fil. 786), FE. 18 (EH.-Fil. 735), FE. 53 (EH.-Fil. 799), FE. 55 (EH.-Fil. 743); 1978: EH.-Fil. 759; 1978/79: EH.-Fil. 801, EH.-Fil. 762, EH.-Fil. 747, EH.-Fil. 752, EH.-Fil. 768, EH.-Fil. 810.

63. For films addressing upper-class Brazilians, see 1973: F. 126 (EH.-Fil. 936); 1978/79: EH.-Fil. 763, EH.-Fil. 804, and EH.-Fil. 808. Those films portray and appeal to the upper class—people who can afford to go on a cruise. For films targeting the lower strata, watch 1976: FI. 49 (EH.-Fil. 777), FI. 27 (EH.-Fil. 709), FI. 46 (EH.-Fil. 774), and FI. 48 (EH.-Fil. 776); 1977: FI. 65 (EH.-Fil. 710) and FE. 20 (EH.-Fil. 724); 1978/79: (EH.-Fil. 757). These films either portray or offer programs for poor people.

64. Under this category this study counted fifty-three (55.8 percent) in total. These films show several classes or they appeal to the general public.

65. The quantitative analysis provides a general overview of topics and their development and is based on the voice-over text provided by the catalogues, along with the limited film material itself. The archive films alone would have provided a very small and uneven sample, since it only contained seven made by the AERP. The analysis was done in two stages. First, I wrote a list of recurrent topics that captured the gist of the film. The catalogues provide the full voice-over text, and most catalogues, at least those of the ARP, also show a picture for each film. Having established categories for the film topics, I attributed a topic to each of the archive films and, finally, the remaining films in the catalogues. For a list of classification criteria, please consult table 2 in appendix 1. Occasionally, when two aspects were equally prominent, I attributed two topics to a single film. Thus films can have a varying number of attributes, and the overall percentage occasionally adds up to more than 100 percent. This proved suitable, as films often addressed more than one main topic. The advantage of this procedure is to produce a clear result (avoiding too many categorizations per film) that, at the same time, is not too generalized either.

66. The percentage does not always add up to 100 percent, since I occasionally attributed more than one topic to a film. The advantage of this method is that it yields more precise results.

67. The years 1978/79 could not be included, since the corresponding catalogues are missing in Camargo's private archive.

68. Galletti ("Propaganda," 67) calls it "realizations."

Chapter 3. Beware! More Propaganda

1. The National Archives in Rio holds documentation from the Agência Nacional. There is little information available about the organ. Dictionary entries and secondary literature have yet to be written.

2. Spínola Castro, *Na tessitura*, 177, 187.

3. Editions of the radio text are available for the years 1968 and 1969. AERP, *Você precisa saber que*, vol. 1, March 31–September 30, 1968 [?]. This section is based on these editions and three selected archive samples: the month of December 1968; the period around the 1964 coup; and the takeover of Médici.

4. ANR/CODEH/Seção CODES/203/DAN/45, 29.04.1964.

5. ANR/CODEH/Seção CODES/Lata 203/PE DAN/SA/54, 06.05.1964.

6. ANR/CODEH/Seção CODES/Lata518/PRIAN: noticiário-rádio dezembro 1968, 02.12.1968, 3; ANR/CODEH/Seção CODES/Lata447/1969/noticiário-imprensa março 1969 1a quinzena, 03.03.1969, 23f.

7. Spínola Castro, *Na tessitura*, 177, 187.

8. AERP, *Você precisa saber*, vol. 1, 20, 22, 41, 45–46, 66, 101, 135; Radiobras, http://www.radiobras.gov.br/estatico/ radio_voz_do_brasil_historia.htm (accessed January 3, 2009).

9. Radiobras, http://www.radiobras.gov.br/estatico/ radio_voz_do_brasil_histo-ria.htm (accessed January 3, 2009). Ethevaldo Siqueira alludes to a joke implying that the program was only of interest to old people: "Avós do Brasil? Não! A voz do Brasil." ["Grandfathers of Brazil? No! The voice of Brazil"] (*Brasil: 500 anos*, 147). In 1980, TV Globo made fun of the program in a commercial that showed a television with the Globo logo and the text "the voice of Brazil," suggesting that Globo was the real voice of the people. See *Propaganda* 285, April 1980, 17.

10. Siqueira, *Brasil: 500 anos*, 148.

11. Newsreels were first produced in Brazil during the New State era (Estado Novo). In 1938, Getúlio Vargas signed a law that made the exhibition of newsreels obligatory within Brazilian cinemas. This law remained in place until 1985. See Machado, *Os anos de chumbo*, 13. For the Médici presidency, see, for example, the newsreels EH.-Fil. 375–78, 441, 454, 456, 458, 459, 465, 477, and 489, and for Geisel, see EH.-Fil. 51, 494, 497, 499, 503, 504, 506, 509, 519, 528, 572, 581, 582, 589, 592, 595, 605, 610, and 632.

12. Interviews with ex-Minister Passarinho, May 9, 2007; Camargo, *A espada virgem*, 182.

13. Interview with Professor Soares, March 20, 2007; Camargo, *A espada virgem*, 182.

14. "Mostrar belezas e riquezas brasileiras bem como realçar a ação paternalista do governo," Camargo, *A espada virgem*, 182.

15. Costa, "Governo e Comunicação social," 9; Garcia, *Sadismo*, 78. See Camargo's critique in *O Estado de São Paulo* and *Diário Brasileiro*, June 17, 1977; Camargo, *A espada virgem*, 189.

16. Abreu, "Jornalistas e jornalismo," 29.

17. Camargo, *A espada virgem*, 188, 190.

18. Education and science during the military regime represents another unexplored field. For a general introduction, see Reznik, "A construção da memória"; Nunes, "As políticas educacionais"; and Fonseca, "O ensino de história." For monographs, consult Cunha and Góes, *O golpe na educação*; and Silva, *A deformação da história*. Mathias, in *A militarização da burocracia*, analyzes the military interference in the Ministry of Education.

19. In line with the regime's aspirations of "modernization" and "progress" for the country, the authoritarian government also undertook a major reform of the Brazilian education system, which established postgraduate studies in Brazil and made schooling mandatory between the ages of four and eight (Law 5.692/71). Nunes, "As políticas educacionais," 351; Filgueiras, "O livro didático," 3377. Cunha and Góes claim that the private education sector benefited substantially from the military regime. The policy was in accordance with the early regime's free-market policies and arguably still has an impact on present-day Brazil (*O golpe na educação*, 42).

20. Anísio Teixeira, the director of the University of Brasília, was dismissed in 1964, and later died under suspicious circumstances, which are presently reinvestigated by both the National Truth Commission and the local truth commission of the University of Brasília (UNB). The famous sociologist Florestan Fernandes was jailed the night before the competition for a position at the University of São Paulo, in order to prevent him from getting the post. He subsequently taught abroad. The local truth commissions instated at the University of Brasília (UNB) and São Paulo (USP) are currently investigating their institutions' history under military rule and may shed more light on these questions. See Cunha and Góes, *O golpe na educação*, 35–38.

21. For pupils in the first four years of education (*primeiro grau*), the subject was called Moral and Civic Education (Educação Moral e Cívica [EMC]), while for graduate students it was called Study of Brazilian Problems (Estudo de Problemas Brasileiros, EPB). See Fonseca, "O ensino de história," 369, 374–75. According to Cunha and Góes, the two main agents engaged in resistance against EMC were Anísio Teixeira and Durmeval Trigueiro, who were forced out of their positions in the Federal Education Council by 1969, opening the way for the eventual implementation of the subject (*O golpe na educação*, 73–74).

22. Interview with Gen. Octávio Pereira da Costa, Rio de Janeiro, March 22, 2007; interview with Gen. José Maria Toledo Camargo, Rio de Janeiro, March 3, 2007; interview with Professor José Cavalieri, Rio de Janeiro, March 27, 2007; Camargo, *A espada virgem*, 142.

23. Fonseca, "O ensino de história," 369.

24. Cunha and Góes, *O golpe na educação*, 73–74.

25. Decree Law No. 869. Fonseca, "O ensino de história," 369; Cunha and Góes, *O golpe na educação*, 73–74; Silva, *A deformação da história*, 53; Filgueiras, "O livro didático," 3375. Humberto Grande had previously authored the book *The Pedagogy of the New State*, and during the military regime he wrote *Civil Education and Work* and

Civic Education for Women. For the CNMC members, see Cunha and Góes, *O golpe na educação*, 75–76.

26. Secretaria de Estado e Educação, Comissão Estadual de Moral e Civismo, Educação moral e cívica, 5.

27. Silva, *A deformação da história*, 54.

28. Abreu and Filho, "A educação," 128.

29. Filgueiras, "O livro didático," 3383.

30. Abreu and Filho, "A educação," 33.

31. Filgueiras, "O livro didático," 3383.

32. Levine and Crocitti, *The Brazil Reader*, 259.

33. Abreu and Filho, "A educação," 126; Silva, *A deformação da história*, 60.

34. Mathias, *A militarização*, 178.

35. Interview with Professor Cavalieri, March 27, 2007; ANB, SNI, ACEN 9123/84, Info No. 506/119/APA/76, 11.08.1976.

36. Interview with Professor Cavalieri, March 27, 2007.

37. C. Simpson, *Science of Coercion*, 11–13.

38. C. Simpson, *Science of Coercion*, 12–13.

39. The Ministry of Justice was responsible for general censorship, and the Ministry of Education and Culture (MEC) for the educational sector. FGV, CPDOC, EG Pr. 1974.04.08, Circular 11.05.1976, microfilm p. 0087.

40. FGV, CPDOC, EG Pr. 1974.03.00, SNI Chefia do Gabinete, 18.11.1974, 1–2.

41. Ventura, *1968*, 285–86. According to the director of the official censorship organ (Divisão de Censura), Rogério Nunes, six films, two prime-time serials (*novelas*), twenty-nine plays, and seventy-four books were censored in the year 1976 (*Jornal do Brasil*, December 30, 1979, 19).

42. Ortiz, *A moderna tradição brasileira*, 114–15; Schwarz, "Cultura e política," 62.

43. Schwarz, "Cultura e política," 62.

44. Schwarz, "Cultura e política," 63.

45. Johnson and Stam, *Brazilian Cinema*, 392–93.

46. For literature, consult Dunn, *Brutality Garden*; Favaretto, *Tropicália*; and Brito, *Tropicalismo*.

47. Schwarz, "Cultura e política," 140; Dunn, *Brutality Garden*, 4; Napolitano, "Historiografia," 194; Ridenti, "Cultura e política," 149.

48. Dunn, *Brutality Garden*, 121, 158–66, 186.

49. Johnson, *Cinema Novo*, 9; King, "Latin American Cinema," 489; Ramos, *Cinema, estado e lutas culturais*, 72–73. According to Fico (*Reinventando*, 102), the AERP had delegates in the INC. Contrary to radio and TV, the film industry, alongside the publishing and theater sectors, was free from the license system. See Xavier, *O cinema*, 56.

50. King, *Companion*, 301.

51. For literature on the regime's cinema politics, consult Johnson, *The Film Industry*, and King, "Latin American Cinema," 503.

52. King, "Latin American Cinema," 503; Johnson, *The Film Industry*, 171–72.

53. King, "Latin American Cinema," 488–89; Johnson and Stam, *Brazilian Cinema*, 43–45; Johnson, *The Film Industry*, 9–12.

54. King, "Latin American Cinema," 509.

55. Johnson and Stam, *Brazilian Cinema*, 43–45.

56. King, "Latin American Cinema," 489.

57. King, *Companion*, 309–10. Later, the so-called Lei do Audiovisual (Audiovisual Law) reintroduced state investment in film production in Brazil, but in a less organized way than EMBRAFILME.

58. King, *Companion*, 310.

59. King, "Latin American Cinema," 489–90; Johnson and Stam, *Brazilian Cinema*, 33; Johnson, *Cinema Novo*, xi, 1, 219. On the long-term influence of Cinema Novo on Brazilian cinema, consult Nagib, *Brazil on Screen*.

60. On Marginal Cinema, see Xavier, *O cinema*, 31–39, and Ramos, *Cinema, estado e lutas culturais*, 67. In *Brazilian Cinema* (39–40), Johnson and Stam explain that Marginal Cinema took up the philosophy of the first phase of Cinema Novo (1960–1964): lonely settings; a focus on poverty rather than the middle class; and use of realism instead of allegory. An important representative of Marginal Cinema was Sganzerla (*O bandido da luz vermelha*, 1968).

61. Ridenti, "Cultura e política," 155.

62. Mattos, "Domestic and Foreign."

63. A. Smith, *A Forced Agreement*, 11, 15, 18, 21.

64. In 1978, almost 3 percent of plays were forbidden. Many films—nearly 1.5 percent of the total production—were prohibited in 1980. See Fico, *Além do golpe*, 90; "A pluralidade," 75; Como *eles agiam*, 172, 177; and "Prezada censura," 18.

65. Fico, "A pluralidade," 76.

66. Marconi, *A censura política*; Aquino, *Censura*, 25; A. Smith, *A Forced Agreement*; Soares, "A censura durante," 21–43. For the newsweekly *Pasquim*, see J. Braga, *O Pasquim e os anos 70*. For an account of the lawsuit of the newsweekly *Opinão* against the state, see J. Machado, *Opinão x censura*.

67. Mattos, "Domestic and Foreign," vii, 101–3, 244, 199; Marconi, *A censura*, 132–35.

68. ANB, SNI, ACEN No. 44502/72, ARJ/SNI, Info No. 3516.15.03.1972; ANB, SNI, ACEN 301/79, Info No. 13/116/ACG/79, 30.10.1979; ANB, SNI, ACE No. 5950/81, Info No. 119/ASP/SNI/1975, and Circular 402/19/AC/75; ANB, SNI, ACE No. 6026/81, Info No. 3217/119/ASP/SNI/1978.

69. Caparelli, *Televisão*, 164; Garcia, *Sadismo*, 76; Mattos, "Domestic and Foreign," 127–28.

70. Mattos, "Domestic and Foreign," 97–98, 101.

71. Mattos, "Domestic and Foreign," 7, 98.

72. Mattos, "Domestic and Foreign," 7.

73. ANB, SNI, ACEN No. 44502/72, ARJ/SNI, Info No. 3516, 15.03.1972, 3.

74. Zimmermann, *Medien im Nationalsozialismus*, 86–90.

75. A. Smith, *A Forced Agreement*, 11, 15, 18, 21.

76. A. Smith, *A Forced Agreement*, 40–41.

77. Fico, *Além do golpe*, 94.

78. Kushnir, "Entre censores," 81.

79. Skidmore, *The Politics of Military Rule*, 135. Today *Veja* is clearly a right-wing magazine. In the 1960s and 1970s it was more centrist than it is now.

80. The *Diário de Notícias* and *Diário Carioca* also had to close. See Capelato, *Imprensa*, 55.

81. A. Smith, *A Forced Agreement*, 90–91, 165.

82. Mattos, "Domestic and Foreign," 107–8.

83. Aquino, *Censura*, 105, 108, 340.

84. A. Smith, *A Forced Agreement*, 167.

85. Fico, *Além do golpe*, 94; Kushnir, "Entre censores," 87–88.

86. "Médici: ninguém segura este país," "Médici: não haverá escalada de repressão," "Médici: democracia acompanham evolução social," "Médici ao povo: revolução fêz o Brasil nascer de nôvo," "Ritmo de progresso supera previsões." Supplement called "Jornal da independência" in *O Globo*, September 7, 1972, 12.

87. Mattos, "Domestic and Foreign," 141; Branco, Martensen, and Reis, *História da propaganda*, 32–33.

88. Mattos, "Domestic and Foreign," 14–12, 145, 227.

89. Tufte, *Living with the Rubbish Queen*, 77.

90. Branco, Martensen, and Reis, *História da propaganda*, 11.

91. Straubhaar, "The Reflection," 63–64.

92. FGV, CPDOC, EG Pr. 1974.04.08, Circular of 21.07.1975, microfilm p. 1703–704.

93. Lima, Priolli, and Machado, *Televisão e vídeo*, 27.

94. Britto and Bolaña, *Rede Globo*, 122. For an overview of the rise of Globo from the perspective of international relations, consult Wilkin, "Global Communication," 93–113, here 101.

95. A substantial body of research exists on Globo's collaboration with the military regime. Besides those mentioned previously, one of the most critical studies is Herz, *A história secreta*. For the newspaper *O Globo*, consult Marconi, *A censura*, and A. Smith, *A Forced Agreement*. For studies on TV, see Mattelart, *El carnaval*; Mattos, "Domestic and Foreign"; and Vink, *The Telenovela*.

96. Herz, *A história secreta*, 90, 93; Lima, Priolli, and Machado, *Televisão e vídeo*, 32; Tufte, *Living with the Rubbish Queen*, 75; Britto and Bolaña, *Rede Globo*, 270; Wilkin, "Global Communication," 99.

97. Branco, Martensen, and Reis, *História da propaganda*, 34. As mentioned previously, Costa told me in an oral history interview (March 2, 2007) that he disapproved of this type of violent propaganda, and he also showed evidence of this in his final report. CAM, AERP, *Relatório*, 32.

98. Wilkin, "Global Communication," 102; Britto and Bolaña, *Rede Globo*, 122–23.

99. Tufte, *Living with the Rubbish Queen*, 86.

100. FGV, CPDOC, EG Pr. 1974.04.08, Circular 15.12.1977 (microfilm 481f. and 681f.); Salles, "Uma lição ainda hoje atual," 22.

101. Memória Globo, *Jornal Nacional*, 159.

102. BBC News, "Brazilian Media Magnate Dies," http://news.bbc.co.uk/2/hi/americas/3130983.stm (accessed May 20, 2006). See also Kucinski, "Roberto Marinho," 52–53.

103. Vincent Bevins, "Brazil's Globo Group Apologizes for Backing Military Government," *Los Angeles Times*, September 4, 2013, http://articles.latimes.com/2013/sep/04/world/la-fg-wn-brazil-globo-network-military-20130904, accessed September 10, 2013.

104. Branco, Martensen, and Reis, *História da propaganda*, 140.

105. Mattos, "Domestic and Foreign," 233, 235–36; Gracioso and Penteado, *Cinquenta anos*, 128.

106. Bechtos, "Não existe falta de veículos de propaganda no Brasil," 91.

107. Mattos, "Domestic and Foreign," 233.

108. Kunsch, "Professional and Academic Institutionalization," paper presented at the annual meeting of the International Communication Association, San Francisco, May 23, 2007, http://www.allacademic.com/meta/p_mla_apa_research_citation/1/7/2/3/4/p172343_index.html (accessed February 1, 2009), 2; Mattos, "Domestic and Foreign," 155–56, 167, 208, 212, 254.

109. At least not as systematically as press censorship. However, the front page of the *Propaganda* 267 (December 1978) congratulates the government on ending censorship for commercial advertisement, suggesting that a kind of informal censorship existed.

110. Diniz, "Empresariado"; Saes, *Classe media*.

111. Gracioso and Penteado, *Cinquenta anos*, 119.

112. Afonso de Souza and Fernando Reis, "A comunicação 1975," 27–31.

113. Gracioso and Penteado, *Cinquenta anos*.

114. *Propaganda* 236 (March 1976), 85.

115. Rodrigues, "MPM Propaganda," 36.

116. Abreu and Paulo, *Dicionário*, 63; *Propaganda* 170 (November 1969), 19–23; *Propaganda* 267 (December 1978).

117. Superior War School (Escoal Superior da Guerra, ESG), Presidência da República, Escola-maior das Fôrças Armadas, Escola Superior de Guerra, "Divulgação Governamental," 1971, 26–27.

118. "Afinal, o que aconteceu em 1968 e 1973?" *Propaganda* 269 (December 1978), 24–46.

119. "The colorful sound." Gracioso and Penteado, *Cinquenta anos*, 149. Unlike Henfil or Jaguar, he was mildly critical of the military regime. Ziraldo was one of the artists whose release from prison Costa helped to secure.

120. The only major agency the AERP worked with was the MPM. Interview with Gen. Octávio Pereira da Costa, June 5, 2009.

121. Interviews with Gen. Octávio Pereira da Costa, March 2, 2007, and June 5, 2009.

122. Costa, "Governo e comunicação social," 12.

123. Interview with Gen. Octávio Pereira da Costa, March 2, 2007; "Otávio Costa diz que AERP obteve entendimento entre o pôvo e o governo," *Jornal do Brasil*, July 7, 1971, 4.

124. Interview with Gen. Octávio Pereira da Costa, March 22, 2007; interview with Professor Cavalieri, March 27, 2007; Ney Peixoto do Vale, "Communication to criate [*sic*] image," 66–69.

Chapter 4. Getting Into Their Heads

1. "Como não condenar previamente um regime político de supressão das liberdades mais elementares? . . . como não presumir uma intenção mascadora por parte da propaganda"; "o simplismo a que as condenações superficiáis induzem," Fico, *Reinventando*, 22.

2. For edited interviews, see D'Araújo, Castro, and Soares, *A volta aos quartéis, Os anos do chumbo*, and *Visões do golpe*; and Biblioteca do Exército, *1964—31 de Março*. Regarding my own interviews, instead of adopting an issue-related approach, I decided to focus on narratives, as this allowed me to explore the interviewees' perspectives and internal contradictions. Interviews with Gen. Octávio Pereira da Costa, Rio de Janeiro, March 2, 2007, March 22, 2007, October 23, 2007, and June 5, 2009.

3. Ginzburg, "Morelli."

4. Médici, *Nova Consciência de Brasil*, 57–82.

5. Interviews with Gen. Octávio Pereira da Costa, Rio de Janeiro, March 2, 2007, and March 22, 2007. "The repression, the subversion increased, the repression continued growing, and the picture did not change. Therefore I stuck to my way of thinking. I started to contribute only with the shipment/dispatch [*remessas*] of social communication."

6. Interview with Gen. Octávio Pereira da Costa, Rio de Janeiro, March 2, 2007. See also the interview with Professor Alberto Rabaça, Rio de Janeiro, March 14, 2007. Rabaça mentions that Leitão de Abreu was one of the hardliners who constantly pressured Costa. See D'Araújo, Castro, and Soares, *A volta aos quartéis*, 140.

7. Interview with Gen. Octávio Pereira da Costa, Rio de Janeiro, March 22, 2007.

8. Interview with Gen. Octávio Pereira da Costa, Rio de Janeiro, March 22, 2007.

9. Interview with Gen. Octávio Pereira da Costa, Rio de Janeiro, March 2, 2007; D'Araújo, Castro, and Soares, *A volta aos quartéis*, 140.

10. Interview with Gen. José Maria Toledo Camargo, Rio de Janeiro, March 7, 2007; Camargo, *A espada virgem*, 153–54.

11. Interviews with Gen. Octávio Pereira da Costa, Rio de Janeiro, March 2, 2007, and March 22, 2007. Costa characterizes the Médici government as a triumvirate comprised of Orlando Geisel, the most powerful man and head of the armed forces, Delfim Netto, leading the economic sector, and Leitão de Abreu as the chief of staff, who is

the highest-ranking member of the executive office of Brazil. It is comparable to the position of a prime minister, yet not quite the same, because Brazil has a presidential system.

12. "He came into the office with a mission to combat subversives. . . . This was more important than anything else. . . . His strategy was to combat subversives whatever the cost. . . . And he did it, did it. But with a terrible result. And we can see it even today, even today. . . . The only reason why we didn't get a worse result was because of the ability of Tancredo Neves and other politicians who managed to bring it to a less detrimental end. But in principle this was his [Médici's] strategy. I was excluded from this strategy." Interview with Gen. Octávio Pereira da Costa, Rio de Janeiro, March 2, 2007.

13. "After so many years, I am convinced that President Médici, who was a good man . . . he had this image of a big repressor . . . but personally he was a good man. He *just* was not a man of vision. He was convinced that his role was to win the war of repression. I think he behaved more like a military commander who wants to win a battle between subversives and repressors. I think he would have allowed a reopening [of the system], had he won against the repression. I think that would have been possible, but for him, his strategy—nowadays I am convinced—his *personal* strategy was to win the war of repression. To crush the subversives. I am convinced that *that* was not the solution. The facts showed that it was not the solution. You definitively do not win anything without concessions from all sides. Nobody crushes the other. You always need to offer a way out to the other. . . . When you are dealing with national unity there are no winners and losers. When you are dealing with the fate of the country it is necessary to resign yourself to making concessions rather than to winning. So I think that he did not share this opinion." Interview with Gen. Octávio Pereira da Costa, Rio de Janeiro, March 2, 2007.

14. Interview with Gen. Octávio Pereira da Costa, Rio de Janeiro, March 22, 2007.

15. "Para criar um clima positivo . . . na esperança que a criação desse clima, levasse a melhores dias. . . . Era *essa* a minha estratégia. E foi dentro dessa estratégia que eu vivì, sofrì, intensamente quatro anos. Com incompreensões de toda parte. . . . E com a incompreensão dos próprios beneficiários. O presidente nunca, nunca deu valor maior ao que eu fiz por ele, nunca." Interview with Gen. Octávio Pereira da Costa, Rio de Janeiro, March 22, 2007.

16. Interviews with Professor João Clemente Baena Soares, Rio de Janeiro, March 20, 2007; Professor José Cavalieri, Rio de Janeiro, March 27, 2007; and Gen. José Maria Toledo Camargo, Rio de Janeiro, March 7, 2007.

17. Interview with Gen. Octávio Pereira da Costa, Rio de Janeiro, March 2, 2007.

18. Interview with Professor José Cavalieri, Rio de Janeiro, March 27, 2007; interview with Professor João Clemente Baena Soares, Rio de Janeiro, March 20, 2007.

19. D'Araújo, Castro, and Soares, *Os anos do chumbo*, 278–79. That is what Médici's son said as well; see Nogueira Médici, *Médici, o depoimento*.

20. Interview with Gen. Octávio Pereira da Costa, Rio de Janeiro, March 22, 2007.

21. Interview with Professor João Clemente Baena Soares, Rio de Janeiro, March 20, 2007.

22. This passage from an article in the *Jornal do Brasil* demonstrates that Costa was being mocked: "And because I know that my fatherland is like this, and because I know . . . the soul of my people, I dare to say words of peace in a time of violence. Even if they consider me a dreamer and an unrealist, I dare to plead that we all shake hands with each other." Costa, *Mundo sem hemisfério*, 146.

23. Interview with Professor Alberto Rabaça, Rio de Janeiro, March 14, 2007.

24. Fico, *Reinventando*, 27–52, 138; Garcia, *Sadismo*, 64.

25. Camargo, *A espada virgem*, 182; interview with Professor João Clemente Baena Soares, Rio de Janeiro, March 20, 2007; interview with Professor Alberto Rabaça, Rio de Janeiro, March 14, 2007.

26. Interview with Gen. Octávio Pereira da Costa, Rio de Janeiro, March 22, 2007.

27. Costa, *Mundo sem hemisfério*, 13. For critical comments regarding exaggerated anticommunism, see, for example, interview with Gen. Octávio Pereira da Costa, Rio de Janeiro, March 22, 2007; D'Araújo, Castro, and Soares, *Visões do golpe*, 78–79, and *A volta aos quartéis*, 205–6.

28. Costa, *Mundo sem hemisfério*, 41.

29. D'Araújo, Castro, and Soares, *Visões do golpe*, 78–79. The writings were strongly influenced by Gabriel Bonnet's *Guerras insurrecionais e revolucionárias*.

30. Interview with Gen. Octávio Pereira da Costa, Rio de Janeiro, March 22, 2007.

31. Costa, *Mundo sem hemisfério*, 41–42; interview with Gen. Octávio Pereira da Costa, Rio de Janeiro, March 22, 2007.

32. Costa, *Mundo sem hemisfério*, 30.

33. "What did we deify? Well, the fatherland, the future, the construction of this country, growth, values—values which make this country a great country." Interview with Gen. Octávio Pereira da Costa, Rio de Janeiro, March 22, 2007.

34. Interview with Professor Alberto Rabaça, Rio de Janeiro, March 14, 2007; interview with Professor José Cavalieri, Rio de Janeiro, March 27, 2007; interview with Professor João Clemente Baena Soares, Rio de Janeiro, March 20, 2007; D'Araújo and Castro, *João Clemente Baena Soares*, 59.

35. "Civic education, or . . . the formation of citizenship . . . through nationalist messages, to give incentives to the organization of society and the participation of the citizens." Interview with Professor João Clemente Baena Soares, Rio de Janeiro, March 20, 2007. See also D'Araújo and Castro, *João Clemente Baena Soares*, 40.

36. One may argue that this applies to many ideologues engaged in propaganda. Yet if we look at Hitler's *Mein Kampf*, we find that many propagandists deliberately lied. Hitler openly claimed that the means justified the ends and that falsification was a legitimate strategy. According to Hitler's vision, the common people were stupid anyway. He came to this conclusion after reading Gustave Le Bon's 1895 study, *La psychologie des foules* [The Crowd: A Study of the Popular Mind].

37. This comrade had fully supported the coup but was sidelined within the armed

forces at a later stage of the military regime. Interview with Gen. Octávio Pereira da Costa, Rio de Janeiro, March 22, 2007.

38. Interview with Gen. Octávio Pereira da Costa, Rio de Janeiro, March 22, 2007.

39. Costa, "Governo e comunicação social," 14; interview with Gen. Octávio Pereira da Costa, Rio de Janeiro, March 2, 2007.

40. Interview with Professor João Clemente Baena Soares, Rio de Janeiro, March 20, 2007; interview with Professor Alberto Rabaça, Rio de Janeiro, March 14, 2007.

41. "Mesmo porque era mais eficaz . . . o que nos faziamos para diminuir o impacto da linha dura, do que discutir com a linha dura. [*laughs*] . . . O nosso trabalho foi muito mais sútil. . . . Foi muito mais inteligente esse resultado do que 'Vamos acabar com a linha dura . . . ' aí teria uma reação, claro." Interview with Professor João Clemente Baena Soares, Rio de Janeiro, March 20, 2007.

42. "Nós estavamos numa ditadura. Não havia diálogo do pôvo com o governo quase nenhum. . . . Então nos sentimos na obrigação de *suprir* esse vazio. E a estratégia do Octávio Costa, que eu adirí totalmente, homem competentíssimo, nós fomos cumprir os caminhos que nos permitiram . . . estabelecer a comunicação com o pôvo. Então utilizemos temas de utilidade pública. Por exemplo, 'amor ao trabalho.' . . . Já que não podiamos falar sobre democracia e ditadura, seria o grande tema na ocasião, seria bloqueado, nós fomos a uma área que nos parecia útil." Interview with Gen. José Maria Toledo Camargo, Rio de Janeiro, March 7, 2007.

43. Interview with Professor Alberto Rabaça, Rio de Janeiro, March 14, 2007; interview with Professor João Clemente Baena Soares, Rio de Janeiro, March 20, 2007; interview with Gen. José Maria Toledo Camargo, Rio de Janeiro, March 7, 2007; D'Araújo and Castro, *João Clemente Baena Soares*, 43. Nazi Germany strictly controlled all film output through the Reichsfilmkammer. The scripts were censored, and the final version was checked as well.

44. *Gorilla* is a derisive term for secret agents from the community of intelligence services or CI (the SNI, CISE, CIA, and CENIMAR). Interview with Professor João Clemente Baena Soares, Rio de Janeiro, March 20, 2007.

45. "Nós não fomos aliados de nenhuma forma da repressão. . . . Se você estimula o sentimento de patriotismo, . . . de autoconfiança da população, se você estimula a população a receber mensagens de educação—ora você esta fazendo uma contra-partida . . . a extremismos. A AERP nunca foi extremista. De jeito algum." Interview with Professor João Clemente Baena Soares, Rio de Janeiro, March 20, 2007.

46. "Nem Octávio nem Camargo endossavam essa situação. Ao contrário, sempre se punham na posição de tentar modificá-la. Hoje e muito fácil falar do passado, mas naquele momento não se sabia da extensão do que estava acontecendo, ou podia acontecer." Interview with Professor João Clemente Baena Soares, Rio de Janeiro, March 20, 2007. See also D'Araújo and Castro, *João Clemente Baena Soares*, 45–46.

47. "Nós não concordavamos com aquela forma de repressão. O grupo do Octávio Costa e ele não concordavamos daquela forma de repressão. Então nos não fomos instrumento auxiliar—absolutamente não, ao contrário! Nós fomos instrumento acredi-

tando que o país precisava de uma coesão social. Precisava de uma integração entre os contrários. Precisava acolher todos." Interview with Professor Alberto Rabaça, Rio de Janeiro, March 14, 2007.

48. "Muito desligado do núcleo duro do governo." Interview with Professor José Cavalieri, Rio de Janeiro, March 27, 2007.

49. "A AERP colaborou para que houvesse uma certa tranquilidade, uma certa paz, um certo equilíbrio. Não digo que isso aí tenha desviado o pôvo—não! Não havia essa intenção. A intenção era exatamente se criar um clima sobre isso que eu disse a você, moral e civismo." Interview with Professor José Cavalieri, Rio de Janeiro, March 27, 2007.

50. "Eu acho que em hipótese alguma o nosso trabalho pôde ser considerado ajudando a repressão. Era o contrário, nós estavamos acompanhando a repressão, e tentamos entrar na comunicação com o pôvo, através de temas nobres. Não acredito que possa ter influido a repressão. Uma coisa que eu nunca teria feito, e não estou de acordo (ria). . . . Agora a minha posição é radicalmente contra essa acusação. Não tem o menor— nós ajudamos nem a repressão nem ao contrário. Nós tentamos buscar uma brecha de comunicação. . . . E conseguimos. Pequena, mas era um absurdo, então quem consegue um pouquinho já é uma vitória. E conseguimos, muita coisa. Tem erros que cometemos. . . . Se isso era feito [ajudar a repressão] seria um fracasso do trabalho, ajudar a repressão. . . . O 'Brasil: Ame-o ou deixe-o' seria exatamente esse vetor que nós não aceitamos nunca." Interview with Gen. José Maria Toledo Camargo, Rio de Janeiro, March 7, 2007.

51. Costa, "Compreensão da revolução brasileira," 73–74, 80.

52. Costa, "Compreensão da revolução brasileira," 82.

53. Costa, "Compreensão da revolução brasileira," 62.

54. As mentioned previously, these articles were edited in Costa, *Mundo sem hemisfério*. Through this work he became friends with famous journalists, including Carlos Castello Branco and Alberto Dines.

55. For an account of the crisis of 1968–69 that considers intramilitary friction, consult J.R.M. Filho, *O pálacio e a caserna*.

56. "A hora e a vez de diplomar." Costa, *Mundo sem hemisfério*, 27–30.

57. Moreira Alves, a member of the opposition party, MDB, demanded a boycott of the national holiday celebrations of Brazilian independence, September 7, and appealed to Brazilian women to refuse to form romantic attachments with military officials. The government consequently demanded that Congress remove his political immunity, but Congress refused to comply with the order. In December the regime passed the notorious Institutional Act 5 (AI 5), which eventually curtailed the power of Congress. Scholars debate whether Moreira Alves' behavior really caused the AI 5 or merely functioned as a pretext.

58. "Esperamos em Deus que o instante seja curto mas fecundo, para que a Revolução de nossos sonhos, a mudança, em verdade, se realize toda em proveito de nosso pôvo, em nome de nosso futuro." Costa, *Mundo sem hemisfério*, 30.

59. This event has been described by a member of the guerrilla group, Fernando Gabeira, who, however, did not play a leading role in this incident. See his bestseller, *O que é isso, companheiro?* This memoir about the left-wing guerrilla movements—the literal translation of the title is "What is this, comrade?"—was turned into a film in 1997 by the Brazilian director Bruno Barreto. For more on the reception of this book, consult Rollemberg, "Esquecimento das memórias," 81–92.

60. J.R.M. Filho, *O palácio e a caserna*, 181–82.

61. Costa, *Mundo sem hemisfério*, 143–46.

62. Costa, *Mundo sem hemisfério*, 144–45.

63. Interview with Gen. Octávio Pereira da Costa, Rio de Janeiro, March 22, 2007; Documentation Center of the Armed Forces (Centro de Documentação do Exército), Brasília, Personal Files of General Octávio Pereira da Costa; D'Araújo, Castro, and Soares, *Visões do golpe*, 74.

64. This question is also raised by Fico (*Reinventando*, 100): why did Costa not leave the regime, if he was as much of an outcast as he says?

65. Costa, "Compreensão da revolução," 63, 67, 80, 82; interview with Gen. Octávio Pereira da Costa, Rio de Janeiro, October 23, 2007.

66. Costa, *Mundo sem hemisfério*, 27.

67. D'Araújo, Castro, and Soares, *Visões do golpe*, 84–85.

68. The ECEME is a traditional military school in Rio de Janeiro that trains officials for top military positions.

69. Costa says that at the time he was "a man he [Orlando] could trust [homem de confiança]." Interview with Gen. Octávio Pereira da Costa, Rio de Janeiro, March 22, 2007.

70. Why Orlando and Ernesto Geisel were in dispute is not clear. It appears that Orlando Geisel was disappointed when he was not appointed to any post during his brother's presidency, Ernesto Geisel ostensibly considering it inappropriate to place a sibling in a position of high command. Yet, personally, I find another explanation more convincing. I wonder whether Ernesto Geisel chose not to appoint his brother, because Orlando Geisel had been the military leader during the years of violent repression. Employing the military official who was largely responsible for acts of torture would have surely undermined the credibility of Ernesto Geisel's project of political opening (*distensão*).

71. "Ele era o homem que aglutinava toda força militar, actuou na área de repressão." Interview with Gen. Octávio Pereira da Costa, Rio de Janeiro, March 22, 2007.

72. Interview with Gen. Octávio Pereira da Costa, Rio de Janeiro, March 2, 2007. He also mentions that Figueiredo criticized him for not being a good soldier.

73. Costa, *Mundo sem hemisfério*, 140. He repeated this to me in our interview (Rio de Janeiro, March 2, 2007), and *Veja* magazine (no. 75, February 11, 1970, 66) reported on it as well.

74. "Convite ao poder," *Veja* 64, October 22, 1969, 23.

75. Interview with Gen. Octávio Pereira da Costa, Rio de Janeiro, March 22, 2007; D'Araújo, Castro, and Soares, *Visões do golpe*, 73–75, 84–85.

76. This article is taken from the compilation of articles "Exército 92/2000," held in the Library of the Senate in Brasília: "General diz que Exército e pôvo querem democracia," *O Estado de São Paulo*, January 27, 1978, 4.

77. This section is based on an interview conducted on March 7, 2007, in Camargo's flat in Rio, on Camargo's autobiography, *A espada virgem*, and on several newspaper articles, including press cuttings found under the keywords "public relations" and "propaganda 74–77" held by the Senate Library in Brasília. Unfortunately, I was unable to interview other ARP staff members. I contacted Professor Claudio Figueiredo, who, at the time, was responsible for the ARP in Rio (the successor to Carlos Rabaça), but he vehemently refused an interview.

78. Camargo, *A espada virgem*, 8, 143, 197–98.

79. Interview with Gen. José Maria Toledo Camargo, Rio de Janeiro, March 7, 2007; Camargo, *A espada virgem*, 184, 186, 232–33.

80. Camargo, *A espada virgem*, 186; interview with Gen. José Maria Toledo Camargo, Rio de Janeiro, March 7, 2007.

81. Interview with Gen. José Maria Toledo Camargo, Rio de Janeiro, March 7, 2007.

82. Camargo, *A espada virgem*, 184–85.

83. "Um so ato de tortura tem malignidade suficiente para comprometer o conjunto." Camargo, *A espada virgem*, 133.

84. "The cruelty of the repression, absolutely unnecessary, managed to transfer the sympathy and the support of the population to the students." Camargo, *A espada virgem*, 121–22.

85. Camargo, *A espada virgem*, 129, 137.

86. Camargo, *A espada virgem*, 132.

87. Camargo, *A espada virgem*, 132.

88. Aarão Reis, *Ditadura*, 42; Fico, *Como eles agiam*, 12; Pereira, *Political (In)justice*, 75, 143.

89. Camargo, *A espada virgem*, 133–34.

90. Camargo, *A espada virgem*, 286–87.

91. Camargo, *A espada virgem*, 289.

92. I am aware that survivors of violent repression and the families of victims may rub their noses on this "grief," but I maintain that it is important to portray the nuances within the system.

93. "Ao amigo Camargo na recordação do desafio que, unidos, soubemos vencer, o abraço de meu agradecimento, Octávio (18.3.74)." CAM, AERP, *Relatório*.

Chapter 5. The End of the Story

1. The document was called "Instructions for the functioning of the A.E.R.P." "Analisar, para o Governo, as possibilidades de reação da Opinião Pública, face a medidas e políticas a executar, assim como interpretar as reações que essa opinião venha a con-

cretizar," CAM, AERP, *Instruções para o funcionamento*, 3, 6 (Art. 7, n), 8 (Art. 9, d and e), 9 (Art. 11, j and l), and 13 (Art. 34).

2. CAM, AERP, *Relatório*, 45. The Rondon project was inaugurated in 1966, and it entailed flying Brazilian students to poor areas in the Amazon region for voluntary teaching positions. In 2005, the project was reinstated. "Uma Campanha," *Propaganda* 191 (April 1972), 52–54.

3. CAM, AERP, *Relatório*, 45–46; interview with Gen. Octávio Pereira da Costa, Rio de Janeiro, March 2, 2007; D'Araújo and Castro, *João Clemente Baena Soares*, 43.

4. Fejes, "Critical Mass Communications," 221; Gurevitch, Bennett, Curran, and Woollacott, *Culture*, 265; Ball-Rokeach and De Fleur, "A Dependency Model," 3, 7.

5. Zaller, *The Nature*, 22.

6. Mutz, "Mass Media," 483–508; Gurevitch, Bennett, Curran, and Woollacott, *Culture*, 241.

7. Gurevitch, Bennett, Curran, and Woollacott, *Culture*, 242–44; Ball-Rokeach and De Fleur, "A Dependency Model," 13; Zaller, *The Nature*, 78.

8. See, for example, Simpson and Pearson, *Critical Dictionary*, 366–67. For a more detailed reflection, consult in particular Stuart Hall's chapter on the processes of encoding and decoding media messages in Hall, *Culture*, 128–38.

9. Lazarsfeld, Berelson, and Gaudet, *The People's Choice*.

10. Simpson and Pearson, *Critical Dictionary*, 368–70; Fish, *Is There a Text*.

11. Hall, *Culture*, 131.

12. By "actual" reception, I mean what in literary criticism is referred to as an "explicit reader," as opposed to the "implicit reader," which is contained in the "text." While Garcia neglects the way in which propaganda was received, because he tends to conceive of propaganda as an all-powerful means, Fico (*Reinventando*, 16, 20) acknowledges that propaganda is not homogeneously accepted by the recipient, but does not investigate it because of methodological problems. O. Lima ("A tentação do consenso," 84–90) analyzes the press coverage of the campaigns.

13. "E quem comunica?" *Veja* 81, March 25, 1970, 84; "Silêncio da melhor," *Veja* 122, January 6, 1971, 60–61; CAM, AERP, *Relatório*, 31, 33. The film was called *You Always Encounter the Sun at the End of the Road* [Você sempre encontra o sol no final do camino].

14. It is possible that both magazines were referring to the same prize. *Veja* magazine does not specify who donated the prize. The jingle "Prá frente Brasil" by Miguel Gustavo was also awarded a prize. *Propaganda* 176 (January 1971), 26, 28.

15. "Você constrói o Brasil," *Propaganda* 188, (January 1972), 13. *Jeitinho* refers to a specific, supposedly Brazilian way of getting results by bypassing normal procedures and rules: "Campanha de Integração Do Governo—provando que não somente ama como todos nós, mas que também conhece o produto que vende, a equipe da AERP uniu os brasileiros. A campanha desenvolvimentista e de integração do Governo mostrou que somos hoje não somente o país de Pelé, do jeitinho e do carnaval, mas também o país que cresce e sabe que cresce. A campanha da AERP nos aproximou da Amazônia, nos colocou mais perto da União e entrosados num esforço comúm que jamais tivemos."

16. "Silêncio da melhor," *Veja* 122, (January 6), 1971, 60–61.

17. Interviews with João Pinto, Rio de Janeiro, July 18, 2007; Clovis, Rio de Janeiro, September 17, 2007; Ricardo Corrêa, Rio de Janeiro, September 8, 2007; and Alberto Rabaça, Rio de Janeiro, March 14, 2007.

18. "'Prevenildo,' o irmão de 'Sujismundo,' vai liderar campanha contra acidente," *Journal do Brasil*, November 21, 1972, 14; "Ceará forma turma 'Sujismundo,'" *Journal do Brasil*, December 1, 1972, 14; "A AERP de volta," *Veja* 382, (December 31, 1975), 22; Carlos Monforte, "Como no sabão, a qualidade é tudo," *O Estado de São Paulo*, October 16, 1977, 8.

19. "Mais livros," *Veja* 169, (December 1, 1971), 57; interview with Alberto Rabaça, Rio de Janeiro, March 14, 2007; "A batalha da imagem," *Visão*, October 10, 1970, quoted in O. Lima, "A tentação do consenso," 100.

20. Interview with Gen. Octávio Pereira da Costa, Rio de Janeiro, March 2, 2007.

21. "É tempo de construir," "Ontém, hoje, sempre Brasil." CAM, AERP, *Relatório*, 31, 36, 53.

22. For example, he clearly states that expositions that had "very poor results" failed. See CAM, AERP, *Relatório*, 44. Fico (*Reinventando*, 103–4) and O. Lima ("A tentação do consenso," 84–100) also believe that the films had a significant, positive influence.

23. "E quem comunica?" *Veja* 81, (March 25, 1970), 84.

24. "Sujismundo—contra ou a favor da sujeira," *Propaganda* 197 (October/November/December 1972), 57.

25. CAM, AERP, *Relatório*, 31.

26. Camargo, *A espada virgem*, 154–55.

27. *Propaganda* 236, (March 1976), 74.

28. The slogan was "Don't make a weapon of your car, you may be the victim" ["Mortes no trânsito preocupam a Aerp"], *O Estado de São Paulo*, October 16, 1977, 8; interview with Alberto Rabaça, Rio de Janeiro, March 14, 2007.

29. Interview with Alberto Rabaça, Rio de Janeiro, March 14, 2007; Camargo, *A espada virgem*, 154; interview with Professor José Cavalieri, Rio de Janeiro, March 27, 2007.

30. "Eu acho que eles partem do princípio de que o povo brasileiro é meio idiotizado." Monforte, "Como no sabão," *O Estado de São Paulo*, October 16, 1977, 8.

31. Monforte, "Como no sabão," *O Estado de São Paulo*, October 16, 1977, 8.

32. "A nova propaganda," *O Estado de São Paulo*, December 30, 1975, quoted in O. Lima, "A tentação do consenso," 102; interview with Professor José Cavalieri, Rio de Janeiro, March 27, 2007; interview with Alberto Rabaça, Rio de Janeiro, March 14, 2007; D'Araújo and Castro, *João Clemente Baena Soares*, 43.

33. O. Lima, "A tentação do consenso," 90. Many of my interviewees quoted this phrase.

34. Interview with Gen. José Maria Toledo Camargo, Rio de Janeiro, March 7, 2007. The films were FE 42 (WWWW), FE 44 (EH.-Fil. 798), FE 46 (EH.-Fil. 796), FE 47 (EH.-Fil. 795), and FE 51 (EH.-Fil. 797).

35. "Propaganda: Anúncio de graça," *Veja*, (May 2, 1973), 62–63; Fico, *Reinventando*, 140–41; "Consumidor não está só," *O Estado de São Paulo*, September 28, 1977, 23.

36. Gaspari, *A didatura encurralada*, 495.

37. See Boberach, *Meldungen aus dem Reich, 1938–1945*.

38. A typical SNI report consists of several standardized headings, one of which is "public opinion." Yet "public opinion" was equivalent to "public discourse." It mainly reported on criticism in the media or by opposition groups and on demonstrations. Comments on the repercussions of statements that were critical of the regime do appear, but they are very vague, and no proof is given. Often a phrase such as "repercussion among some sectors of public opinion" is used. A report from Manaus mentions a nationwide investigative project. Another denounces the negative public opinion in Porto Alegre in the first half of 1978. While these files form a valuable qualitative source for exploring the reasons behind public dissent, they do not yield any information about the propaganda reception. National Archives Brasília (ANB), Acervo do SNI, AC A092692/76, "Informação à Agência Central" (13.5.1976), 2; ANB, SNI, ACEN 3300/83, "Informação No. 0814/70/AMA/74" (02.9.1974); ANB, SNI, ACEN 643/79, "Informação para o SNI AC" (10.9.1979).

39. State Archive São Paulo, DEOPS, OP 1115, No. 246, 1.

40. Bibliotéca do Senado, Brasília, Recortes de jornais da pasta "Opinião Pública 81"; "Brasileiro após 9 anos deixa de ser antes de tudo otimista," *Jornal do Brasil*, February 6, 1977.

41. Ernesto Geisel Pr. 1974.11.25, Resenha Semanal No. 16, No. 68, and No. 113; "Analisando prestígio do Executivo em pesquisa Gallup," *O Globo*, January 25, 1977; Biblioteca do Senado, Brasília, Recortes de jornais da pasta "Opinião Pública 81-"; "Gallup culpa reformas pela queda de prestígio de Geisel," *Jornal do Brasil*, May 26, 1977; "Prestígio de Geisel cai, revela pesquisa," *O Estado de São Paulo*, May 26, 1977, 4; ANB, SNI, ACEN 3300/83, "Informação No. 0814/70/AMA/74" (02.9.1974), 3; ANB, SNI, ACEN 643/79, "Informação para o SNI AC" (10.9.1979), 1–2; FGV, CPDOC, EG Pr. 1974.03.00, Apreciação Sumária No. 15/74, 18.11.1974, 2; FGV, CPDOC, EG Pr. 1974.00.00; letter from Mauro Salles, December 5, 1978, 2; Lamounier and Cardoso, *Os partidos*, 44.

42. The study was conducted by the Center for Political Studies at the Institute for Social Research at the University of Michigan and the Instituto Universitário de Pesquisas do Rio de Janeiro at Candido Mendes University. Cohen defines politicization as "a process by which individuals become interested and acquire knowledge about politics and develop strong identifications with groups or ideas of a political nature." In comparison, in the United States the number of unpoliticized people in 1968 was half as much, at 44 percent. See Cohen, "Popular Support," iii, 2–3, 11–12, 108.

43. Cohen, "Popular Support," 25, 46–47.

44. See, for example, Cole, *International Encyclopedia of Propaganda*, 623.

45. Albrecht, *Nationalsozialistische Filmpolitik*.

46. Lowry, *Pathos*; Zimmermann, *Medien im Nationalsozialismus*, 163.

47. Zimmermann, *Medien im Nationalsozialismus*, 163–64. Sabine Hake has also pointed to the complexity and ambivalence of film material. See Hake, *German National Cinema*.

48. See his *Film in the Third Reich*. Hull even emphasized a certain power to resist, in the case of the famous actor Heinz Rühmann, who had a Jewish wife.

49. Rentschler, "Deutschland"; Zimmermann, *Medien im Nationalsozialismus*, 171–72.

50. The propaganda intended to "conceal the dictatorial character of the government" [ocultar o caráter ditatorial do governo]. Fico, *Reinventando*, 21.

51. Fico, *Reinventando*, 94–95. The founders of the AERP "were conscious of the propaganda's capacity to reach out to Brazilian society. The 'decent' topics relating to family, the 'national character,' etc., thus represented an acceptable means of producing propaganda, because a more strictly political way of elevating the regime . . . would certainly have been rejected" [Os criadores da AERP sabiam do alcance da propaganda para o restante da sociedade brasileira. Os temas "decorosos" sobre família, o "caráter nacional" etc., portanto, eram a forma possível de fazer essa propaganda, que se assumisse um vies estritamente político, de enaltecimento do regime, do governo ou dos governantes, certamente seria rejeitada, . . . mas que, nem por isso, deixariam de perceber o grotesco de tal pretensão]. See also 146.

52. CAM, AERP, *Documentos fundamentais*, 1.

53. FGV, CPDOC, EG Pr. 1974.03.00, SNI Chefia do Gabinete, 18.11.1974, 1; FGV, CPDOC, EG Pr. 1974.04.08, Circular 11.05.1976, microfilm 0087.

54. Martins, "Ditadura militar," 87–88.

55. Rentschler, "Deutschland."

Conclusion

1. Ridenti, "Cultura e política," 155.

Glossary

ABIN (Agência Brasileira de Inteligência). Current Brazilian intelligence organ that in 1999 (Law No. 9.883) succeeded the former SNI. The ABIN donated the SNI documents to the National Archive in Brasília.

ABI (Associação Brasileira de Imprensa). Brazilian Press Association located in Rio. It has defended the interests of journalists and the press since 1908.

Abreu, Hugo Leitão de (1913–1992). Official from the elite troop of the Brazilian Air Force Para-Sar, who held the position of chief of staff, similar to the post of a prime minister, under President Médici. A notorious hardliner, he fiercely criticized Golbery in his memoirs and sided with General Frota, who had been dismissed in 1977 after an attempt to seize power from Geisel. Abreu consistently attacked AERP leader Costa and replaced him as Médici's speechwriter.

Academia Brasileira de Letras. The Brazilian Academy of Literature is a nonprofit literary society founded on December 15, 1896, and today made up of forty members.

AERP (Assessoria Especial de Relações Públicas). Special public relations consultancy, founded on January 15, 1968 (Decree No. 62,119) under President Arthur da Costa e Silva and initially headed by Colonel Hernani D'Aguiar. After 1969, the AERP was led by Colonel Octávio Costa until its dissolution in 1974. It was a small propaganda organ that systematically developed subtle and highly professional propaganda campaigns to enhance the regime's reputation, contracting with private publicity agencies to produce these. Its means were manifold, but short films and radio programs were its most important productions.

Agência Nacional. Official news agency created as a successor to the Department of Press and Propaganda (DIP). Since 1971, it has been in charge of news about federal administrative acts, government institutions, and "public interest." In addition to its newsreel production (*Cine Jornal*

Informativo and *Brasil Hoje*) and providing information to the press, it has also produced news synopses, which were sent to the president and leading politicians. The Agência Nacional had a different propaganda philosophy than the AERP, constructing enemies such as the "dangerous communist" or the "chaotic student protester."

aggressive propaganda. The most negatively connoted and repressive kind of propaganda. Aggressive propaganda hails the military regime by promoting violence, clearly constructing enemies, creating a personality cult around leading military figures, and praising repressive organs. Aggressive propaganda is closely related to psychological war propaganda, which used intimidating propaganda in addition to physical violence. In the sources this is also called "revolutionary war."

AIRP (Assessoria de Imprensa e Relações Públicas). Founded in January 1975 under Geisel, the press and public relations consultancy succeeded the AERP and preceded the ARP. It combined the presidential press service and governmental PR but did not run propaganda campaigns.

AI 5 (Ato Institucional No. 5). The notorious "Revolutionary Law," which overruled basic democratic rights, Institutional Act Number 5 was officially decreed on December 13, 1968, after Congress refused to withdraw the immunity of MDB deputy Márcio Moreira Alves. Most scholars, however, regard that incident as mere pretext. The AI 5 empowered the president to (1) adjourn Congress; (2) suspend political rights for ten years; (3) dismiss state officials, including judges; (4) declare a state of emergency; (5) defer habeas corpus in cases of offenses against National Security; (6) transfer civilian trials to military courts; and (7) rule by decree. Some scholars argue that the AI 5 was an inherent strategy of "hardliners." Many people regard the AI 5 as a "coup within the coup," but this theory is contested, because moderates also accepted it and dictatorial measures were introduced prior to 1968. A prominent myth about the AI 5 is that it was a reaction to armed dissident groups. The AI 5 was finally revoked in 1979.

Alves, Márcio Moreira. Deputy of the opposition party, MDB. In 1968, he demanded a boycott of the national holiday celebrations of September 7, Brazil's Independence Day, and appealed to Brazilian women to refuse to go out with military officials. The government consequently demanded that Congress retract his political immunity, which Congress refused to do. In December 1968, the regime passed the notorious Institutional Act 5 (AI 5), which eventually curtailed the power of Congress. Scholars debate whether Alves' behavior really caused the AI 5 or whether it merely functioned as a pretext. Alves managed to go into exile, where he continued to denounce the regime's human-rights abuses (for details, consult Green's *We Cannot Remain Silent*). He died in April 2009. Alves' sister, Maria Helena Moreira Alves, wrote one of the best historical accounts of the regime.

Amnesty Law (Law No. 6683). Ratified in 1979 under military president Figueiredo, the Amnesty Law grants general amnesty to officials of the former repressive organs but only partial amnesty to former members of the armed struggle. The so-called *anistia recíproca* (reciprocal amnesty) was neither granted to political prisoners sentenced for trying to reestablish illegal parties nor to militants involved in the armed struggle or charged with what the regime labeled "blood crimes." While this law has long been the subject of debate, it has been increasingly questioned since the proceedings of the Ustra trial in 2007. Human-rights advocates, including UN officials, have long demanded that former torturers be punished, and in late 2010 the Inter-American Court on Human Rights (IACHR) condemned the Brazilian state for granting impunity to the perpetrators of the Araguaia massacre. Still, to this day, no civilian government has revoked the law; to the contrary, in April 2010 the Brazilian Supreme Court ruled to maintain the amnesty law. Some legal professionals, including Hélio Bicudo, have argued that the current law simply needs to be properly interpreted.

Araguaia. Brazilian river in the southern part of the state of Pará, which gave its name to a rural guerrilla group that operated in this region between 1972 and 1975. The Araguaia guerrilla movement was founded by militants from the Communist Party of Brazil (PC do B) in 1966 and mobilized local residents to stimulate a revolution to overthrow the Brazilian military government. The Araguaia guerrillas were eradicated by government troops, comprising the largest group of victims between 1964 and 1985, with a total of sixty-four murders (according to the 2007 report; numbers may rise in the truth commission's final report). The event was reported to the Inter-American Court on Human Rights (IACHR) in 1995. In late 2010, the IACHR condemned the Brazilian state for failing to clarify the circumstances of murder and for granting impunity to the perpetrators. Araguaia has been a key subject in the "memory struggle" over the military regime. Most of the victims were "disappeared"; their bodies are still missing.

ARENA (Aliança Renovadora Nacional). The National Renewal Alliance has been the official government party since the introduction of a two-party system (Institutional Act Number 2) in 1965. The party was supposed to obey the regime, but the relationship was occasionally tense. For example, in late 1966, ARENA refused to give its consent to the withdrawal of political rights (*cassações*) of federal deputies, and in 1968, it withheld its vote for the disenfranchisement of a MDB deputy. While ARENA collaborated well with the regime during Médici's presidency, friction between the party and the government reemerged early in Geisel's term in office.

ARP (Assessoria de Relações Públicas). The public relations consultancy was created in February 1976 under Geisel, in order to improve ARENA's showing in the electoral results. The successor organ to the AERP, it was led by Camargo Toledo, who had also worked for the AERP. ARP organized subtle campaigns using the same methods as the AERP. It also outsourced propaganda, but produced a larger volume than AERP, and the style of its campaigns differed slightly.

bilhetinhos (little notes). Euphemistic term for censorship notes accompanying prohibited topics. After the introduction of the AI 5 in 1968, they were sent out to the media by the Ministry of Justice. The number of *bilhetinhos* was drastically reduced in 1975 under the Geisel presidency.

blunt propaganda. A form of propaganda that directly praises the arbitrary regime, mentions the names of agents even to the extent of creating a personality cult, directly hails government programs and actions, and uses myths and stereotypes. It is a form of obvious pro-regime propaganda or, in Portuguese, *chapa branca*.

Brasil Grande (Great Brazil). A type of propaganda produced by the early leader of the AERP, Colonel D'Aguiar, and Amaral Netto in his program *Amaral Netto Repórter*. Propaganda à la "Great Brazil" emphasized the natural resources of Brazil and encouraged patriotism by pointing out the untapped potential of the country. This type of "ufanistic" (boastful) propaganda was rejected by the AERP and ARP.

Brasil Hoje. Newsreel produced by the official news agency, Agência Nacional. Another newsreel was *Cine Jornal Informativo*.

Brasil Nunca Mais (BNM). First major report on torture published in 1985 by the archdiocese of São Paulo that turned into an instant bestseller. Based on the documentation of the Military Supreme Court (STM), this project was of historic importance, since it first described the systematic use of torture in the absence of a truth commission. The archive has a remarkable history: for six years a group of activists secretly copied the files of nearly two thousand cases of torture, reaching more than a million pages (equivalent to five hundred rolls of microfilm). The BNM is hosted by the Edgar Leuenroth Archive in Campinas, and since July 2013 available online at http://bnmdigital.mpf.mp.br/#!/.

Brazilian miracle (milagre Brasileiro). Rapid economic growth on a spectacular scale between 1969 and 1973. Culminated in nearly 14 percent expansion of GDP in 1973, which remains the highest rate in the history of Brazil. The miracle was based upon the "cake theory": the bigger the cake, the bigger the portion for everybody. Yet the flip side of the miracle, described by Draibe as "social indebtedness," increasing social inequality, was enormous and still haunts Brazil. The miracle myth is still prevalent today. Many Brazilians look back nostalgically on that period, despite the repression that accompanied it.

Burnier, João Paulo (1919–2000). Extreme radical brigadier with the Royal Air Force, who worked for the repressive organs and was described by several interviewees as a "scoundrel" for denouncing his own comrades. Burnier, the prototype of a sadistic torturer, threw his enemies into the open sea from a helicopter. This action was denounced by a military officer (called Macaco), who faced severe punishment after his denunciation, which indicates that Burnier was a powerful man. Burnier's hit list included Jarbas Passarinho and General Mourão Filho.

carioca. Inhabitant of Rio de Janeiro.

cassações. Loss of political rights for ten years, including the right of political mandate and franchise. Important means for threatening and disempowering critics of the regime. Prominent persons who lost their rights were the former president Juscelino Kubitschek and the politician Carlos Lacerda.

CCC (Comando de Caça aos Comunistas). Right-wing terrorist group, literally Command to Hunt Down Communists. Launched several attacks, including bombings, on students, journalists, and artists.

CDOCEx (Centro de Documentação do Exército). Documentation center of the armed forces, located in the military headquarters in Brasília. According to a military expert, this archive was closed down on December 30, 2011, by the Brazilian Supreme Command of the Armed Forces (Regulation No. 797)

CENIMAR. Intelligence service of the Marines. The Brazilian Truth Commission has recently discovered documentation of the CENIMA that formerly was said to be missing.

Chefe da Assessoria da Imprensa (leader of the press consultancy).
Official name for the post of the official spokesman for the president,
which Camargo occupied between 1977 and 1978.

chefe da casa civil (chief of staff). The highest-ranking member of the
executive office of Brazil and a senior aide to the president holding the
rank of minister. A member of the president's cabinet. It is comparable to
the position of prime minister, but not quite the same, because Brazil has a
presidential system.

CI (Communidade de Inteligência). Common word for the entire system
of intelligence organs including the CIE, CISA, Cenimar, and the SNI,
including its subsections.

CIE (Centro de Informações do Exército). Army intelligence center,
created in 1967. It was involved in counterterrorist activities and was
responsible for torture and murder. Dominated by hardliners, the CIE
increasingly became uncontrollable and antagonistic toward President
Geisel. It failed to install Army Minister Frota as Geisel's successor.

Cine Jornal Informativo. Name of the newsreel produced by the Agência
Nacional. This type of official news film was produced before and after
the military regime. The films are held in the National Archives in Rio.
Another newsreel produced by the Agência Nacional was *Brasil Hoje.*

Cinema do Lixo (Rubbish Cinema). This most radical cultural movement,
also called Marginal Cinema (Cinema Marginal), rejected the
commercialization of cinema and demanded the acceptance of Brazil's
"underdevelopment," poverty, and "rubbish." It was diametrically opposed
to the ideas perpetuated by the AERP, as it undermined the miracle myth.

Cinema Novo (New Cinema). Between the 1960s and 1980s, Brazilian
cinema was dominated by the Cinema Novo, a heterogeneous movement
that demanded social change, rejected the "neo-colonial cultural system,"
and tried to promote independent Brazilian art. Its most prominent
representative was Glauber Rocha.

CISA (Centro de Informações de segurança da Aeronaútica). Founded
in May 1970, the Center of Security Information of the Air Force is that
military branch's intelligence unit.

class. Social category used in a nonpejorative, neutral way. The category's
meaning changes over time; therefore, it should be enclosed in quotation
marks. In this work, the term "upper class" is loosely defined as wealthy
citizens without social problems or the need to work, for example, large

estate owners (*latifundistas*), business owners, and high-ranking managers. I use "middle class" as an umbrella term for groups from different professions and people from various social backgrounds including lawyers, doctors, engineers, public servants, bank officials, members of the new middle class, and the lower technical and administrative sector of huge thriving companies encompassing managers and service personnel. (This definition is based on that of Angela Maria de Castro Gomes and Décia Saes.) Lastly, "working class" or "lower class" is a nonpejorative term for people whose salaries are close to or below the minimum wage and who struggle to make ends meet, such as residents of the slums, street traders, domestic laborers, construction workers on small salaries, and so forth.

CODI-DOI (Centro de Operações de Defesa Interna–Destacamento de Operações de Informações). Created in 1970 as the successor organ of the OBAN, the Center of Internal Defense Operations–Detachment of Intelligence Operations was a repressive body responsible for torture and murder during the military regime. In the literature it is also called DOI-CODI; however, formally the DOI was under the CODI.

Comissão Especial sobre Mortos e Desaparecidos Políticos. The Special Commission of the Families of the Dead [Killed] and Disappeared Political Activists was the primary agency to influence public memory discourse and to press for punishment of those involved in torture. Founded in 1995 in order to investigate the circumstances of murder during the military regime, the commission helped publish a final report, which came out in 2007, entitled "Direito à Memória e à Verdade: Comissão Especial sobre Mortos e Desaparecidos Políticos." This was the first official report about the regime's human-rights crimes and predecessor of the truth commission's final report, expected in 2014.

Communição Social **(literally "social communication").** Term used in the documents of the AERP and ARP for their campaigns. Synonym for public relations work, or propaganda, albeit in a neutral sense.

CONTEL (Conselho Nacional de Telecomunicações). National Telecommunication Council, founded in 1962 with the purpose of modernizing the Brazilian communications system. Its executive unit was the Department of National Telecommunications.

Coup of 1964. Scholars' explanations of this overthrow vary, but it can be described as the result of different economic, social, and ideological predispositions on a micro- and macro-political scale. Some (often

Marxist-informed) scholars emphasize the role of the "bourgeoisie," national and multinational entrepreneurs, and the United States (Dreifuss, Gorender), while others regard the Brazilian military as the leading force (Soares). However, the coup was largely supported and celebrated by civilian actors, including large sections of the upper and middle classes, businessmen, and the press, turning it into a civilian-military coup (Reis Filho). The term "civilian-military coup" has, however, frequently been misused by revisionists who continue to legitimize the illegal overthrow by reference to the "public demand." The armed forces and their civilian allies launched the coup with the stated intention to prevent Goulart's reforms, to avert "chaos" and "communism," and to restore the principle of hierarchy.

CPDOC (Centro de Documentação e Pesquisa). The Center for Research and Documentation of Contemporary Brazilian History Unit of the Getúlio Vargas Foundation (FGV) in Rio de Janeiro has held manuscripts, photos, and documents since the 1930s. The CPDOC pioneered a series of oral history interviews with important military figures and is one of the leading research centers on the military regime.

Costa e Silva, Artur da (1899–1969). Secretary of the armed forces under Castello Branco and later president (1967–1969), who died suddenly from a stroke during his presidency. Under his presidency the AI 5 was passed, although some witnesses argue that he opposed the law and only ratified it because of pressure from hardliners. Although he is often called a hardliner, he was not a radical and did not support violence like the officials who worked for the repressive organs did and therefore, in the view of the author, should be given yet another classification. Before he died, he gave his consent for the foundation of the AERP, initially led by his friend Colonel D'Aguiar.

CSN (Conselho de Segurança Nacional). National Security Council. The main executive organ under the regime, which had the right to elect the president.

DCDP (Divisão de Censura e Diversões Públicas). Although comparable censorship organs had existed previously, the Division for Censorship and Public Entertainment was created on June 2, 1972 (Decree No. 70,665). The DCDP applied mainly prior censorship and censored television, radio, cinema, theater productions, and song lyrics according to "moral" criteria (sexuality, religion, profanity). A clear-cut distinction between moral and political censorship, however, is problematic (Fico).

DOI-CODI. See CODI-DOI.

DEOPS (Departamento Estadual de Ordem Política e Social). The State Department of Political and Social Order was a repressive organization created in 1924 to control political and social opposition movements in the state of São Paulo.

Developmentalism (Desenvolvimentismo). Name of a political development strategy under President Juscelino Kubitschek (1956–1961). This pro-capitalist ideology emphasized national greatness, social equality, order, and security, and regarded foreign capital as indispensable to overcoming underdevelopment. It followed democratic and Christian traditions, anticommunism, and nationalism. Several developmentalist values were adopted by the military regime.

DIP (Departmento de Imprensa e Propaganda). The Department of Press and Propaganda was the first systematic Brazilian institution for propaganda and censorship (1939–1945), which diffused the ideology of the Estado Novo and created a personality cult around Vargas. The DIP controlled the mass media, produced books, journals, and pamphlets, and was responsible for cultural politics. It introduced the radio-propaganda show *Hora do Brasil* which was later renamed *A Voz do Brasil* and used as a propaganda organ by the military regime. *A Voz do Brasil* (the *Voice of Brazil*) continues to be broadcast today. The primary means of dissemination favored by the DIP propaganda was the press. Whereas the AERP and ARP hired private media organizations and "outsourced" propaganda, the DIP produced propaganda itself; 60 percent of the press content was directly produced by the DIP.

Diretas-Já. Strong popular movement that took to the streets in 1983/84 demanding the re-democratization of Brazil and direct presidential elections.

Distensão (literally "depressurization"). Political liberalization (not democratization) project of President Geisel, which was riddled with inconsistencies. Its stated goal was to gradually transfer power into civilian hands. Arguably, the *distensão* was meant to restore military unity and elevate the regime's popularity.

DOPS (Departamento de Ordem Política e Social). Created in 1924, the Department of Political and Social Order was a repressive organ established to control political and social opposition movements in Brazil.

DSI (Divisão de Segurança Interna). The Division of Internal Security was a subsection of the SNI, which was set up in each federal ministry to place state officials under surveillance. The documents of the DSI of the Ministry of Justice are currently being processed and can already be partially accessed in the National Archives in Rio. The Brazilian National Truth Commission is currently reinvestigating the DSI.

economic propaganda films. Films that exclusively sell "development" and "progress." They deal with topics such as export and inflation and often show workers and machines.

EMBRAFILME. Cinema institution created in 1969 (the second state institution to regulate cinema production after the INC) that increasingly functioned as a state-controlled cinema monopoly. First, EMBRAFILME distributed films internationally. Starting in 1975, it also exhibited them within Brazil and produced films. In the 1970s, EMBRAFILME distributed 30 percent of all Brazilian films and controlled between 25 and 50 percent of total film production.

EMBRATEL (Brazilian Enterprise for Telecommunication). Built in 1965 and later subordinated to the Department of Communication, this agency gradually improved the infrastructure for postal services, telecommunications, and radio and television services, developing networks for television and radio.

EMC (*Educação Moral e Cívica* [moral and citizenship education]). This subject became obligatory in Brazilian schools and universities from September 12, 1969 (Decree No. 869), and only ended in 1993. For pupils in the first four years (*primeiro grau*) it was called moral and civic education (EMC), while for graduate students it was called study of Brazilian problems (Estudo de Problemas Brasileiros).

Escola do Estado Maior (ECEME, General Staff School). Traditional military school in Rio de Janeiro that trains officials for leading military positions.

ESG (Escola Superior da Guerra). The Superior War College, a military school, gained power from the early 1960s onward. It provided the revolution's key ideology, the National Security Doctrine (NSD), and functioned as a "network of influence," as many civilian and military leaders during the dictatorship were ESG graduates. While strongly influenced by French military philosophies, it was also related to the U.S. War College. The ESG's key ideologist was Golbery.

Falcão Law. Legislation of 1976 that severely restricted electoral propaganda in order to put the opposition party, MDB, at a disadvantage.

FEB (Força Expedicionária Brasileira). The Brazilian Expeditionary Force was a military regiment of approximately twenty-five thousand soldiers sent to Italy to fight the fascists and the Nazis in 1944. Nearly one thousand soldiers died on this mission. Many former FEB officials occupied leading positions during the military regime.

FIESP. Commercial Association of São Paulo, which in the late 1960s and late 1970s frequently criticized the economic policies of the military regime, since foreign multinationals benefited from them more than Brazilian businesses.

Filho, Olympio Mourão (1900–1972). General who launched the coup in 1964, when he gave his infantry division the order to march toward Rio. Later, he became the leader of the Military Supreme Court (STM). In his memoirs he attacks the arbitrariness of the military regime and declares that his intention was to disempower Goulart, not to establish a dictatorship.

filmete. Technical term for the propaganda short films produced by the AERP and ARP. Usually the films lasted approximately one minute, were accompanied by music, and contained minimal text or dialogue.

Frente Ampla (Broad Front). Political anti-regime alliance founded in 1966 by Goulart, Kubitschek, and Lacerda, which failed because it did not combine with the various other opposition groups at the time (students, workers, clergy, lawyers). The regime prohibited the Frente Ampla in 1968.

Frota, Sylvio (1910–1996). General regarded as a hardliner. Served as army minister under Ernesto Geisel and attempted to instigate a coup against Geisel, which failed. Frota was dismissed in 1977. This was the first time that the friction between hardliners and moderates became publicly apparent.

Geisel, Ernesto (1907–1996). Commander of the military in Brazil in 1961, chief of the military cabinet of the president in 1961 and 1964–1967, minister of the Superior Military Tribunal 1967–1969, president of Petrobrás (state-owned oil company) 1969–1973, and president of Brazil, 1974–1979. Partly educated in the United States, he belonged to the moderate faction within the military. Although he announced a policy of slow, gradual, and secure decompression (*distensão*), the repressive organs continued operating under his presidency, and he defended them publicly. Geisel liberalized the elections and ended prior censorship; however, he did not democratize the regime. Following the principles of the NSD, he continued to defend the Security State. In contrast to his predecessor, he adopted a centralizing stance and did not delegate authority to others. Geisel produced more propaganda than the hardliner Médici. Before his death in 1996, he allowed the CPDOC to interview him and donated his private archive to the CPDOC.

Geisel, Orlando (1905–1979). Military general and brother of Ernesto Geisel. Served as secretary of the armed forces under President Médici and was thus chiefly responsible for the repression that occurred during those years.

gorilla. Derisive term for military and intelligence officials of the military regime.

Goulart, João Belchior Marques. Vice president 1956–1961; president 1961–1964. Also called Jango. Some scholars regard the instability during the last months of his presidency as a key reason for the civilian-military coup. Goulart died in exile in Argentina under circumstances that as of this writing remain unclear, but started being reexamined by the Brazilian Truth Commission in 2013.

Grupo de Estudos sobre a ditadura militar (GEDM). Study group about the military dictatorship based at the Federal University of Rio (UFRJ), led by Professor Carlos Fico and Professor Paula Nascimento D'Araújo (available at http://www.gedm.ifcs.ufrj.br/).

guerra psicológica (psychological warfare). The so-called *guerra psicológica* propaganda was based on radical anticommunism that, although to a certain extent represented a tradition within the Brazilian armed forces, had been sharpened in the context of the Cold War and the Goulart crisis.

hardliner (*linha dura*). Like "moderate," a problematic category that denotes military officials or civilians who supported repression and favored the continuation of military rule. Usually associated with Costa e Silva, Médici, and Frota. In my view, however, these individuals were less radical than those officers working in the repressive organs, such as Brigadier Burnier.

IACHR (Inter-American Commission on Human Rights). Autonomous division of the Organization of American States (OAS) for the promotion and protection of human rights and the investigation of human-rights abuses.

IACHR (Inter-American Court on Human Rights). Established in 1979, the Inter-American Court of Human Rights, in San José, Costa Rica, is an autonomous judicial institution of the Organization of American States (OAS). Its objective is the application and interpretation of the American Convention on Human Rights from 1978 and other treaties concerning this matter. In late 2010, the IACHR condemned the Brazilian state for granting impunity to perpetrators of the crimes in the Araguaia region.

IBAD (Instituto Brasileiro de Ação Democrática). Founded in 1959 with the help of the CIA, the Brazilian Institute for Democratic Action, together with the IPÊS, launched huge propaganda campaigns against Goulart in the early 1960s in order to persuade Brazilians to support the coup.

IBOPE (Instituto Brasileiro de Opinião Pública e Estatística). The Institute of Brazilian Public Opinion, created in 1942, was the first opinion-poll institute in the history of Brazil. While it is one of the few sources on public opinion in the 1960s and 1970s, evidence suggests that its statistics were manipulated at the time.

INC (Instituto Nacional do Cinema). National film institute founded in 1966. Via the INC, the state invested in cinema, with the aim of strengthening the national film output.

indirect propaganda. Whereas the term "political propaganda" is used to refer to films that explicitly mention and praise the government or its programs, indirect propaganda films mention or explain programs without explicitly praising them. The viewer associates these films with the government.

IPEA (Instituto de Pesquisa Econômica Aplicada). The Institute of Applied Economic Research was a government-led research institution set up to advise the government on economic issues. Founded in 1964, the IPEA still exists today. See http://www.ipea.gov.br.

IPÊS (Instituto de Pesquisas e Estudos Sociais). The Institute of Social Research and Studies was officially a "civilian" association (1962–1971), which represented the interests of the upper and middle classes. Together with the IBAD, the IPÊS ran propaganda campaigns against Goulart in the early 1960s and prepared the way for the coup. Its archives were later used by the SNI. While the IPÊS branch in São Paulo closed down in 1970, the Rio branch was deactivated in March 1972.

IPÊS films. Propaganda films produced by IPÊS. The most important campaigns were produced before the coup, in order to dissuade the Brazilian population, particularly the middle classes, from supporting Goulart. This type of propaganda was characterized by the construction of a clearly defined enemy, primarily Goulart but also communism. For example, communists were compared with Hitler in one film. These film productions were often longer, lasting up to an hour.

ISEB (Instituto Superior de Estudos Brasileiros). The Superior Institute of Brazilian Studies was officially created in 1955 as part of the Ministry of Education and Culture. It was responsible for the study of social sciences and the elaboration of ideas for national development. Between 1954 and 1964, it was the think tank of developmentalists integrating different ideological camps. At its core lay demands for the end of class distinctions, social pacification, and the realization of the "common good" in order to overcome political, cultural, and economic underdevelopment and achieve national unity. The state was expected to lead this development. In the early 1960s most *isebianos* found themselves on the political left and supported Goulart's idea of "basic reforms" (*reformas de base*). After the coup, the ISEB was destroyed by the military.

Itamaraty. Brazilian Foreign Office in Brasília.

Jango. Nickname for João Belchior Marques Goulart, vice president 1956–1961 and president 1961–1964.

jôgo de verdade **(truth game).** Recurrent metaphor employed by President Médici, which he used in his very first speech after receiving the presidential nomination. It describes his paradoxical ideal of strictly combating "subversion" on the one hand while granting "full freedom" on the other.

Kubitschek, Juscelino (1902–1976). Also known as JK, Kubitschek was president from 1956 to 1961, during which time he built the city of Brasília. JK was famous for his so-called developmentism (*desenvolvimentismo*), an economic strategy designed to build up a national industry, in particular the motor industry. During the military regime, JK lost his political rights and was forced into exile. His political alliance against the regime, Frente Ampla, founded in 1966, was prohibited and failed. He died in a car accident in 1976, yet another conspicuous death currently being reinvestigated by the Brazilian National Truth Commission. Many Brazilians commemorated his death, and scholars have read this as a condemnation of the military regime.

lower class. See **class**.

luta armada **(armed struggle).** Umbrella term for left-wing guerrilla groups that fought against the military regime using all available means, including violence, with the purpose of establishing a socialist or communist society. The different guerrilla groups pursued diverging revolutionary projects. They included the ALN (Aliança Libertadora Nacional [National Liberation Action]) under Carlos Marighella, the VPR (Vanguarda Popular Revolucionário [Popular Revolutionary Vanguard]) led by Carlos Lamarca, the MR8 (Movimento Revolucionário Oito de Outubro [Revolutionary Movement 8th October]), to which the renowned historian Daniel Aarão Reis Filho belonged, and Var-Palmares (Vanguarda Armada Revolucionária Palmares [Palmares Armed Revolutionary Vanguard]), a guerrilla group in which President Dilma Roussef participated.

Maré. Slum in the north of Rio de Janeiro.

MDB (Movimento Democrático Brasileiro). The Brazilian Democratic Movement has been the official opposition party since the implementation of a two-party system under the Institutional Act No. 2 (AI 2) in 1965. When Brazil returned to democracy in 1985, the party was renamed PMDB.

MEC (Ministério de Educação e Cultura). During the Médici government, the Ministry of Education and Culture was led by Jarbas Passarinho. The MEC paid for copies of the AERP films but had no influence on content and strategy.

Médici, Emilio Garrastazú (1905–1985). Chief of the SNI 1967–1969; commander of the Third Battalion in 1969; president 1969–1974. Médici took part in the Revolution of 1930, when the armed forces deposed President Washington Luís. He was educated in the United States for two years. Most people consider him a hardliner, as he ruled during the so-called years of lead, one of the most violent periods in Brazilian history. He disempowered parliament and governed by decree-law. In 1970–71, he eradicated the urban guerrillas. While Médici is associated with repression, high rates of economic growth and low inflation—phenomena of the so-called miracle—are remembered positively by many Brazilians. His propaganda presented Brazil as an already developed country, although social inequality continued to rise under his rule.

Merenda Escolar. Fifty-year-old program for free meals in Brazilian schools that is still running today.

middle class. See **class.**

Ministério do Exército (ministry of the armed forces). Being responsible for the armed forces, this department was extraordinarily powerful during the military regime. In 1999, this department was replaced by the Secretary of Defense, placing the armed forces under civilian control.

Ministro do Exército (Army Minister). During the military regime, this was a very powerful position. Some people, including the AERP leader Octávio Costa, argue that, particularly during the Médici presidency, the army minister, Orlando Geisel, was chiefly responsible for the violent acts of repression.

MNC. Multinational corporation.

moderates (moderado). Heuristic classification for civilians and military officials. This term needs to be used with care. Moderates were also authoritarian but rejected systematic, long-term repression and ultimately intended to hand over power to civilians. However, as exemplified by Ernesto Geisel, moderates were by no means liberal or democratic; they were simply less radical than the hardliners. Sometimes also called softliners (*castellistas*).

MPB (Música Popular Brasileira). Brazilian popular music is rooted in the Tropicália movement.

National Integration (*integração nacional*). Propaganda slogan and regime policy to build infrastructure (communication, roads) in all Brazilian regions and connect areas of the vast country together. An example was the Transamazon Highway.

newsreels. Official films usually lasting several minutes and depicting news about official state procedures—for example, that the president had opened a bridge or signed a new law. Newsreels were produced by the Agência Nacional during the military regime and thus form another type of official film propaganda, alongside the AERP and ARP films. They were, however, not invented under military rule, but had been produced since the Vargas era.

NSD (National Security Doctrine). Also called Doutrina de Segurança Nacional, or DSN. An ideology that originally evolved after the military dismantled the empire in 1889 and promoted the belief that it was responsible for the good of the nation. At the beginning of the twentieth century, the NSD held that the army was the only force capable of overcoming regional differences and solving the nation's problems. In the 1950s, in the Cold War context, a new version of the NSD spread throughout Latin America. Its main novel feature was the idea of a constant threat posed by "internal enemies," which formed the basis of the repression. The new role of the military institution was not to moderate but to defy potential enemies, who were believed to psychologically infiltrate people's minds.

OAS (Organization of American States). The OAS was established in 1948 with the signing of the Charter of the OAS, in order to achieve among its member states "an order of peace and justice, to promote their solidarity, to strengthen their collaboration, and to defend their sovereignty, their territorial integrity, and their independence." Also called the Inter-American System, it is the oldest international institutional system. Headquartered in Washington D.C., its main pillars are democracy, human rights, security, and development.

OBAN (Operação Bandeirantes). Created July 1, 1969, the Operation Bandeirantes was the first special force for violent repression and a predecessor of the notorious CODI-DOIs. Financed by local and multinational industrialists, the OBAN already operated in close association with the Second Army in São Paulo.

Pacote de Abril. A series of laws passed by Ernesto Geisel in 1977. Geisel closed Congress in order to pass the laws, which did not have sufficient support from Congress. This incident showed once more that Ernesto Geisel did not intend to reinstate democracy but that his political opening was a strategy to remain in power and regain public consent.

Passarinho, Jarbas. Ex-colonel who has been federal minister four times. Passarinho is regarded as the unofficial spokesman of the armed forces who frequently defends the military regime and attacks what he calls "revanchism." He signed the AI 5 and was the secretary of education and culture under President Médici. Although ostensibly defensive of the regime in his press articles, Passarinho was often attacked by hardliners, and, surprisingly, he later maintained cordial intellectual relations with numerous ex-guerillas.

Passeata dos cem mil (March of the One Hundred Thousand). Huge manifestation of the heterogeneous public opposition movement against the regime on June 26, 1968, in Rio de Janeiro. Comprised of students, intellectuals, workers, progressive clergymen, people from the liberal professions, and the public.

PCB (Partido Comunista Brasileiro). Brazilian Communist Party; Soviet ideology.

PC do B (Partido Comunista do Brasil). Communist Party of Brazil; Maoist ideology.

Planalto. The building in Brasília where the president and the government are based.

PND (Plano Nacional de Desenvolvimento). National Development Plan, deployed in two stages: PND I (1972–1974), under Médici, and PND II (1974–1979), under Geisel. The latter acknowledged that only specific sectors of the population, and not the whole of society, benefited from economic growth.

PNDH-3 (National Program of Human Rights Number Three). The program was developed by ex-Minister of Human Rights Paulo Vannuchi in dialogue with civil society representatives. It follows earlier programs set up under ex-president Fernando Henrique Cardoso. One of the most important suggestions to come out of it was the creation of a National Truth Commission. This and other aspects of the PNDH-3 have been criticized by different agents, including the armed forces, the secretary of defense, the Church, and large parts of the press.

pornochanchadas. Erotic film genre that emerged in the 1970s, when filmmakers were politically constrained in their film content and wanted to criticize the box office system as a criterion for state funding.

Porões (basement). A term used metaphorically to describe the places where acts of torture were committed. A synonym for organs involved in acts of repression. Daniel Aarão Reis Filho, however, has rightly criticized this term, since it undermines the fact that torture was a systematic procedure during the military regime.

propaganda. The exact meaning of this term is debated. While the AERP and ARP sources use the neutral term *communicação social* (social communication), in this study I refer to propaganda in a negative sense yet to varying degrees. This study uses attributes to describe a spectrum of negatively connoted propaganda: subliminal, blunt, and aggressive pro-regime propaganda. Subliminal is seemingly apolitical and nonviolent propaganda; blunt propaganda directly praises the regime or its policies; and aggressive propaganda hails violence, constructs enemies, and intimidates.

More specifically, **political propaganda** is the deliberate attempt by a political power to strengthen, alter, or form public opinion through the monopolization and transmission of ideas and values, with the intention of making the populace react in the way desired by the propagandist. These ideas might be rational or irrational and epistemologically true or false. Propaganda is limited to the "field of signification"; it principally comprises the mass media and symbols, such as flags, but excludes political acts such as murder.

repression. In the case of the military regime, this term refers to an arbitrary legal system that violated basic rights, distorted elections, suspended political rights for ten years (*cassações*), forced retirements of civil servants and military officials, and, most importantly, constituted political repression in the form of exile, imprisonment, torture, "disappearance," and murder.

revanchism (revanchismo). Key term in the military and civilian discourse that accuses predominantly the press but also other critics of the military regime of being wholly negative. Some right-wing officials use it as a synonym for "left-wing." As Heloísa Amélia Greco has pointed out, "revanchism" is a politically biased term, because it implies personal vengeance, while in fact it is used with reference to a public and political, and not a private, sphere. However, the term has also been used by former victims of the regime, including President Dilma Rousseff and former minister Paulo Vannuchi.

Revolution. Euphemistic term for the military coup. Also used as a synonym for the military regime installed after 1964.

Riocentro. Concert hall in Rio that became famous when a right-wing terrorist group planned a bomb attack there in 1981 that failed and instead killed one of the right-wing terrorists and injured the other. An official investigation ordered by President Figueiredo confirmed the false allegation of the surviving criminal that the bomb had been planted by left-wing subversives. This incident—considered a ridiculous farce—led many military officials to turn their backs on the armed forces, among them Golbery, Costa, and Camargo. The Riocentro bombing and a bomb attack in the OAB building were key right-wing terrorist acts during the regime. Yet, even more recently, right-wing terrorists tried to threaten the work of the local truth commission in Rio, alluding to these past acts of violence. On March 7, 2013, a small bomb was launched at the headquarters of the Brazilian Lawyers Organization (Ordem dos Advogados) with no injuries, alluding to the right-wing terror in the past. Apparently, military reserve soldiers were retaliating against the new president of the truth commission of the state of Rio de Janeiro.

School of the Americas (SOAS). Military school in the United States which trained tens of thousands of Latin American military officials between 1964 and 2001, including Hugo Bánzer and several generals of the Pinochet regime.

SECOM (Secretaria Especial de Comunicação, Special System of Communication). Propaganda organ that succeeded the ARP in May 1979. It was a much bigger institution, led by General Said Farhat, which, however, had already been closed down in December 1980.

Secretaria Especial dos Direitos Humanos (SEDH). The Special Department for Human Rights was created in 2003 and is responsible for the protection of human rights. Between 2005 and 2010 it was led by Paulo Vannuchi, who has implemented the Direito à Memória e à Verdade project. This project published the final commission report from the Comissão Especial sobre Mortos e Desaparecidos Políticos and established several monuments honoring victims of the left-wing resistance to the military regime. The SEDH has been a key agent in the new politics of memory of the state championing an active culture of memory. Since 2011 it has been headed by Maria do Rosário Nunes.

Semana da Pátria. Bank holiday week celebrating Brazilian Independence Day (September 7). Traditionally commemorated with military parades.

Sesquicentenario. Celebration in 1972 commemorating one hundred fifty years of independence from Portugal.

SNI (Serviço Nacional de Informação). The National Intelligence Service (1964–1999) was created in June 1964 by Decree No. 4,341 with the purpose of supervising and coordinating Brazilian intelligence in the interest of national security. It provided the president and the National Security Council with information. Led by Golbery do Couto e Silva (1964–1967), Médici (1967–1969), Carlos Alberto da Fontoura (1969–1974), João Batista Figueiredo (1974–1978), and Otávio de Medeiros (after 1978). As of December 2005, SNI material can be accessed in the National Archives in Brasília.

Souza, Ivan de. Leader of the SNI under President Figueiredo. Among the generals who vehemently attacked torture committed during the regime.

STM (Superior Tribunal Militar). Military Supreme Court. Historically, the STM is the supreme court concerned with military trials. During the military dictatorship, the tribunal also dealt with civilian personnel. The first major report on systematic cases of murder and torture, "Brasil Nunca Mais," is based on STM files.

subliminal propaganda. Campaigns that reiterate specific values designed to stabilize the military regime (order, security, patriotism, striving for economic development) but neglect to mention violence, the arbitrary regime, and the regime's agents. Subliminal propaganda is indirect and hidden; it is only recognizable as propaganda with knowledge of its specific historical context. It appears apolitical and features everyday topics.

subversão (literally "subversives"). This umbrella term was applied during (and even before) the military regime, by both military and civilian personnel, to denounce people who represented any form of opposition. The term is politically biased, as it was not exclusively used for members of the armed struggle, but also applied to journalists, artists, workers and labor representatives, and clergymen. The word occurred in official speeches and newspaper articles but most of all in reports produced by the intelligence community (SNI, CODI-DOI, CIE, CISA, Cenimar). The word even occurs in SNI files of the early 1980s, when the military regime was heading toward a political opening.

Tortura Nunca Mais Group (Torture Never Again). One of the key organizations representing the interests of political prisoners of the military regime and victims of torture and their families. Founded in 1985, the nationwide organization, whose headquarters are in Rio, has denounced human-rights violations and offered juridical and psychological assistance to victims of the dictatorship, as well as contemporary human-rights victims. One of the key agents demanding remembrance of the history of the military regime.

Tropicália. Cultural movement that emerged in 1967–68 and was mostly associated with music but also influenced theater, poetry, and visual art. The movement was an aesthetic and ideological "rupture" and is sometimes called a "counterculture." Scholars interpret Tropicálismo differently, but its defining characteristic is its use of allegory. Several musicians belonging to the Tropicália movement temporarily went into exile, most prominently Chico Buarque, Caetano Veloso, and Gilberto Gil. The Tropicália movement was short-lived and soon gave way to Brazilian Popular Music (MPB).

TSE (Tribunal Superior Eleitoral). Situated in Brasília, the Superior Electoral Tribunal is the organization that deals with Brazilian elections and publishes the election results.

ufanism. The word "ufanistic" means "boastful nationalism" or "chauvinism." In the case of Brazil, it alludes to the natural richness of the country.

UNE (União Nacional de Estudantes). Student association banned during the military regime, which played an important role in the organization of student protests.

upper class. See **class**.

Ustra trial. Court case involving the Almeida Teles family versus Colonel Carlos Alberto Brilhante Ustra, leader of the São Paulo branch of the CODI-DOI between 1970 and 1974. Represented an important stage in the memory struggle, for this was the first time that a member of the military regime in Brazil had been tried. In October 2008 and August 2012, he was declared responsible for torture and "morally and politically condemned." This case was particularly upsetting, because it involved the kidnapping and imprisonment of (at the time) four- and five-year-old children Edson and Janaína Teles, who were used to extract information from their captured and brutally tortured parents, Maria Amélia de Almeida and César Teles. While some members of the government demanded his punishment, others have protected Ustra on the grounds of the Amnesty Law of 1979. Renowned state attorneys from São Paulo, including Marlon Weichert and Eugênia Augusta Gonzaga Fávero, are currently bringing criminal charges against Ustra, trying to sidestep the Amnesty Law.

Vargas, Getúlio Dornelles (1882–1954). Brazilian president (1930–1945 and 1951–1954). Led a coup in November 1937, dissolved Congress, passed a new constitution, and ruled Brazil for seven years as a dictator. In 1945, the armed forces coerced him into standing down. In 1950, was reelected as president by 48.7 percent of total votes. His popularity among the Brazilian population partly derived from his new labor legislation that first granted basic workers rights. Vargas committed suicide in 1954, after the armed forces exerted pressure on him to resign. The propaganda organ, DIP, created a personality cult around Vargas. His face even appeared on Brazilian bank notes. Presidents of the military dictatorship tried to construct themselves as different from Vargas, because he was considered totalitarian.

The Voice of Brazil (*A Voz do Brasil*). A radio program that broadcast government propaganda every day between 7 and 8 p.m. Successor to *Brazilian Hour*, the radio propaganda program of the former dictator, Getúlio Vargas.

years of lead (*anos do chumbo*). Period comprising the end of the presidency of Costa e Silva, the three-month triumvirate (*junta militar*), and the whole term of Médici's presidency (1968–1974). The years of lead were characterized by repression and the peaking of hardliners' power, as well as by left-wing guerrilla activity.

Bibliography

Archives

Archive of the Navy (Arquivo da Marinha), Rio de Janeiro. (MAR)
Arquivo Histórico do Exército (Palácio Duque de Caxias), Rio de Janeiro. (AHEX)
Arquivo Público do Estado do Rio de Janeiro. Rio de Janeiro. (APERJ)
Documentation Center of the Armed Forces (Centro de Documentação do Exército), Brasília. (CDOCEX) This archive was closed down in 2008.
Edgar Leuenroth Archive (Arquivo Edgar Leuenroth), Campinas, São Paulo. (AEL)
Getúlio Vargas Foundation, O Centro de Pesquisa e Documentação de História Contemporânea do Brasil, Ernesto Geisel Archive, Rio de Janeiro. (EG)
Library of the Escola Superior de Marketing, Rio de Janeiro. (ESPM)
Library of the Planatalto (Bibliotéca do Planatalto), Brasília. (BP)
National Archive (Arquivo Nacional), Rio de Janeiro. (ANR)
National Archive Brasília, Acervo Gabinete de Segurança Institucional/Serviço Nacional de Informações (GSI/SNI). (ANB)
National Archives London, Foreign and Commonwealth Records. (NAL)
National Library (Bibliotéca Nacional), Rio de Janeiro. (BN)
Private Archive of General José Maria Toledo Camargo. (CAM)
Senate Library (Bibliotéca do Senado), Brasília. (BS)
State Archive São Paulo (Arquivo Estadual de São Paulo). (AESP)
Superior War School (Escola Superior da Guerra), Rio de Janeiro. (ESG)
TV GLOBO Archive, Central Globo de Comunicação, Rio de Janeiro. (CGCOM)

References

Abrão, Paulo, and Torelly, Marcelo D. "As dimensões da Justiça de Transição no Brasil, a eficácia da Lei de Anistia e as alternativas para a verdade e a justiça." In *A anista na era da responsibilização: o Brasil em perspectiva internacional e comparada*, edited by Leigh A. Payne, Paulo Abrão, and Marcelo D. Torelly, 212–48. Brasília and Oxford: Ministry of Justice and Oxford University, 2011.
Abreu, Alzira Alves de. "Os anos de chumbo: Memória da guerrilha." In *Entre-vistas: Abordagens e usos da história oral*, edited by M. de Morães Ferreira, 14–32. Rio de Janeiro: Editora Fundação Getúlio Vargas, 1998.

————. "Jornalistas e jornalismo econômico na transição democrática." In *Mídia e política no Brasil: Jornalismo e ficção*, edited by Alzira Alves de Abreu, Fernando Lattman-Weltman and Mônica Almeida Kornis, 29. Rio de Janeiro: Editora Fundação Getúlio Vargas, 2003.

————, ed. *Dicionário histórico-biográfico brasileiro, pós-1930*. Vol. 2. Rio de Janeiro: Editora Fundação Getúlio Vargas, CPDOC, 2001.

Abreu, Alzira Alves de, and Christiane Jalles de Paulo, eds. *Dicionário histórico-biográfico da propaganda no Brasil*. Rio de Janeiro: Editora Fundação Getúlio Vargas, ABP, 2007.

Abreu, Alzira Alves de, Fernando Lattman-Weltman, and Mônica Almeida Kornis, eds. *Mídia e política no Brasil: jornalismo e ficção*. Rio de Janeiro: Editora Fundação Getúlio Vargas, 2003.

Abreu, Hugo. *O outro lado do poder*. Rio de Janeiro: Nova Fronteira, 1979.

Abreu, Vanessa Kern de, and Geraldo Inácio Filho. "A Educação Moral e Cívica— doutrina, disciplina e prática educativa." *Revista HISTEDBR On-line* 24 (2006): 125–34.

Albrecht, Gerd. *Nationalsozialistische Filmpolitik: Eine soziologische Untersuchung über die Spielfilme des Dritten Reiches*. Stuttgart: Ferdinand Enke Verlag, 1969.

Alves, Maria Helena Moreira. *State and Opposition in Military Brazil*. Austin: University of Texas Press, 1985.

Aquino, Maria Aparecida de. *Censura, imprensa, estado autoritário (1968–1978): O exercício cotidiano da dominação e da resistência, O Estado de São Paulo e Movimento*. São Paulo: EDUSC, 1999.

————. "A especifidade do regime militar brasileiro: Abordagem teórica e exercício empírico." In *Intelectuais, história e política: Séculos xix e xx*, edited by Daniel Aarão Reis, 271–89. Rio de Janeiro: Viveiros de Castro, 2000.

————. "Estado autoritário brasileiro pós-64: Conceituação, abordagem historiográfica, ambiguidades, especifidades." In *21 anos de regime militar balanços e perspectivas*, edited by Gláucio Ary Dillon Soares and Maria Celina de Araújo, 55–70. Rio de Janeiro: Editora Fundação Getúlio Vargas, 1994.

Aquino, Maria Aparecida de, Marco Aurélio Vannucchi Leme de Mattos, and Walter Cruz Swensson, eds. *No coração das trevas: O DEOPS/SP visto por dentro*. São Paulo: Arquivo de Estado, 2001.

Arquidiocese de São Paulo. *Um relato para a história. Brasil: Nunca mais*. Petrópolis: Vozes, 1985.

Arquivo Público do Estado do Rio de Janeiro. *Os arquivos das polícias políticas: Reflexos de nossa história contemporânea*. Rio de Janeiro: APERJ, 1994.

————. *Dops: A lógica da desconfiança*. Rio de Janeiro: Secretaria de Justiça/APERJ, 1996.

Assessoria Especial de Relações Públicas. *Catálogo de peças produzidas—Out. 69/Mar 74*. Rio de Janeiro: [1969?].

————. *Catálogo de peças produzidas 1974/1975*. Rio de Janeiro: [1977?].

————. *Documentos fundamentais. Planejamento desenvolvido.* Rio de Janeiro: [1969?].

————. *Encontro de Brasília 27 a 31 de julho de 1970.* Brasília: AERP, 1970.

————. *1° Seminário de relações públicas do executivo, instruções para o funcionamento da A.E.R.P., 30 de setembro a 5 de outubro de 1968, Guanabara.* Brasília: AERP, 1968.

————. *Manual de serviço de 1969 a 1974.* Rio de Janeiro: AERP, 1969.

————. *O processo revolucionário brasileiro.* Brasília: AERP, 1968.

————. *Relatório de comunicação social (governo e opinião pública).* Brasília: AERP, [1974?].

————. *Você precisa saber que. . . .* Vol. 1. March 31–September 30, 1968. Brasília: [1968?].

Assessoria de Relações Públicas. *Catálogo de peças produzidas 1976.* Rio de Janeiro: [1976?].

————. *Catálogo de peças produzidas 1977.* Rio de Janeiro: [1977?].

Assis, Denise. *Propaganda e cinema a serviço do golpe, 1962–1964.* Rio de Janeiro: MAUAD, 2001.

Bacchus, Wilfred A. "Development under Military Rule: Factionalism in Brazil." *Armed Forces and Society* 12, no. 3 (1986): 401–18.

————. "Long-Term Military Rulership in Brazil: Ideologic Consensus and Dissensus, 1963–1983." *Journal of Political and Military Sociology* 13 (1985): 99–123.

Ball-Rokeach, S. J., and M. L. De Fleur. "A Dependency Model of Mass-Media Effects." *Communication Research* 3, no. 1 (1976): 3–20.

BBC News. "Brazilian Media Magnate Dies." Accessed May 20, 2006, http://news.bbc.co.uk/2/hi/americas/3130983.stm.

————. "Brazil Probes Human Rights Atrocities." Accessed May 20, 2006, http://news.bbc.co.uk/2/hi/americas/753908.stm.

Bechtos, Ramona. "Não existe falta de veículos de propaganda no Brasil, mas nenhum pode ser considerado de âmbito nacional." *Propaganda* 203 (June 1973): 88–91.

Belmonte, Laura. *Selling the American Way: U.S. Propaganda and the Cold War.* Philadelphia: University of Philadelphia Press, 2008.

————. "Selling Capitalism: Modernization and U.S. Overseas Propaganda, 1945–1959." In *Staging Growth: Modernization, Development, and the Global Cold War,* edited by David C. Engerman, Nils Gilman, and Mark H. Haefele, 107–28. Amherst and Boston: University of Massachusetts Press, 2003.

Bevins, Vincent. "Brazil's Globo Group Apologizes for Backing Military Government." *Los Angeles Times,* September 4, 2013. Accessed September 10, 2013, http://articles.latimes.com/2013/sep/04/world/la-fg-wn-brazil-globo-network-military-20130904.

Biblioteca do Exército. *A revolução de 31 de Março.* Rio de Janeiro: Biblioteca do Exército, 1966.

————. *31 de Março 1964–1978: A nação que se salvou a si mesma.* Rio de Janeiro: Biblioteca do Exército, 1978.

Boberach, Heinz. *Meldungen aus dem Reich 1938–1945: Die geheimen Lageberichte des Sicherheitsdienstes der SS.* Vol. 1–17. Hersching: Pawlak Verlag, 1984.

Bourdieu, Pierre. "Understanding." *Theory, Culture and Society* 13 (1996): 17–37.

Braga, Geraldo de Araújo Ferreira, ed. *Manual do sistema do arquivamento e recuperação de documentos para informação*. Brasília: SNI, 1984.

Braga, José Luiz. *O Pasquim e os anos 70: Mais pra êpa que pra ôba*. Brasília: UNB, 1991.

Branco, Carlos Castelo. *Os militares no poder*. Vols. 1–3. Rio de Janeiro: Editora Nova Fronteira, 1979.

Branco, Renato Castelo, Rodolfo Lima Martensen, and Fernando Reis. *História da propaganda no Brasil*. São Paulo: T. A. Queiros, 1990.

"The Brazilian Communications Media." *Propaganda* 214 (May 1971): 31–34.

Brecht, Berthold. *Gesammelte Werke*. Frankfurt am Main: Suhrkamp, 1967.

Brito, Alexandra B. de. "Truth, Justice, Memory, and Democratization in the Southern Cone." In *The Politics of Memory: Transitional Justice in Democratizing Societies*, edited by Alexandra B. de Brito, Carmen Gonzalez-Enriquez, and Paloma Aguila, 119–61. Oxford: Oxford University Press, 2001.

Brito, Antonio Carlos. *Tropicalismo: Sua estética, sua história*. Rio de Janeiro: Vozes, 1972.

Britto, Valério Cruz, and César Ricardo Siquiera Bolaña. *Rede Globo: 40 anos de poder e hegemonia*. São Paulo: Editora Paulas, 2005.

Bruller, Jean. *Le silence de la mer*. München: Langenscheidt, 1987.

Brunner, Otto. "Propaganda." In *Geschichtliche Grundbegriffe*, edited by Otto Brunner, 69–112. Stuttgart: Klett, 1984.

Burke, Peter. *Augenzeugenschaft: Bilder als historische Quellen*. Berlin: Wagenbach, 2003.

———. *Varieties of Cultural History*. Cambridge: Polity Press, 2004.

Camargo, José Maria Toledo. *A espada virgem: Os passos de um soldado*. São Paulo: Ícone, 1995.

Caparelli, Sérgio. *Televisão e capitalismo no Brasil: com dados da pesquisa da ABEPEC*. Porto Alegre: L&PM, 1982.

Capelato, Maria Helena. *Imprensa e história do Brasil*. São Paulo: Editora Contexto, 1988.

———. *Multidões em cena: Propaganda política no Varguismo e no Peronismo*. Campinas: Papyrus, 1998.

Cardoso, Fernando H. *O modelo político brasileiro e outros ensaios*. São Paulo: Difusão Européia do Livro, 1973.

Carrilho, Kleber Nogueira. "A legitimação da ditadura: Imprensa e propaganda na eleição e posse do presidente Médici." Master's thesis, Methodist University of São Paulo, 2005.

Castro, Celso. "The Military and Politics in Brazil: 1964–2000." May 29, 2006. Accessed May 10, 2007, http://www.brazil.ox.ac.uk/workingpapers/celso10.pdf.

Castro, Celso, and Maria Celina de Araújo, eds. *Dossiê Geisel*. Rio de Janeiro: Editora Fundação Getúlio Vargas, 2002.

———, eds. *Militares e política na Nova República*. Rio de Janeiro: Editora Fundação Getúlio Vargas, 1998.

Castro, Maria Céres Pimenta Spínola. *Na tessitura da cena, a vida: Comunicação, sociabilidade e política*. Belo Horizonte: Editora UFMG, 1997.

Catálogo da Coleção Audiência da TV Brasileira. *Dados sistematizados de audiência nas cidades de São Paulo e Rio de Janeiro para as décadas de 1950 a 1980*. Vols. 1–3. Campinas: CESOP, UNICAMP, 2005.

Catela, Ludmila da Silva. "Do segredo à verdade . . . processos sociais e políticos na abertura dos arquivos da repressão no Brasil e na Argentina." In *Desarquivando a ditadura: Memória e justiça no Brasil*, vol. 2, edited by Cecilia MacDowell Santos, Edson Teles, and Janaína de Almeida Teles, 444–71. São Paulo: Aderaldo and Rothschild Editores, 2009.

———. "Em nome da pacificação nacional: Anistias, pontos finais e indultos no cone sul." In *Democracia e forças armadas no Cone Sul*, edited by Maria Celina D'Araújo and Celso Castro, 293–328. Rio de Janeiro: Editora Fundação Getúlio Vargas, 1998.

———. "Violencia política y dictadura en Argentina: De memorias dominantes, subterráneas y denegadas." In *Ditadura e democracia na América Latina: Balanço histórico e perspectivas*, edited by Carlos Fico, Maria Paula Nascimento Araujo, Marieta de Morães Ferreira, and Samantha Viz Quadrat, 179–200. Rio de Janeiro: Editora Fundação Getúlio Vargas, 2008.

Centro de Pesquisa e Documentação de História Contemporânea do Brasil (CPDOC). "A propaganda brasileira: trajetórias e experiências dos publicitários e das instituições de propaganda." [Interviews with Mozart Dos Santos Melo, Petrônio Corrêa, Luiz Vicente Goulart Macedo, Carlos Alberto da Fontoura, Altino João de Barros, Sérgio Graciotti, Deoclécio Lima de Siqueira, Hilda Ulbrich Schuetzer, Edeson Ernesto Coelho, Roberto Duailibi, Sérgio Ferreira, Alex Periscinoto.] Accessed March 30, 2006, http://www.cpdoc.fgv.br/comum/htm/.

Chirio, Maud. *A política nos quartéis: revoltas e protestos de oficiais na ditadura militar brasileira*. Rio de Janeiro: Zahar, 2012.

Christenson, Reo M., and Robert O. McWilliams, eds. *Voice of the People: Readings in Public Opinion and Propaganda*. New York: McGraw-Hill, 1962.

Cohen, Youssef. "Popular Support for Authoritarian Governments: Brazil under Médici." PhD diss., University of Michigan, Ann Arbor, 1979.

Coimbra, Cecília Maria Bouças. "Tortura ontém e hoje: Resgatando uma certa história." *Psicologia em Estudo* 6, no. 2 (2001): 11–19.

Cole, Philip M. *International Encyclopedia of Propaganda*. Chicago and London: Fitzroy Dearborn, 1998.

Comissão Estadual de Moral e Civismo, *Educação Moral e Cívica*. São Paulo: Secretaria de Estado e Educação., n.d.

Comissão Nacional de Moral e Civismo. *Educação moral e cívica como disciplina obrigatória nos três níveis de ensino*. Brasília: Ministério da Educação e Cultura, 1970.

Cony, Carlos Heitor. *O ato e a fato: crônicas políticas*. Rio de Janeiro: Civilização Brasileira, 1964.

Costa, Otávio. "Compreensão da Revolução Brasileira." In *A nação que se salvou a si mesma*, ed. Clarence W. Hall, 61–83. Rio de Janeiro: Reader's Digest, 1964 (originally published in a supplementary issue of the *Jornal do Brasil*, June 21, 1964).

Costa, Otávio. "Comunicar é dizer a verdade." *Revista do Gas* 7 (1971): 16–17.

———. "O engenheiro e soldado." *A Defesa Nacional* 743 (May 1989): 80–98.

———. "General-de-Divisão Otávio Pereira da Costa." In *1964–31 de março: O movimento revolucionário e sua história*, 2: 43–92. Rio de Janeiro: Biblioteca do Exército, 2003.

———. "Governo e comunicação social." Presidência da República, Escola-maior das Fôrças Armadas, Escola Superior de Guerra, C116-123-70, 1970.

———. *Mundo sem hemisfério*. Rio de Janeiro and São Paulo: Record, n.d.

———. *Trinta anos depois da volta*. Rio de Janeiro: Biblioteca do Exército, 1976.

Couto, Ronaldo Costa. *História indiscreta da ditadura e da abertura—Brasil: 1964–1985*. Rio de Janeiro and São Paulo: Record, 2003.

Cunha, Luiz Antônio, and Moacyr de Góes. *O golpe na educação*. Rio de Janeiro: Jorge Zahar, 1991.

D'Araújo, Maria Celina. "Ouvindo os militares: imagens de um poder que se foi." In *Entre-vistas: Abordagens e usos da história oral*, edited by Marieta de Morães Ferreira, 147–72. Rio de Janeiro: Editora Fundação Getúlio Vargas, 1998.

D'Araújo, Maria Celina, and Celso Castro, eds. *Ernesto Geisel*. Rio de Janeiro: Editora Fundação Getúlio Vargas, 1997.

———, eds. *João Clemente Baena Soares: Sem medo da diplomacia*. Rio de Janeiro: Editora Fundação Getúlio Vargas, 2006.

D'Araújo, Maria Celina, Celso Castro, and Gláucio Ary Dillon Soares. *Visões do golpe: A memória militar sobre 1964*. Rio de Janeiro: Relume Dumará, 1994.

D'Araújo, Maria Celina, Celso Castro, and Gláucio Ary Dillon Soares, eds. *Os anos do chumbo: A memória militar sobre a repressão*. Rio de Janeiro: Relume Dumará, 1994.

———, eds. *A volta aos quartéis: A abertura*. Rio de Janeiro: Relume Dumará, 1995.

D'Araújo, Maria Paula Nascimento. "Estratégias de resistência e memória da luta contra o regime militar no Brasil (1964–1985)." In *O golpe de 1964 e o regime militar: Novas perspectivas*, edited by João Roberto Martins Filho, 93–104. São Carlos: Edufscar, 2006.

———. "Memories of the Resistance in Brazil in the 60s, 70s, and 80s." Accessed August 18, 2007, www.ppghis.ifcs.ufrj.br/media/paula_memories_resistance.pdf.

Davis, Sonny B. "Brazil: National Security Doctrine." In *Encyclopedia of Latin American History and Culture*, edited by Barbara A. Tenenbaum, 1: 442. New York: Macmillan, 1996.

DeFleur, Melvin L., and Sandra J. Ball-Rokeach. *Theories of Mass Communication*. New York and London: Longman, 1989.

Diniz, Eli. "Empresariado, regime autoritário e modernização capitalista." In *21 anos de regime militar balanços e perspectivas*, edited by Gláucio Ary Dillon Soares and Maria Celina d'Araújo, 198–231. Rio de Janeiro: Editora Fundação Getúlio Vargas, 1994.

Draibe, Sônia Miriam. "As políticas sociais do regime militar brasileiro: 1964–84." In *21 anos de regime militar balanços e perspectivas*, edited by Gláucio Ary Dillon Soares and Maria Celina d'Araújo, 271–307. Rio de Janeiro: Editora Fundação Getúlio Vargas, 1994.

Dreifuss, René A. *1964, a conquista do estado: Ação política, poder e golpe de classe.* Rio de Janeiro: Vozes, 1981.

———. "State, Class, and the Organic Elite: The Formation of an Entrepreneurial Order in Brazil 1961–1965." PhD diss., University of Glasgow, 1980.

Driencourt, Jacques. *La propaganda: Nouvelle force politique.* Paris: Collin, 1950.

Drosdoff, Daniel. *Linha dura no Brasil: O governo Médici 1969–1974.* São Paulo: Global, 1986.

Dunn, Christopher. *Brutality Garden: Tropicália and the Emergence of a Brazilian Counterculture.* Chapel Hill: University of North Carolina Press, 2001.

Dupont, Waldir. *Geraldo Alonso: O homem, O mito.* São Paulo: Global, 1991.

Eagleton, Terry. *Ideology: An Introduction.* London and New York: Verso, 1991.

Ellul, Jacques. *Propaganda: The Formation of Men's Attitude.* New York: Alfred A. Knopf, 1965.

Éluard, Paul. *Poésie et vérité.* Paris: Éditions de la main à la plume, 1942.

Engerman, David C., Nils Gilman, and Mark H. Haefele, eds. *Staging Growth: Modernization, Development, and the Global Cold War.* Amherst and Boston: University of Massachusetts Press, 2003.

Fausto, Boris, and Sérgio Buarque de Holanda, eds. *O Brasil republicano.* Vol. 10, *Sociedade e política (1930–1964).* História geral da civilização brasileira. Rio de Janeiro: Betrand Brasil, 2007.

Favaretto, Celso. *Tropicália: Alegoria, alegria.* São Paulo: Brasiliense, 1979.

Fejes, Fred. "Critical Mass Communications Research and Media Effects: The Problem of the Disappearing Audience." *Media, Culture and Society* 6 (1984): 219–32.

Ferreira, Marieta de Morães, ed. *Entre-vistas: Abordagens e usos da história oral.* Rio de Janeiro: Editora Fundação Getúlio Vargas, 1998.

Fico, Carlos. *Além do golpe: Versões e controvérsias sobre 1964 e a ditadura militar.* Rio de Janeiro and São Paulo: Record, 2004.

———. *Como eles agiam: Os subterrâneos da ditadura militar: Espionagem e polícia política.* Rio de Janeiro and São Paulo: Record, 2001.

———. "A pluralidade das censuras e das propagandas da ditadura." In *O golpe e a ditadura militar: Quarenta anos depois (1964–2004),* edited by Daniel Aarão Reis, Marcelo Ridenti, and Rodrigo Patto Sá Motta, 71–79. Rio de Janeiro: 7 Letras, 2004.

———. "'Prezada censura': cartas ao regime militar." *Topoi-Revista de História* 5 (2002): 251–86.

———. *Reinventando o otimísmo: Ditadura, propaganda e imaginário social no Brasil.* Rio de Janeiro: Editora Fundação Getúlio Vargas, 1997.

———. "Versões e controvérsias sobre 1964 e a ditadura military." *Revista Brasileira de História* 24, no. 47 (2004): 29–60.

Fico, Carlos. "Dos anos do chumbo à globalização." In *Brasiliana da Biblioteca Nacional: Guia das fontes sobre o Brasil,* organized by Paulo Roberto Pereira, 349–68. Rio de Janeiro: Editora Nova Fronteira, 2001.

Fico, Carlos, and Maria Paula Araújo, orgs. *1964–2004, 40 anos do golpe: Ditadura militar e resistência no Brasil*. Rio de Janeiro: 7 Letras, 2004.

Fico, Carlos, Marieta de Morães Ferreira, Maria Paula Nascimento Araújo, and Samantha Viz Quadrat, eds. *Ditadura e democracia: Balanço e perspectivas*. Rio de Janeiro: Editora Fundação Getúlio Vargas, 2008.

Fiechter, Georges-André. *Brazil since 1964: Modernisation under a Military Regime*. London and New York: Macmillan, 1975.

Filgueiras, Juliana Miranda. "O livro didático de educação moral e cívica na didatura de 1964: A construção de uma disciplina," May 17, 2007. Accessed May 23, 2008, http://www.faced.ufu.br/colubhe06/anais/arquivos/302JulianaMirandaFilgueiras.pdf.

Filho, João Roberto Martins. "A ditadura revisitada: Unidade ou desunião?" In *O golpe e a ditadura militar: Quarenta anos depois (1964–2004)*, edited by Daniel Aarão Reis, Marcelo Ridenti, and Rodrigo Patto Sá Motta, 125–39. Bauru: EDUSC, 2004.

———, ed. *O golpe de 1964 e o regime militar: Novas perspectivas*. São Carlos: Edufscar, 2006.

———. *O palácio e a caserna: A dinâmica militar das crises políticas na ditadura (1964–1969)*. São Carlos: Edufscar, 1995.

———. "The War of Memory: The Brazilian Military Dictatorship According to Militants and Military Men." *Latin American Perspectives* 36, no. 5 (2009): 89–107.

Filho, Luís Viana. *O governo Castelo Branco*. Rio de Janeiro: José Olympio, 1975.

Filho, Olympio Mourão. *Memórias: A verdade de um revolucionário*. Porto Alegre: L&PM, 1978.

Fiorin, José Luiz. *O regime de 1964: Discurso e ideologia*. São Paulo: Atual Editora, 1988.

Fish, Stanley. *Is There a Text in This Class? The Authority of Interpretive Communities*. Cambridge, Mass.: Harvard University Press, 1980.

Flynn, Peter. "Authoritarianism and Class Control." *Journal of Latin American Studies* 6, no. 2 (1974): 315–33.

Fonseca, Selva Guimarães. "O ensino de história e o golpe militar de 1964." In *1964–2004, 40 anos do golpe: Ditadura militar e resistência no Brasil*, organized by Carlos Fico and Maria Paula Araújo, 364–77. Rio de Janeiro: 7 Letras, 2004.

Frank, Anne. *Tagebuch*. Frankfurt am Main: Fischer, 1996.

Freyre, Gilberto. *The Masters and the Slaves—Casa-Grande and Senzala: A Study in the Development of Brazilian Civilization*. New York: Knopf, 1970.

Fried, Erich. *Warngedichte*. Frankfurt am Main: Fischer, 1964.

Furtado, Celso. *Formação econômica do Brasil*. Rio de Janeiro: Editôra Fundo de Cultura, 1964.

Galletti, Maria Luiza Mendonça. "Propaganda e legitimação do poder: Brasil, 1970–1978." Master's thesis, University of Brasília, 1980.

Garcia, Nelson Jahr. *O Estado Novo: Ideologia e propaganda política*. São Paulo: Edições Loyola, 1982.

———. *Sadismo, sedução e silêncio: Propaganda e controle ideológico no Brasil, 1964–1980*. São Paulo: Edições Loyola, 1990.

Gaspari, Elio. *A didatura encurralada*. São Paulo: Companhia das Letras, 2004.

———. *A didatura escancarada*. São Paulo: Companhia das Letras, 2002.

Geisel, Ernesto. *Discursos*. Vol. 1, *1974*. Brasília: Assessoria de Imprensa e Relações Públicas, 1975.

———. *Discursos*. Vol. 2, *1975*. Brasília: Assessoria de Imprensa e Relações Públicas, 1976.

———. *Discursos*. Vol. 3, *1976*. Brasília: Assessoria de Imprensa e Relações Públicas, 1977.

———. *Discursos*. Vol. 4, *1977*. Brasília: Assessoria de Imprensa e Relações Públicas, 1978.

Ginzburg, Carlo. "Morelli, Freud, and Sherlock Holmes: Clues and Scientific Method." *History Workshop Journal* 9 (1980): 5–36.

Gomes, Angela de Castro. "Classe media na crise política." In *O Brasil republicano, sociedade e política (1930–1964)*, edited by Boris Fausto and Sérgio Buarque de Holanda, 10: 594–602. Rio de Janeiro: Betrand Brasil, 2007.

———. "Liberdade não é de graça." *Revista de História da Biblioteca Nacional* 18 (2007): 48–53.

Gorender, Jacob. *Combate nas trevas*. São Paulo: Ática, 1998.

Gracioso, Francisco, and J. Roberto Whitaker Penteado. *Cinquenta anos de vida e propaganda brasileiras*. São Paulo: Mauro Ivan Marketing Editorial Ltd., 2001.

Gramsci, Antonio. *Selections from the Prison Notebooks*. London: Lawrence and Wishart, 1971.

Grandin, Greg. *The Last Colonial Massacre: Latin America in the Cold War*. Chicago and London: University of Chicago Press, 2004.

Green, James N. *We Cannot Remain Silent: Opposition to the Brazilian Military Dictatorship in the United States*. Durham, N.C.: Duke University Press, 2010.

Gurevitch, Michael, Tony Bennett, James Curran, and Janet Woollacott, eds. *Culture, Society, and the Media*. London and New York: Routledge, 1992.

Hagopian, Frances. "After Regime Change: Authoritarian Legacies, Political Representation, and the Democratic Future of South America." Review. *World Politics* 45, no. 3 (1993): 464–500.

Hake, Sabine. *German National Cinema*. London and New York: Routledge, 2002.

Hall, Stuart, ed. *Culture, Media, Language: Working Papers in Cultural Studies, 1972–79*. London and New York: Routledge, 1992.

Hanhimaki, Jussi M., and Arne Westad Odd, eds. *The Cold War: A History in Documents and Eyewitness Accounts*. Oxford, UK: Oxford University Press, 2003.

Harrison, Hope M. "Teaching and Scholarship on the Cold War in the United States." *Cold War History* 8, no. 2: 259–84.

Herman, Edward S., and Noam Chomsky. *Manufacturing Consent: The Political Economy of the Mass Media*. New York: Pantheon, 2002.

Herz, Daniel. *A história secreta da Rede Globo*. Porto Alegre: Tchê!, 1988.

Heymann, Luciana Quillet. "O 'devoir de memoire' na França contemporânea: Entre memória, história, legislação e direitos." In *Direitos e cidadania: memória, política e cultura*, organized by Angela de Castro Gomes, 14–43. Rio de Janeiro: Editora Fundação Getúlio Vargas, 2007.

Hobsbawm, Eric J. "In Defence of History: It is fashionable to say 'my truth is as valid as yours.' But it's not true." *The Guardian*, January 15, 2005. Accessed December 10, 2009, http://www.guardian.co.uk/books/2005/jan/15/news.comment.

Hobsbawm, Eric J., and Terence Ranger, eds. *The Invention of Tradition*. Cambridge, UK: Cambridge University Press, 1983.

Holden, Robert H., and Eric Zolov, eds. *Latin America and the United States: A Documentary History*. New York and Oxford, UK: Oxford University Press, 2000.

Huggins, Martha K. "Legacies of Authoritarianism: Brazilian Torturers' and Murderers' Reformulation of Memory." *Latin American Perspectives* 27, no. 57 (2000): 57–78.

Hull, David Stewart. *Film in the Third Reich: A Study of German Cinema 1933–1945*. Berkeley: University of California Press, 1969.

Huxley, Aldous. "Notes on Propaganda." In *Voice of the People: Readings in Public Opinion and Propaganda*, edited by Reo M. Christenson and Robert O. McWilliams, 324–31. New York: McGraw-Hill, 1962.

Ianni, Octavio. *O colapso do populismo no Brasil*. Rio de Janeiro: Civilização Brasileira, 1978.

Jelin, Elizabeth. "La justicia después del juicio: legados y desafíos en la Argentina postdictatorial." In *Ditadura e democracia: Balanço e perspectivas*, edited by Carlos Fico, Marieta de Morães Ferreira, Maria Paula Nascimento Araújo, and Samantha Viz Quadrat, 341–60. Rio de Janeiro: Editora Fundação Getúlio Vargas, 1998.

Johnson, Ollie. *Brazilian Party Politics and the Coup of 1964*. Gainesville: University Press of Florida, 2001.

Johnson, Randal. *Cinema Novo x 5: Masters of Contemporary Brazilian Film*. Austin: University of Texas Press, 1984.

———. *The Film Industry in Brazil: Culture and the State*. Pittsburgh: University of Pittsburgh Press, 1987.

Johnson, Randal, and Robert Stam. *Brazilian Cinema*. London and Toronto: Associated University Presses, 1995.

Jowett, Garth S. "Propaganda and Communication: The Re-emergence of Research Tradition." *Journal of Communication* 31, no. 1 (1987): 97–114.

Katz, Elihu, and George Wedell. *Broadcasting in the Third World: Promise and Performance*. London: Macmillan, 1978.

King, John. "Latin American Cinema." In *The Cambridge History of Latin America*, edited by Leslie Bethell, 10: 455–518. Cambridge, UK: Cambridge University Press, 1995.

———, ed. *The Cambridge Companion to Modern Latin American Culture*. Cambridge, UK: Cambridge University Press, 2004.

Klein, Lucia, and Marcus Figueiredo. *Legitimidade e coação no Brasil pós-64*. Rio de Janeiro: Forense Universitária, 1978.

Krieger, Daniel. *Desde as missões . . . saudades, lutas, esperanças.* Rio de Janeiro: José Olympio, 1976.

Kucinski, Bernardo. "Roberto Marinho." *Index on Censorship* 23, nos. 4–5 (1994): 52–53.

Kunsch, Margarida M. "Professional and Academic Institutionalization of Public Relations in Brazil and Latin America." Paper presented at the annual meeting of the International Communication Association, San Francisco, Calif., May 23, 2007. Accessed January 2, 2009, http://www.allacademic.com/meta/p_mla_apa_research_citation/1/7/2/3/4/p172343_index.html.

Kushnir, Beatriz. "Entre censores e jornalistas: Colaboração e imprensa nos pós-64." In *21 anos de regime militar balanços e perspectivas,* edited by Gláucio Ary Dillon Soares and Maria Celina d'Araújo, 80–92. Rio de Janeiro: Editora Fundação Getúlio Vargas, 1994.

LaFeber, Walter. *Inevitable Revolutions: The United States in Central America.* New York and London: W. W. Norton, 1984.

Lamounier, Bolivar. *Voto de desconfiança: eleições e mudança na política no Brasil, 1970–1979.* Petrópolis: Vozes, 1980.

Lamounier, Bolivar, and Fernando Henrique Cardoso, eds. *Os partidos e as eleições no Brasil.* Rio de Janeiro: Paz e Terra, 1975.

Lazarsfeld, Paul F., Bernard Reuben Berelson, and Hazel Gaudet. *The People's Choice: How the Voter Makes Up His Mind in a Presidential Campaign.* New York: Duell, Sloan, and Pearce, 1944.

Leacock, Ruth. "JFK, Business, and Brazil." *Hispanic American Historical Review* 59, no. 4 (1979): 636–73.

Leslie, Michael. "Representation of Blacks on Commercial Television in Brazil: Some Cultivation Effects." *Intercom* 18, no. 1 (1995): 94–107.

———. "Representation of Blacks on Prime Time Television in Brazil." *Howard Journal of Communications* 4, nos. 1–2 (1992): 1–9.

Levine, Robert M., ed. *Historical Dictionary of Brazil.* Metuchen: Scarecrow Press, 1979.

Levine, Robert M., and John J. Crocitti, eds. *The Brazil Reader: History, Culture, Politics.* Durham, N.C.: Duke University Press, 1999.

Lima, Fernando Barbosa, Gabriel Priolli, and Arlindo Machado. *Televisão e Vídeo.* Rio de Janeiro: Jorge Zahar, 1985.

Lima, Odair de Abreu. "A tentação do consenso: o trabalho da AERP e o uso dos meios de comunicação como fontes de legitimação dos governos militares (1964–1974)." Master's thesis, Pontifícia Universidade Católica, São Paulo, 1998.

Lima, Rui Barbosa Moreira. "Major-Brigadeiro-do-Ar Rui Barbosa Moreira Lima." In *1964, 31 de Março: O movimento revolucionário e a sua História,* vol. 12, edited by Biblioteca do Exército, 37–90. Rio de Janeiro: Biblioteca do Exército, 2003.

Lobo, Amílcar. *A hora do lobo, a hora do carneiro.* Petrópolis: Vozes, 1989.

Lopes, Moacir Araújo. *Moral e civismo: Palestras realizadas em diferentes oportunidades.* São Paulo: CIA Editora Nacional, 1971.

Lowry, Stephen. *Pathos und Politik. Ideologie in Spielfilmen des Nationalsozialismus.* Tübingen: Niemeyer, 1991.

Machado, Arlindo. *Os anos de chumbo: Mídia, poética e ideologia no período de resistência ao autoritarismo militar (1968–1985)*. Porto Alegre: Sulina, 2006.

Machado, José Antônio Pinheiro. *Opinão x censura: Momentos da luta de um jornal pela Liberdade*. Porto Alegre: L&PM Editores, 1978.

Marconi, Paulo. *A censura política na imprensa brasileira*. São Paulo: Global Editora, 1980.

Martins, Ricardo Constante. "Ditadura militar e propaganda política: A revista Manchete durante o governo Médici." Master's thesis, Universidade Federal de São Carlos, 1999.

Mathias, Suzeley Kalil. *A militarização da burocracia: A participação militar na administração federal das comunicações e da educação 1963–1990*. São Paulo: Editora UNESP, 2003.

Matos, Heloiza. "Discursos e imagens das instituições militares no regime democrático." In *Comunicação pública*, edited by Maria José da Costa Oliveira, 117–29. Campinas: Alínea Editora, 2004.

———. "Modos de olhar o discurso autoritário no Brasil (1969–74): O noticiário de primeira página na imprensa e a propaganda governamental na televisão." Master's thesis, School of Communication and Art, São Paulo, 1989.

Mattelart, Michèle. *El carnaval de las imágenes: La ficción brasileña*. Madrid: Akal, 1988.

Mattos, Sérgio Augusto Soares. "Domestic and Foreign Advertising in Television and Mass Media Growth: A Case Study of Brazil." PhD diss., Michigan University, Ann Arbor, 1983.

Medhurst, Martin J., Robert L. Ivie, Philip Wander, and Robert L. Scott, eds. *Cold War Rhetoric: Strategy, Metaphor, and Ideology*. Westport: Greenwood Press, 1990.

Médici, Emilio Garrastazú. *Discurso de posse na Presidência da República*. Brasília: AERP, 1969.

———. *O jôgo de verdade*. Brasília: Departamento de Imprensa Nacional, 1970.

———. *Nosso caminho*. Rio de Janeiro: Secretaria de Imprensa Da Presidência da República, 1972.

———. *Nova consciência de Brasil*. Brasília: Departamento de Imprensa Nacional, 1970.

———. *O povo não esta só*. Rio de Janeiro: Secretaria de Imprensa Da Presidência da República, 1972.

———. *O sinal do amanhã*. Brasília: Departamento de Imprensa Nacional, 1972.

———. *Tarefa de todos nós*. Rio de Janeiro: Secretaria de Imprensa Da Presidência da República, 1972.

———. *A verdadeira paz*. Rio de Janeiro: Secretaria de Imprensa Da Presidência da República, 1972.

Médici, Roberto Nogueira. *Médici, o depoimento*. Rio de Janeiro: MAUAD, 1995.

Memória Globo. *Jornal Nacional: A notícia faz história*. Rio de Janeiro: Jorge Zahar, 2004.

Mezarobba, Glenda. "Brazil." In *Encyclopedia of Transitional Justice 3*, edited by Lavinia Stan and Nadya Nedelsky, 67–73. Cambridge: Cambridge University Press, 2013.

Montero, Alfred P. *Brazilian Politics*. Cambridge: Polity Press, 2005.

Moraes, João Quartim de. "O colapso da resistência militar ao golpe de 64." In *1964: Visões críticas do golpe: Democracias e reformas no populismo*, edited by Caio Navarro de Toledo, 117–33. Campinas: Editora Unicamp, 1997.

Mutz, Diana C. "Mass Media and the Depoliticization of Personal Experience." *American Journal of Political Science* 36, no. 2 (1992): 483–508.

Nagib, Lúcia. *Brazil on Screen: Cinema Novo, New Cinema, Utopia*. London and New York: I. B. Tauris, 2007.

Napolitano, Marcos. "Historiografia, memória e história do regime militar brasileiro." *Revista de Sociologia e Política* 23 (2004): 193–96.

Nars, Edson Luiz. "Um olhar sobre o Brasil pelas lentes de Jean Manzon: de JK a Costa Silva." Master's thesis, Universidade Estadual Paulista (UNESP), Araraquara, 1996.

Niskier, Arnaldo. *Nosso Brasil: Estudos de problemas brasileiros*. Rio de Janeiro: Bloch, 1973.

Nunes, Clarice. "As políticas educacionais pós-64 e o conflito de representações de uma educação voltada para o trabalho." In *1964–2004 40 anos do golpe: Ditadura militar e resistência no Brasil*, organized by Carlos Fico and Maria Paula Araújo, 351–63. Rio de Janeiro: 7 Letras, 2004.

Oberlaender, Ricardo. *História de propaganda no Brasil*. Rio de Janeiro: Shogun Editora e Arte, 1984.

O'Donnell, Guillermo. *Modernización y autoritarismo*. Buenos Aires: Paidos, 1972.

———. "Reflections on the Patterns of Change in the Bureaucratic-Authoritarian State." *Latin American Research Review* 13, no. 1 (1978): 3–38.

Oliva, Oswaldo Muniz. "A comunicação social na revolução de 1964." In "A legitimação da ditadura: imprensa e propaganda na eleição e posse do presidente Médici," by Kleber Carrilho. Master's thesis, Methodist University of São Paulo, 2005.

Oliveira, Eliezer Rio de. "As forças armadas: Política e ideologia no Brasil (1964–1969)." Master's thesis, University of Campinas, 1976.

Oliveira, Francisco de. "Dilemas e perspectivas da economia brasileira no pré-64." In *1964: Visões críticas do golpe: Democracias e reformas no populismo*, edited by Caio Navarro de Toledo, 23–28. Campinas: Editora Unicamp, 1997.

Ortiz, Renato. *A moderna tradição brasileira: Cultura brasileira e indústria cultural*. São Paulo: Brasiliense, 1989.

Orwell, George. *1984*. London and New York: Penguin, 1983.

Pereira, Anthony W. "Brazil." In *Encyclopedia of Human Rights*, edited by David P. Forsythe. E-reference edition. Oxford, UK: Oxford University Press, 2009.

———. *Political (In)justice: Authoritarianism and the Rule of Law in Brazil, Chile, and Argentina*. Pittsburgh: Pittsburgh University Press, 2005.

———. "An Ugly Democracy? State and the Rule of Law in Postauthoritarian Brazil." In *Democratic Brazil: Actors, Institutions, and Processes*, edited by Peter R. Kingstone and Timothy J. Power, 217–35. Pittsburgh: Pittsburgh University Press, 2000.

Petrobrás. *Petrobrás 1979–1984*. Rio de Janeiro: Serviço de Comunicação Social, 1984.

Philip, George. "The Military Institution Revisited: Some Notes on Corporatism and Military Rule in Latin America." *Journal of Latin American Studies* 12, no. 2 (1980): 421–36.

———. "Re-Thinking Military Politics: Brazil and the Southern Cone." Review. *Journal of Latin American Studies* 21, no. 2 (1989): 345–46.

Pinto, Ivan S. "The Brazilian Media Scene." *Propaganda* 203 (June 1973): 64–68.

Presidência da República Brasil. *Metas e bases para a ação de governo: Síntese.* Rio de Janeiro: Fundação IBGE, 1970.

Qualter, Terence H. *Propaganda and Psychological Warfare.* New York: Random House, 1968.

Rabe, Stephen G. *Eisenhower and Latin America: The Foreign Policy of Anticommunism.* Chapel Hill: University of North Carolina Press, 1988.

———. *The Most Dangerous Area in the World: John F. Kennedy Confronts Communist Revolution in Latin America.* Chapel Hill: University of North Carolina Press, 1999.

Ramos, José Mário Ortiz. *Cinema, estado e lutas culturais: Anos 50/60/70.* Rio de Janeiro: Paz e Terra, 1983.

Ramos, Ricardo. *Um éstilo brasileiro de propaganda.* São Paulo: LR Editores, 1983.

———. *Do reclame à comunicação: Pequena história da propaganda no Brasil.* São Paulo: Atual Editora, 1987.

Ramos, Ricardo, and Pyr Marcondes. *200 anos de propaganda no Brasil: Do reclame ao cyber-anúncio.* São Paulo: Meio and Mensagem, 1995.

Reis, Daniel Aarão. *Didatura militar, esquerdas e sociedade.* Rio de Janeiro: Jorge Zahar, 2000.

———. *A revolução faltou o encontro: Os comunistas no Brasil.* São Paulo: Editora Brasiliense, 1990.

Reis, Daniel Aarão, Elio Gaspari, César Benjamin, Franklin Martins, Vera Sílva Magalhães, Helena Salem, Paulo Moreira Leite, Jorge Nahas, Marcelo Ridenti, Alipio Freire, et al., eds. *Versões e ficções: O sequestro da história.* São Paulo: Perseu Abramo, 1997.

Reis, Daniel Aarão, Marcelo Ridenti, and Rodrigo Patto Sá Motta. *O golpe e a ditadura militar: Quarenta anos depois (1964–2004).* Bauru: EDUSC, 2004.

Rentschler, Eric. "Deutschland: Das 'Dritte Reich' und die Folgen." In *Geschichte des Internationalen Films,* edited by Geoffrey Nowell-Smith, 338–46. Stuttgart: Metzler, 2006.

Reznik, Luís. "A construção da memória no ensino da história." In *1964–2004, 40 anos do golpe: Ditadura militar e resistência no Brasil,* organized by Carlos Fico and Maria Paula Araújo, 339–50. Rio de Janeiro: 7 Letras, 2004.

Richter, Hans Peter. *Damals war es Friedrich.* München: Deutscher Taschenbuchverlag, 1980.

Ridenti, Marcelo. "Cultura e política: Os anos 1960–1970 e sua herança." In *O tempo da ditadura: Regime militar e movimentos sociais em fins do século XX,* edited by Jorge Ferreira and Lucilia de Almeida Neves Delgado, 4: 133–66. Rio de Janeiro: Civilização Brasileira, 2007.

———. "Resistência e mistificação da resistência armada contra a ditadura: Armadilhas para pesquisadores." In *O golpe e a ditadura militar: Quarenta anos depois (1964–2004)*, edited by Daniel Aarão Reis, Marcelo Ridenti, and Rodrigo Patto Sá Motta, 53–64. Bauru: EDUSC, 2004.

———. "Resistência e mistificação da resistência armada contra a ditadura: Armadilhas para pesquisadores." In *21 anos de regime militar balanços e perspectivas*, edited by Gláucio Ary Dillon Soares and Maria Celina de Araújo, 140–50. Rio de Janeiro: Editora Fundação Getúlio Vargas, 1994.

Rodrigues, Andre Ibure. "MPM Propaganda: a história da agência dos anos de ouro da publicidade brasileira." Master's thesis, Universidade Federal do Rio Grande do Sul, 2002.

Rollemberg, Denise. "Esquecimento das memorias." In *O golpe de 1964 e o regime militar: Novas perspectivas*, edited by João Roberto Martins Filho, 81–92. São Carlos: Edufscar, 2006.

———. "História, memória e verdade: em busca do universo dos homens." In *Desarquivando a ditadura: Memória e justiça no Brasil*, vol. 2, edited by Cecilia MacDowell Santos, Edson Teles, and Janaína de Almeida Teles, 569–77. São Paulo: Aderaldo and Rothschild Editores, 2009.

Saes, Décio. *Classe média e sistema político no Brasil*. São Paulo: T. A. Queiroz, 1985.

Safatle, Vladimir, and Edson Teles, eds. *O que resta da ditadura: A exceção brasileira*. São Paulo: Boitempo, 2010.

Salles, Mauro. "Uma lição ainda hoje atual." *Revista da Escola Superior de Propaganda e Marketing* 3 (2003): 22.

Samuel, Raphael, and Paul Thompson, eds. *The Myths We Live By*. London: Routledge, 1990.

Santos, Andrea Paula dos. "À esquerda das forças armadas brasileiras: História oral de vida de militares nacionalistas de esquerda." Master's thesis, University of São Paulo, 1998.

Santos, Cecília Macdowell. "A justiça ao serviço da memória: Mobilização jurídica transnacional, direitos humanos e memória da ditadura." In *Desarquivando a ditadura: Memória e justiça no Brasil*, vol. 2, edited by Cecilia MacDowell Santos, Edson Teles, and Janaína de Almeida Teles, 472–95. São Paulo: Aderaldo and Rothschild Editores, 2009.

Santos, Cecília Macdowell, Edson Teles, and Janaína de Almeida Teles, eds. *Desarquivando a ditadura: Memória e justiça no Brasil*. 2 vols. São Paulo: Aderaldo and Rothschild Editores, 2009.

Santos, Maria de Lourdes dos. "Debatendo 40 anos de Rede Globo: História e perspectivas na política, mercado e cultura." *Revista de Economía Política de las Tecnologías de la Información* 8, no. 6 (2005). Accessed April 4, 2006, http://www.eptic.com.br/arquivos/Revistas/VII,n.3,2005/MariaSantos.pdf.

Santos, Sergio Denicoli dos. "A TV Globo e os fluxos de comunicação." Paper for the course "Políticas da comunicação," Universidade do Minho, Portugal. Accessed

April 4, 2009, http://bocc.ubi.pt/pag/denicoli-sergio-tv-globo-fluxos-comunica-cao.pdf.

Scartezini, Antonio Carlos. *Segredos de Médici*. São Paulo: Marco Zero, 1985.

Schneider, Nina. "Breaking the 'Silence' of the Military Regime: New Politics of Memory in Brazil?" *Bulletin of Latin American Research* 30, no. 2 (2011): 198–212.

———. "Impunity in Post-Authoritarian Brazil: The Supreme Court's Recent Verdict on the Amnesty Law." *European Review of Latin American and Caribbean Studies* 90, no. 1 (2011): 39–54.

———. "Legitimisations of a Military Regime: The Propaganda of President Médici and Geisel, Brazil 1969–1979." PhD diss., University of Essex, Colchester, UK, 2011.

———. "'This Is a Country That Advances'—The Official Propaganda of the Military Regime in Brazil, 1968–1979." Master's thesis, University of Essex, Colchester, UK, 2006.

———. "Truth No More? The Struggle over the National Truth Commission in Brazil." *Iberoamericana* 42 (2011): 164–70.

Schneider, Ronald. *The Political System of Brazil: Emergence of a Modernizing Authoritarian Regime, 1964–1970*. New York: Columbia University Press, 1971.

Schramm, Wilbur. *Mass Media and National Development*. Stanford: Stanford University Press, 1964.

Schwarz, Roberto. "Cultura e política, 1964–1969." In *O pai de família e outros estudos*, edited by Roberto Schwarz, 61–92. Rio: Paz e Terra, 1978.

Secretaria Especial dos Direitos Humanos da Presidência da República. *Direito à memória e à verdade: Comissão Especial sobre Mortos e Desaparecidos Políticos*. Brasília, 2007.

Secretaria de Planejamento, Secretaria de Imprensa e Divulgação. *A comunicação social na Presidência da República*. Brasília, 1984.

———. *Legislação brasileira de comunicação social*. Brasília, 1982.

Secretaria de Planejamento, Secretaria de Modernização e Reforma Administrativa (SEMOR). *Cadastro da Administração Federal*. Brasília, 1978.

Senado Federal. "Decreto-LEI no. 869, de 12 de Setembro de 1969." Accessed May 15, 2007, www6.senado.gov.br/legislacao/ListaPublicacoes.action?id=195811.

Serbin, Kenneth P. "Critical Debates: Memory and Method in the Emerging Historiography of Latin America's Authoritarian Era." *Latin American Politics and Society* 48, no. 3 (2006): 185–98.

Shaw, Tony. *Hollywood's Cold War*. Edinburgh: Edinburgh University Press, 2007.

Siepman, Charles A. "Propaganda Techniques." In *Voice of the People: Readings in Public Opinion and Propaganda*, edited by Reo M. Christenson and Robert O. McWilliams, 332–40. New York: McGraw-Hill, 1962.

Silva, Carla Luciana. "Anticomunismo brasileiro: Conceitos e historiográfica." *Tempos Históricos* 2, no. 1 (2000): 195–228.

Silva, Hélio. *A vez e a voz dos vencidos: Militares x militares*. Petrópolis: Vozes, 1988.

Silva, José Luiz Werneck da. *A deformação da história: Ou para não esquecer*. Rio de Janeiro: Jorge Zahar, 1985.

Silva, Luisa Maria N. de Moura. "Segurança e desenvolvimento—a comunicação do governo Médici." *Intercom* 55 (1986): 35–54.

Simpson, Christopher. *Science of Coercion: Communication Research and Psychological Warfare, 1945–1960*. New York and Oxford, UK: Oxford University Press, 1994.

Simpson, Philip, and Roberta E. Pearson, eds. *Critical Dictionary of Film and Television Theory*. London: Routledge, 2001.

Singer, Paul. "O significado do conflito distributivo no golpe de 64." In *1964: Visões críticas do golpe: Democracias e reformas no populismo*, edited by Caio Navarro de Toledo, 15–21. Campinas: Editora Unicamp, 1997.

Siqueira, Ethevaldo. *Brasil, 500 anos de comunicações: A eterna busca da Liberdade*. São Paulo: BCP Telecomunicações and Dezembro Editorial, 2000.

Sirkis, Alfredo. *Os carbonários: Memórias da guerrilha perdida*. São Paulo: Global, 1980.

Skidmore, Thomas E. *Black into White: Race and Nationality in Brazilian Thought*. New York: Oxford University Press, 1974.

———. "Politics and Economic Policy Making in Authoritarian Brazil, 1937–71." In *Authoritarian Brazil: Origins, Policies, and Future*, edited by Alfred Stepan, 3–46. New Haven and London: Yale University Press, 1973.

———. *The Politics of Military Rule in Brazil, 1964–95*. New York: Oxford University Press, 1988.

———. "Raízes de Gilberto Freyre." *Journal of Latin American Studies* 34 (2002): 1–20.

Smith, Anne-Marie. *A Forced Agreement: Press Acquiescence to Censorship in Brazil*. Pittsburgh: University of Pittsburgh Press, 1997.

Smith, Steve. "Two Cheers for the 'Return of Ideology.'" *Revolutionary Russia* 17, no. 21 (2004): 119–35.

Soares, Gláucio Ary Dillon. "A censura durante o regime autoritário." *Revista Brasileira de Ciências Sociais* 4, no. 10 (1989): 21–43.

———. "O Golpe de 64." In *21 anos de regime militar balanços e perspectivas*, edited by Gláucio Ary Dillon Soares and Maria Celina de Araújo, 9–51. Rio de Janeiro: Editora Fundação Getúlio Vargas, 1994.

Soares, Gláucio Ary Dillon, and Maria Celina de Araújo, eds. *21 anos de regime militar balanços e perspectivas*. Rio de Janeiro: Editora Fundação Getúlio Vargas, 1994.

Soares, João Clemente Baena. *Coleção gente: Baena Soares*. Rio de Janeiro: Editora Rio, 2003.

Sodré, Muniz. *Claros e Escuros: Identidade, povo e mídia no Brasil*. Petrópolis: Vozes, 1999.

———. "O negro e os meios de informação." *Revista Cultura Vôzes* 73, no. 3 (1979): 37–42.

Souza, Afonso de, and Reis, Fernando. "A comunicação 1975—uma síntese." *Propaganda* 234 (January 1976): 27–31.

Stepan, Alfred. *Authoritarian Brazil: Origins, Policies, and Future*. New Haven and London: Yale University Press, 1973.

———. "Political Leadership and Regime Breakdown: Brazil." In *The Breakdown of*

Democratic Regimes: Latin America, edited by Juan J. Linz and Alfred Stepan, 110–37. Baltimore and London: Johns Hopkins University Press, 1978.

———. *Rethinking Military Politics: Brazil and the Southern Cone.* Princeton, N.J.: Princeton University Press, 1988.

Strasser, Todd. *The Wave.* New York: Laurel Leaf Books, 1981.

Straubhaar, Joseph D. "The Reflection of the Brazilian Political Opening in the Telenovela, 1974–1985." *Studies in Latin American Popular Culture* 7 (1988): 59–76.

———. "Television and Video in the Transition from Military to Civilian Rule in Brazil." *Latin American Research Review* 14, no. 1 (1989): 140–54.

Taylor, Richard. *Film Propaganda: Soviet Russia and Nazi Germany.* London: I. B. Tauris, 1998.

Toledo, Caio Navarro de. *ISEB: Fábrica de ideologias.* São Paulo: Ática, 1977.

———, ed. *1964: Visões críticas do golpe: Democracias e reformas no populismo.* Campinas: Editora Unicamp, 1997.

Trindade, Hélgio. "O radicalismo militar em 64 e a nova tentação fascista." In *21 anos de regime militar balanços e perspectivas*, edited by Gláucio Ary Dillon Soares and Maria Celina d'Araújo, 123–41. Rio de Janeiro: Editora Fundação Getúlio Vargas, 1994.

Tufte, Thomas. *Living with the Rubbish Queen: Telenovelas, Culture, and Modernity in Brazil.* Luton, UK: University of Luton Press, 2000.

Tulloch, John. *Television Drama: Agency, Audience, and Myth.* New York: Routledge, 1990.

Ustra, Carlos Alberto Brilhante. *Rompendo o silêncio: OBAN DOI/CODI 29 set. 70–23 Jan. 74.* Brasília: Editerra, 1987.

Vale, Ney Peixoto do. "Communication to criate [sic] image as done in 1973 Brazil." *Propaganda* 203 (June 1973): 66–69.

Vasconcelos, Cláudio Beserra. "As análises da memória sobre a ditadura: Balanço e possibilidades." *Estudos Históricos* 22, no. 43 (2009): 65–84.

Ventura, Zuenir. *1968, o ano que não terminou: A aventura de uma geração.* Rio de Janeiro: Nova Fronteira, 1988.

Vink, Nico. *The Telenovela and Emancipation: A Study on TV and Social Change in Brazil.* Amsterdam: Koninklijk Institut voor de Tropen, 1988.

Waisbord, Silvio. "When the Cart of Media Is Before the Horse of Identity: A Critique of Technology-Centered Views on Globalization." *Communication Research* 25, no. 4 (1998): 377–98.

Wanderley, Guilherme. "Desenvolvimentismo: Ideologia dominate." *Revista Tempo Brasileiro* 2 (1962): 155–92.

Ward, Peter M. "Social Policy in a Non-Democratic Regime: The Case of Public Housing in Brazil." Review. *Journal of Latin American Studies* 24, no. 1 (1992): 229–30.

Weber, Maria Helena. *Communicação e espetáculos da política.* Porto Alegre: Editora UFRGS, 2000.

Welch, David. *Propaganda and the German Cinema: 1933–1945.* Oxford, UK: Clarendon Press, 1983.

Westad, Odd Arne. *The Global Cold War: Third World Interventions and the Making of Our Times*. Cambridge, UK: Cambridge University Press, 2007.

———. "The New International History of the Cold War: Three (Possible) Paradigms." *Diplomatic History* 24 (2000): 551–65.

Wickerhauser, Hilda. "O cinema como veículo publicitário." *Propaganda* 230 (September 1975): 14–16.

Wilcken, Patrick. "The Reckoning: Investigating Torture in Brazil." *New Left Review* 78 (2012): 62–78.

Wilkin, Peter. "Global Communication and Political Culture in the Semi-Periphery: The Rise of the Globo Corporation." *Review of International Studies* 34, special issue (2008): 93–113.

Xavier, Ismail. *O cinema brasileiro moderno*. São Paulo: Paz e Terra, 2001.

Zahar, Mariana, ed. *Dicionário da TV Globo: Programa de dramaturgia e entretenamiento*. Vol. 1. Rio de Janeiro: Jorge Zahar, 2003.

Zaller, John R. *The Nature and Origins of Mass Opinion*. Cambridge, UK: Cambridge University Press, 2003.

Zimmermann, Clemens. *Medien im Nationalsozialismus: Deutschland, Italien und Spanien in den 1930er und 1940er Jahren*. Wien: Böhlau, 2007.

Zirker, Daniel. "Civilization and Authoritarian Nationalism in Brazil: Ideological Opposition within a Military Dictatorship." *Journal of Political and Military Sociology* 14 (1986): 263–76.

Zweig, Stefan. *Brazil: Land of the Future*. London: Cassell, 1942.

Index

Page numbers in italics indicate illustrations.

CISA. *See* Centro de Informações de segurança da Aeronaútica

Civilian-military coup, 5, 130n26, 167

Class, 110, 166–67; lower, 60–61; middle, 5, 60, 81, 143n62; upper, 5, 61, 143n63

CNMC. *See* Comissão Nacional de Moral e Civismo

CNP. *See* National Propaganda Council

CODI-DOI. *See* Centro de Operações de Defesa Interna–Destacamento de Operações de Informações

Coercion, 75

Cohen, Youssef, 110, 157n42

Cold War, 5–6, 176; aggressive propaganda and, 12; national security and, 2; press censorship and, 77

COLINA. *See* Comando de Libertação Nacional

Colored Brazilians, 60

Comando de Caça aos Comunistas (CCC), 72, 96, 165

Comando de Libertação Nacional (COLINA), 96

Comissão Especial sobre Mortos e Desaparecidos Políticos (Special Commission of the Families of the Dead and Disappeared Political Activists), 129n10, 167, 180

Comissão Geral de Investigações (CGI), 133n68

Comissão Nacional de Moral e Civismo (CNMC), 69

Commercial Association of São Paulo. *See* Federação das Indústrias do Estado de São Paulo

Commercial propaganda, 27, 80–84, 115

Commissão Nacional da Verdade. *See* National Truth Commission

Communição social (social communication), 9, 91, 167

Communidade de Intelligência (CI), 166

Communist Party of Brazil. *See* Partido Comunista do Brasil

Conselho de Segurança Nacional (CSN), 3, 96, 168

Conselho Federal de Educação (CFE), 69

Conselho Nacional de Telecomunicações (CONTEL), 167

Correio Brasiliense (newspaper), 75

Correio da Manhã (journal), 77

Costa, Octávio, 9, 16, 85, 106–7, 112, 126, 152n22, 161, 175; AERP and, 15, 18, 87–91; audience and, 59; credibility of, 94–100; EMC and, 69; Médici and, 20, 86, 88–89; public relations and, 17; publicity and, 83–84; Schramm and, 23; SECOM and, 25; as speech ghostwriter, 87–94; as teacher and soldier, 91–93

Costa e Silva, Artur da, 14, 96, 97, 161, 168, 183

Coup (1964), 4–5, 95, 167–68

Couto e Silva, Golbery do, 6, 180

CPDOC. *See* Centro de Documentação e Pesquisa

Criptogoverno, 100

CSN. *See* Conselho de Segurança Nacional

Cultural production, 72–73

Cultura Política (newspaper), 9

D'Aguiar, Hernani, 14–15, 89, 161

D'Araújo, Maria Celina, 7

D'Araújo, Paula Nascimento, 172

DCDP. *See* Divisão de Censura e Diversões Públicas

DEOPS. *See* Departamento Estadual de Ordem Política e Social

Departamento de Ordem Política e Social (DOPS), 133n68, 169

Departamento Estadual de Ordem Política e Social (DEOPS), 133n68, 169

Departmento de Imprensa e Propaganda (DIP), 16–17, 161, 169; divisions of, 132n57; Vargas and, 9, 66, 77, 114

Desenvolvimentismo. *See* Developmentalism

Development, 51–59, 61–63, 82, 98, 142n51

Developmentalism (*desenvolvimentismo*), 6, 169, 174

Dictatorship and the Repression of Workers and the Trade Union Movement. *See* Ditadura e repressão aos trabalhadores e ao movimento sindical

Dines, Alberto, 92, 134, 154n54

Diniz, Eli, 59, 81

DIP. *See* Departamento de Imprensa e Propaganda

"Direito à Memória e à Verdade: Comissão Especial sobre Mortos e Desaparecidos Políticos," 167, 180

Diretas-Já, 80, 169

Distensão (depressurization), 1, 169, 171

Ditadura e repressão aos trabalhadores e ao movimento sindical (Dictatorship and the Repression of Workers and the Trade Union Movement), 141n49

Divisão de Censura e Diversões Públicas (DCDP), 75, 146n41, 168

Divisão de Segurança Interna (DSI), 170

DOI-CODI. *See* Centro de Operações de Defesa Interna–Destacamento de Operações de Informações

DOPS. *See* Departamento de Ordem Política e Social

Doutrina de Segurança Nacional. *See* National Security Doctrine

Draibe, Sônia Miriam, 176

Dreifuss, René, 7–8, 130n26

Driencourt, Jacques, 10

DSI. *See* Divisão de Segurança Interna

Duabili, Roberto, 109
Dunn, Christopher, 73

Eagleton, Terry, 10, 111, 133n64
ECEME. *See* Escola do Estado Maior
Economic miracle (short film), 52
Economic propaganda, 31, 36–38, 170
Educação moral e cívica (EMC), 9, 68–71, 145n21, 170
Education, 57, 61, 68–71, 145n18, 145n19, 145n21; programs for, 66
Elbrick, Charles, 97
Elections, 29–31
Ellul, Jacques, 10, 30–31
EMBRAFILME, 73–74, 170
EMBRATEL. *See* Brazilian Enterprise for Telecommunication
EMC. See *Educação moral e cívica*
Emptiness of legitimacy, 6
EPB. See *Estudo de problemas Brasileiros*
Epistemological truth, 10–11, 111
Ernesto Geisel Archive, 70
Escola do Estado Maior (ECEME), 92, 99, 170
Escola Superior da Guerra (ESG), 20, 83, 92, 170; EMC and, 70; ideology of, 131n29, 132n43; NSD and, 5
O Estado de São Paulo (newspaper), 68, 76–78, 96, 107–9
Estado Novo (New State), 68–69, 75
Estudo de problemas Brasileiros (EPB), 145n21
Evaristo Arns, Paulo, 86
Explicit readers, 157n12

Falcão, Armando, 30
Falcão Law, 171
Farhat, Said, 25, 180
Fávero, Eugênia Augusta Gonzaga, 182
FEB. *See* Força Expedicionária Brasileira
Federação das Indústrias do Estado de São Paulo (FIESP), 8, 171
Federal Council of Education. *See* Conselho Federal de Educação
Federal University of Rio (UFRJ), 172
Fernandes, Florestan, 145n20
FGV. *See* Getúlio Vargas Foundation
Fico, Carlos, 15, 18, 85, 87, 94, 116, 131, 133n68, 157n12, 168, 172; on authoritarian utopia, 7; on civilization discourse, 54; Costa, O., and, 112; on ufanism, 135n11
Field of signification, 11, 178
FIESP. *See* Federação das Indústrias do Estado de São Paulo

Figuereido, João Batista, 25, 180
Filho, Olímpio Mourão, 4, 165, 171
Filmetes, 16, 21–22, 27, 28–30, 31, 116, 171; addressees of, 59–61; aesthetics of, 38–51; analysis of, 30–61; animated, 41–45; development and, 51–59; series, 45–48; story of, 38–51; topics of, 61–64, 62, 63, 64
Fish, Stanley, 105
Folha da Tarde (magazine), 78
Fonseca, Selva Guimarães, 69
Fontoura, Carlos Alberto da, 180
Força Expedicionária Brasileira (FEB), 99, 171
Franco, Itamar, 71, 74
Frankfurt School, 105
Freddy, Sérgio, 16, 20
Frente Ampla (Broad Front), 171, 174
Freyre, Gilberto, 45
Frota, Sylvio, 171
Functional truth, 10–11, 111

Gabeira, Fernando, 155n59
Galletti, Maria Luiza Mendonça, 63
Garcia, Nelson Jahr, 134n1, 157n12
GEDM. *See* Grupo de Estudos sobre a ditadura militar
Geisel, Ernesto, 59, 63–64, 73, 110, 112, 128, 155n70, 171–72; ARP and, 23–24; Camargo and, 100; *distensão* and, 1; Pacote de Abril and, 177; public relations and, 68; production volume and, 28–30; torture and, 130n23
Geisel, Orlando, 99, 150n11, 155n70, 172, 176
General Investigation Commission. *See* Comissão Geral de Investigações
General Staff School. *See* Escola do Estado Maior
Getúlio Vargas Foundation (FGV), 8, 138n2, 168
Gil, Gilberto, 73, 181
Global monitoring, 20
Globo (TV network), 12, 76, 84, 115, 144n9, 148n50; repression and, 79; SNI and, 80
O Globo (journal), 76, 78
Goebbels, Joseph, 85
Gorillas, 68, 93, 153n44, 172
Goulart, João Belchior Marques "Jango," 4, 5, 7, 59, 172
Government programs, 61–62
Gracioso, Francisco, 81
Great Brazil. *See* Brasil Grande
Greco, Heloísa Amélia, 179
Green, James N., 129n1, 163
Group for Public Relations, 14
Grupo de Estudos sobre a ditadura militar (GEDM), 172

Nina Schneider is a Marie Curie Postdoctoral Fellow at the Zukunftskolleg at the University of Konstanz, Germany.